DONG-HYUK KIM, Ph.D., Yale University (2011), is a lecturer in Hebrew Bible and Christianity at several universities and seminaries in Korea, including Methodist Theological University, Ewha Womans University, and Myongji University.

Early Biblical Hebrew, Late Biblical Hebrew,
and Linguistic Variability

Supplements

to

Vetus Testamentum

VOLUME 156

The titles published in this series are listed at brill.com/vts

Early Biblical Hebrew, Late Biblical Hebrew, and Linguistic Variability

A Sociolinguistic Evaluation of the Linguistic Dating of Biblical Texts

By

Dong-Hyuk Kim

BRILL

LEIDEN • BOSTON
2013

Bible translations are from the New Revised Standard Version Bible, copyright 1989, Division of Christian Education of the National Council of the Churches of Christ in the United States of America. Used by permission. All rights reserved.

Library of Congress Cataloging-in-Publication Data

Kim, Dong-Hyuk.
    Early Biblical Hebrew, late Biblical Hebrew, and linguistic variability : a sociolinguistic evaluation of the linguistic dating of Biblical texts / by Dong-Hyuk Kim.
        p. cm. — (Supplements to Vetus Testamentum ; v. 156)
    Includes bibliographical references and index.
    ISBN 978-90-04-23560-1 (hardback : alk. paper)—ISBN 978-90-04-23561-8 (e-book)
 1. Hebrew language—History. 2. Hebrew language—Variation. 3. Bible. O.T.—Language, style.
 4. Bible. O.T.—Criticism, Textual. I. Title.

PJ4545.K56 2012
492.4'7—dc23

2012027752

This publication has been typeset in the multilingual "Brill" typeface. With over 5,100 characters covering Latin, IPA, Greek, and Cyrillic, this typeface is especially suitable for use in the humanities. For more information, please see www.brill.com/brill-typeface.

ISSN 0083-5889
ISBN 978-90-04-23560-1 (hardback)
ISBN 978-90-04-23561-8 (e-book)

This book is printed on acid-free paper.

MIX
Paper from
responsible sources
FSC
www.fsc.org   FSC® C004472

PRINTED BY DRUKKERIJ WILCO B.V. - AMERSFOORT, THE NETHERLANDS

For my parents

CONTENTS

ACKNOWLEDGMENTS

The present book is a revision of my Ph.D. dissertation submitted to Yale University in 2011. It is the harvest not only of my doctoral program at Yale but also of the ten-year-long, overseas journey I undertook with my family, who left home and parents for the unkown city of New Haven, Connecticut, in the summer of 2001. Hardships, joys, and disappointments abounded, but now I understand a little more fully that in this blessed journey all things have worked together for good—thanks to the grace of God and the many people who have helped and guided me, some of whom I would like to mention by name.

I must first express my deep gratitude to the congregation of my mother church, The Cheonghak Methodist Church of Incheon, Korea, for their unceasing support, through prayer and resources, during my years at Yale. I also wish to thank both Yale Divinity School and Yale Graduate School of Arts and Sciences for their generous financial support of me and my family.

My humble and respectful thanks are due to my dissertation advisor, Professor Robert R. Wilson. He guided me with his keenness of mind and kindness of heart, both during my years in the master's program and through to the completion of the dissertation. For the last decade, whenever I stumbled, Professor Wilson was there to help, not only with his scholarly wisdom but also with his warm encouragement.

Two other professors at Yale guided my work and shared their expertise with me from the very beginning of my life in New Haven. Professor John J. Collins was an unfailing well of knowledge and assurance, whose scholarship and enthusiasm both informed and inspired me. Like many who know him, I hope to emulate his life and professionalism even partially. To Professor Carolyn J. Sharp is also due my heartfelt gratitude. Her technical skill, impassioned expertise, and spirituality have had a profound impact on me. I sincerely hope that they will shape my life as a scholar.

It was my great blessing that Professor Joel S. Baden joined the faculty at Yale Divinity School during the years of my Ph.D. program. He meticulously read, critiqued, and commented on versions of each of the chapters, and, when it turned out that my initial research would make a smaller contribution to the scholarship than I had hoped, he encouraged me to return to my original method (i.e., sociolinguistics) and apply it more vigorously. His acute comments led to revisions in the whole dissertation, as well as to the addition of a new chapter (chapter 4).

I thank Professor Tai-il Wang of Methodist Theological University, Seoul, Korea, who introduced me to the world of Hebrew Bible studies and directed me to the linguistic study of Classical Hebrew. When I was hunting for a topic for my M.Div. thesis, he handed me Mark Rooker's 1990 monograph *Biblical Hebrew in Transition.* Who could have known at the time that this tiny event was a signpost?

I wish to express my special thanks to two Hebrew Bible colleagues at Yale. Alison Acker Gruseke thoroughly reviewed and commented on a significant part of the work before and after the submission of the dissertation, and Julie Faith Parker, now a professor at Fordham University, helped me through her constant prayer and care. For a decade or so, Julie and Alison have been like my "big sisters." I also feel grateful to my other brilliant colleagues and friends at Yale Graduate School and Yale Divinity School, Antonios Finitsis, John Ahn, Samuel Adams, Matthew Neujahr, Tracy Lemos, Ryan Stokes, Kyong Jin Lee, Robb Young, Stewart Moore, and Ojin Kwon. All of them have been a persistent reminder that this journey was not a lone one.

Hyoungbae Lee, my friend for twenty years and Korean Studies Librarian of Princeton University, read and commented on chapter 3 at an early stage of the project. His service helped me to clarify the method. He also assisted me with the premodern English sentences that appear in chapter 4. Chang-Ho Lee and his family (Eun-Young Park, and the girls Sue-Ah and Jin-Ah) and Haeil Park were like a family while my family was in New Haven. And they still are now that all of us are back in Korea.

I express my sincere gratitude to Professor Christl M. Maier and Professor Hugh G. M. Williamson for accepting my dissertation for the Supplements to Vetus Testamentum series. They made critical comments on my dissertation, which improved the manuscript greatly. Liesbeth Hugenholtz and Willy de Gijzel, the editors of Brill, have helped me through the process of publication. Without their help I would have been like a lost child.

No words can fully express my thankfulness to those who are closest. The love and prayers of my mother and father have been a means of grace during my long stay away from them. My brother and his wife, Dong-Hwan and Ari, helped me with their prayers. My daughters, Heejoo and Yunjoo, the rewards of God to our family, have been the joy of our lives, and helped me overcome the difficult moments of our ten-year sojourn. Finally, to my beloved wife, Eun-young Kwak, I owe the greatest debt of gratitude: without her faithful love, our journey could never have reached the present happy juncture.

LIST OF FIGURES

LIST OF TABLES

ABBREVIATIONS

Technical

ABH	Archaic Biblical Hebrew
BH	Biblical Hebrew
CBH	Classical Biblical Hebrew
DSS	Dead Sea Scrolls
DtrH	The Deuteronomistic History
EBH	Early Biblical Hebrew
inf. const.	infinitive construct
LBH	Late Biblical Hebrew
MH	Mishnaic Hebrew
MT	Masoretic Text
NRSV	New Revised Standard Version
QH	Qumran Hebrew
SBH	Standard Biblical Hebrew
syn.	synoptic

Bibliographical

AB	Anchor Bible
ABD	*Anchor Bible Dictionary.* Edited by David Noel Freedman. 6 vols. New York: Doubleday, 1992
AbrNSup	Abr-Nahrain: Supplement Series
ANES	*Ancient Near Eastern Studies*
ANESSup	Ancient Near Eastern Studies Supplement
AOS	American Oriental Series
ATANT	Abhandlungen zur Theologie des Alten und Neuen Testaments
BA	*Biblical Archaeologist*
BDB	Brown, Francis, S. R. Driver, and Charles A. Briggs. *The Brown-Driver-Briggs Hebrew and English Lexicon of the Old Testament.* Boston: Houghton, 1906. Repr., Peabody, Mass.: Hendrickson, 1997
BETL	Bibliotheca ephemeridum theologicarum lovaniensium
Bib	*Biblica*
BO	*Bibliotheca orientalis*

BSOAS   *Bulletin of the School of Oriental and African Studies*
BZAW   Beihefte zur Zeitschrift für die alttestamentliche Wissenschaft
CahRB   Cahiers de la Revue biblique
CBET   Contributions to Biblical Exegesis and Theology
CEEC   *Corpus of Early English Correspondence.* Compiled by Terttu
           Nevalainen, Helena Raumolin-Brunberg, Jukka Keränen,
           Minna Nevala, Arja Nurmi, and Minna Palander-Collin. Hel-
           sinki: Department of English, University of Helsinki, 1998
DBI   *Dictionary of Biblical Interpretation.* Edited by John H. Hayes. 2
           vols. Nashville: Abingdon, 1999
EncJud²   *Encyclopaedia Judaica.* Edited by Michael Berenbaum and
           Fred Skolnik. 22 vols. 2nd ed. Detroit: Macmillan, 2007
FAT   Forschungen zum Alten Testament
FRLANT   Forschungen zur Religion und Literatur des Alten und Neuen
           Testaments
GKC   *Gesenius' Hebrew Grammar.* Edited and enlarged by E. Kautzsch.
           Translated and revised by A. E. Cowley. 2nd ed. Oxford: Clar-
           endon, 1910
HA   *Hebrew Abstracts*
HALOT   Koehler, Ludwig, Walter Baumgartner, and Johann Jakob
           Stamm. *The Hebrew and Aramaic Lexicon of the Old Testa-
           ment.* Translated and edited under the supervision of M. E. J.
           Richardson. 5 vols. Leiden: Brill, 1994–2000
HAR   *Hebrew Annual Review*
HC   *Helsinki Corpus of English Texts.* Compiled by the Helsinki Cor-
           pus project team. Helsinki: Department of English, University
           of Helsinki, 1991
HS   *Hebrew Studies*
HSM   Harvard Semitic Monographs
HSS   Harvard Semitic Studies
HTR   *Harvard Theological Review*
Int   *Interpretation*
JANES   *Journal of the Ancient Near Eastern Society*
JANESCU   *Journal of the Ancient Near Eastern Society of Columbia
           University*
JBL   *Journal of Biblical Literature*
JHS   *Journal of Hebrew Scriptures*
JQR   *Jewish Quarterly Review* (new series)

JSOTSup	Journal for the Study of the Old Testament: Supplement Series
NCB	New Century Bible
NICOT	New International Commentary on the Old Testament
OLA	Orientalia lovaniensia analecta
OTE	*Old Testament Essays*
OTL	Old Testament Library
RBL	*Review of Biblical Literature*
SBLMasS	Society of Biblical Literature Masoretic Studies
SBLMS	Society of Biblical Literature Monograph Series
SJOT	*Scandinavian Journal of the Old Testament*
SOTSMS	Society for Old Testament Study Monograph Series
STAT	Suomalainen Tiedeakatemian Toimituksia (= Annales Academiae Scientiarum Fennicae)
STDJ	Studies on the Texts of the Desert of Judah
SubBi	Subsidia biblica
Text	*Textus*
VT	*Vetus Testamentum*
VTSup	Supplements to Vetus Testamentum
WBC	Word Biblical Commentary
WMANT	Wissenschaftliche Monographien zum Alten und Neuen Testament
WTJ	*Westminster Theological Journal*
ZAH	*Zeitschrift für Althebräistik*
ZAW	*Zeitschrift für die alttestamentliche Wissenschaft*

CHAPTER ONE

INTRODUCTION

1. *The Problem*

Can we date biblical texts only on the basis of linguistic evidence? Until the turn of the millennium, the answer had been an almost unanimous yes. This situation owed much to Avi Hurvitz, the most prominent scholar in the subject of Late Biblical Hebrew (= LBH).[1] Hurvitz had (and has) consistently argued the following: first, that *linguistic change in Biblical Hebrew (= BH) during the exile was so decisive as to render the postexilic biblical writers unable to write Early Biblical Hebrew (= EBH) of the pre-exilic period*; and, second, that, since LBH of the postexilic period was a linguistic body distinct from EBH both in form and in chronology, *one can date biblical texts solely on the basis of linguistic data.* While Hurvitz's first point is firmly rooted in the traditional understanding of BH, the second point represents Hurvitz's most significant contribution to scholarship. Since the beginning of his career in the 1960s, Hurvitz has established the primary method of defining LBH features on the basis of which one can decide whether a particular text is written in LBH or not.[2] Not only Hurvitz, but also some other scholars, who may be legitimately called Hurvitz's students, have vigorously used his method in dating those biblical texts whose dates are considered problematic. For Hurvitz himself and those other scholars, Hurvitz's method was a reliable mathematical formula: the input of linguistic data would produce the output of either LBH or EBH. Aside from those who actively employed Hurvitz's method, many other biblical scholars whose main interests did not lie in philology also accepted Hurvitz's method and the results that derived from it. A few scholars disagreed, for example, Philip R. Davies, but Davies's critique of

---

[1] Late Biblical Hebrew designates, in general, Biblical Hebrew after the exile. The contrasting term, Early Biblical Hebrew, generally refers to the Biblical Hebrew of the preexilic period. For a fuller discussion of these terms, see chapter 2.

[2] See further chapter 2, which is a survey of scholarship, where I will detail Hurvitz's method, studies that employ it, and arguments that challenge it.

Hurvitz was not thorough.[3] Until about a decade ago, few scholars had made a serious case against Hurvitz, and Hurvitz's conclusions remained practically unchallenged.

Then the situation changed suddenly and radically. From 2003 to 2006, the subject of the linguistic dating of biblical texts was extensively discussed in one essay collection and sections of two consecutive volumes of a journal; parts of these works were contributions by those who disagree with Hurvitz.[4] In 2008, the subject was fully treated and critiqued in a two-volume collaborative book; the authors may properly be called the "challengers" of Hurvitz and of the (hitherto) consensus.[5] Not only did these publications multiply readings in the subject, but they also complicated the discussion. In these works, the challengers' arguments are elaborate, thorough, and, most importantly, data-based; they constitute a formidable challenge to Hurvitz's enterprise.

While the challengers' discussions are quite complex and deal comprehensively with many issues of the subject, their main ideas are precisely the opposite of the traditional understanding. First, although the challengers accept that EBH and LBH are different, they believe that *EBH and LBH are not as distinct in form and in chronology* as Hurvitz and his followers argue. Second, for this reason and others that will be discussed below, *EBH and LBH should rather be considered stylistic options from which the postexilic (and possibly preexilic) biblical writers were free to choose.*[6] The corollary is, of course, that *it is impossible to date biblical texts*

---

[3] That is, when Davies wrote *In Search of 'Ancient Israel'* (first edition in 1992; the references here are from the second edition [London: Sheffield Academic Press, 1995], the revision of which is limited mostly to typographical errors). Davies spends five pages (pp. 97–101) critiquing Hurvitz. Later, he developed a more elaborate argument in his "Biblical Hebrew and the History of Ancient Judah: Typology, Chronology and Common Sense," in *Biblical Hebrew: Studies in Chronology and Typology* (ed. Ian Young; JSOTSup 369; London: T&T Clark, 2003), 150–63. See further chapter 2 of the present study.

[4] Ian Young, ed., *Biblical Hebrew: Studies in Chronology and Typology* (JSOTSup 369; London: T&T Clark, 2003); *HS* 46 (2005): 321–76; and *HS* 47 (2006): 83–210.

[5] Ian Young, Robert Rezetko, and Martin Ehrensvärd, *Linguistic Dating of Biblical Texts* (2 vols.; London: Equinox, 2008). I will use the term 'challengers' to designate those scholars who object to the linguistic dating of BH texts (in most cases, they are Young, Rezetko, and Ehrensvärd). This is in accord with Ziony Zevit, who, in his review of Young (ed.), *Biblical Hebrew,* coined the term 'challenger arguments' to refer to the arguments proposed by those who disagree with Hurvitz and who believe that it is impossible to date biblical texts only by using linguistic evidence. Zevit, review of Young (ed.), *Biblical Hebrew, RBL* 6 (2004): 7. Online: http://bookreviews.org/pdf/4084_3967.pdf.

[6] For the challengers, the terms 'EBH' and 'LBH' may be misleading, as they do not represent the early and late stages of BH but its two contemporary styles. For want of better terms, however, they use the term EBH for the Hebrew style of the Pentateuch

solely on the basis of linguistic data. I will survey many facets of the challengers' argument in chapter 2. Here, I will focus on its one major aspect: the problem of "postexilic EBH," a term which the challengers would call the language of postexilic prophets such as Isaiah 40–66, Haggai, Zechariah, and Malachi.

The language of Isaiah 40–66, Haggai, Zechariah, and Malachi has long been considered to be similar to EBH. Martin Ehrensvärd, one of Hurvitz's prominent challengers, however, goes further and argues that their language *is* EBH, despite the books' postexilic provenance (and, in the case of Isaiah 40–55, late exilic).[7] His argument rests on the following points. First, using Hurvitz's own method of defining LBH, Ehrensvärd argues that "no clear LBH features are shown to occur in these books, and the limited number of LBH features that scholars point to in the books can at best only tentatively be ascribed to LBH." Second, even if we accept that there is a limited number of LBH features in these postexilic prophets, the texts should still be considered EBH texts because "EBH texts contain LBH features, occasionally even clear LBH features."[8] The implication is that EBH did not end with the exile, but was used alongside LBH during the postexilic period.

Hurvitz and the proponents of the chronological understanding of BH, on the other hand, argue that EBH did *not* coexist with LBH even for a short period. "When properly examined," Hurvitz declares, "the misleading 'classical' [i.e., EBH] appearance [of postexilic prophets] turns out to be nothing more than an external façade."[9] Books such as Haggai, Zechariah, and Malachi "*do* contain unmistakable imprints of Late Biblical Hebrew," however meager they are.[10] Therefore, for Hurvitz, EBH did not extend its life beyond the exilic period, and LBH completely replaced EBH at the start of the Second Temple period.

The debate between Hurvitz and his followers and Hurvitz's challengers will be treated more extensively in the next chapter. The main issue, however, is hinted at in the preceding paragraphs: that is, the distinction

---

and the Deuteronomistic History and the term LBH for the Hebrew style of undisputed postexilic books. See Young, Rezetko, and Ehrensvärd, *Linguistic Dating*, 1:4 and chapter 2 of the present study.

[7] Martin Ehrensvärd, "Linguistic Dating of Biblical Texts," in Young (ed.), *Biblical Hebrew*, 175–86.

[8] Ehrensvärd, "Linguistic Dating," 176.

[9] Hurvitz, "The Recent Debate on Late Biblical Hebrew: Solid Data, Experts' Opinions, and Inconclusive Arguments," *HS* 47 (2006): 204–5.

[10] Hurvitz, "Recent Debate," 206–7. Emphasis original.

between EBH and LBH is not one of exclusive choice but of *frequency* or *tendency*. Many, if not all, early texts *do* contain LBH features; *all* late texts preserve what Hurvitz and his followers would identify as EBH features. And the two groups of scholars disagree as to how much accumulation of LBH features is sufficient to make a text an LBH text or how little accumulation of LBH features is negligible so that a text may still be identified as an EBH text. For example, in the case discussed above, whereas one scholar sees "unmistakable imprints" of LBH in the postexilic prophets, the other considers the evidence "tentative" and thus to be dismissed. The decision of taking or dismissing the evidence is made by individual scholars rather than by formal criteria. Our question, therefore, is obvious. *Can we establish empirical criteria with which to evaluate the evidence of a mixed nature, that is to say, the evidence that is not categorical?*

2. *Variation and the Variationist Approach*

To begin with, it does not seem reasonable to choose 'yes' or 'no' for a problem that involves data that are not categorical (i.e., ambiguous). But is there a third way to tackle the problem? This is where I believe this study will make a contribution. Quite a few cases of the mixed use of EBH features and contrasting LBH features are summarized thus: meaning A is expressed by form B or form C; form B is used more frequently in preexilic literature and form C in postexilic literature. Accordingly, the traditionalists would understand that form B is a marker of EBH and form C a marker of LBH; the challengers, on the other hand, would argue that, since both forms were available through the biblical period, the relationship of the two forms is no more than a matter of free style. Let us take an example. The roots צעק and זעק express the same meaning "to cry (out)." Each of the two forms is found in both the earlier and the later biblical books. However, the earlier books use צעק more frequently than זעק, while the later books use זעק more frequently than צעק. The traditional understanding is that צעק is a marker of EBH and זעק a marker of LBH, whereas the challengers argue that the use of the two forms does not have any chronological implications.[11]

---

[11] See further chapter 5 for a more extensive analysis of צעק and זעק. There are other types of contrasts between EBH and LBH, as discussed by the advocates of linguistic dating. To take a few examples: (1) the usage or meaning of one word changed from EBH to LBH; (2) a word or expression that was absent from EBH was invented in or borrowed

This kind of relationship between the purported EBH feature and the purported LBH feature is a good example of *linguistic variation*.[12] A central subject matter of sociolinguistics, linguistic variation refers to the situation in which a linguistic item has alternate realizations that are linguistically (i.e., grammatically) equivalent. For example, one person may say "I am singing," and another may say "I am singin'"; or an individual may say "I don't know nothing" on one occasion, whereas on another occasion the same individual may say "I do not know anything." Each pair expresses grammatically identical meaning, although any native English speaker will be able to tell the social and stylistic (i.e., non-linguistic) differences between the first and the second sentences of each pair. The two forms of each pair constitute an example of linguistic variation.

Earlier linguists understood variation to be incoherent and confusing. They called it *free*, implying that variation was arbitrary and insignificant.[13] In today's linguistics, especially in sociolinguistics, however, a fresh view on linguistic variation has emerged and is gaining wider acceptance. Robert Bayley, a sociolinguist, states it lucidly:

> The central ideas of this approach [i.e., the variationist approach] are that an understanding of language requires an understanding of variable as well as categorical processes and that the variation that we witness at all levels of language is not random. Rather, linguistic variation is characterized by orderly or "structured heterogeneity." That is, speakers' choices between variable linguistic forms are systematically constrained by multiple linguistic and social factors that reflect underlying grammatical systems and that both reflect and partially constitute the social organization of the communities to which users of the language belong.[14]

Linguistic variation bears linguistic and social significance, and variation analysis (or the variationist approach) seeks to identify linguistic and social factors and conditions that are integral to the process of the

---

to LBH; and (3) a word or expression that was used in EBH disappeared from LBH. The present study chooses to examine only those cases in which one meaning is considered to be expressed by two different forms in accordance with the proposed linguistic shift from EBH to LBH. See further below for the rationale of this decision.

[12] For a fuller discussion of this term, see chapter 3 of the present study.

[13] R. L. Trask, *Historical Linguistics* (London: Arnold, 1996), 269.

[14] Robert Bayley, "The Quantitative Paradigm," in *The Handbook of Language Variation and Change* (ed. J. K. Chambers, Peter Trudgill, and Natalie Schilling-Estes; Malden, Mass.: Blackwell, 2002), 117. The idea of "orderly heterogeneity" was originally suggested by Uriel Weinreich, William Labov, and Marvin I. Herzog, "Empirical Foundations for a Theory of Language Change," in *Directions for Historical Linguistics: A Symposium* (ed. W. P. Lehmann and Yakov Malkiel; Austin: University of Texas Press, 1968), 95–195 (esp. 99–100).

speaker's choice of a variation. Conversely, given specific linguistic and social factors and conditions, variation analysis will explain the speaker's choice.[15]

I will devote more space to explicating this important subject in chapter 3, where I will discuss the method of the present study. In this introductory chapter, I will briefly illustrate how variation analysis can be helpful for understanding language. The following is a summary of a study by Peter Trudgill, who is one of the earliest sociolinguists.

3. *The Variationist Approach and the Variation* -ing *vs.* -in' *in Norwich*

Peter Trudgill, a British sociolinguist, conducted a wide-ranging investigation of variations in the speech of Norwich, England.[16] In one experiment, Trudgill looked at the variation between two types of pronunciation of the verb ending *-ing*. In Norwich, as elsewhere, the ending may be pronounced with the velar nasal, as in the word 'thing', or with the /n/ sound, typically spelled as *-in'*.

Trudgill collected data by tape-recording his subjects. In doing so, he used a special scheme. On the one hand, each subject was assigned to one of five classes: the *middle middle class* (MMC), the *lower middle class* (LMC), the *upper working class* (UWC), the *middle working class* (MWC), and the *lower working class* (LWC). On the other hand, each subject spoke and was recorded in four linguistically different contexts: *word-list speech* (WLS), in which the subject read aloud a list of written words, one at a time; *reading-passage speech* (RPS), in which the subject read aloud from a written text; *formal speech* (FS), the self-conscious speech of a formal interview; and *casual speech* (CS), in which the subject was engaging in ordinary, relaxed conversation.

Each subject used both pronunciations, and it was generally impossible to predict which style a speaker would use on the next occasion. However, when Trudgill sorted the data according to each class and each context, a striking pattern emerged (Table 1 and Figure 1).

---

[15] The two adjectives in the definition of the variationist approach—'linguistic' and 'social'—constitute, of course, the term 'sociolinguistics'. Thus Trask says, "Sociolinguistics may be usefully defined as the study of variation in language." Trask, *Historical Linguistics,* 269.

[16] Peter Trudgill, *The Social Differentiation of English in Norwich* (Cambridge Studies in Linguistics 13; Cambridge: Cambridge University Press, 1974). My presentation of Trudgill's study of *-ing* and *-in'* depends on Trask, *Historical Linguistics,* 277–78.

Table 1. The use of *-in'* in Norwich by class and style (percentages)

Style Class	WLS	RPS	FS	CS
MMC	0	0	3	28
LMC	0	10	15	42
UWC	5	15	74	87
MWC	23	44	88	95
LWC	29	66	98	100

Source: Trudgill, *Social Differentiation of English*, 92. Used by permission of Cambridge University Press.

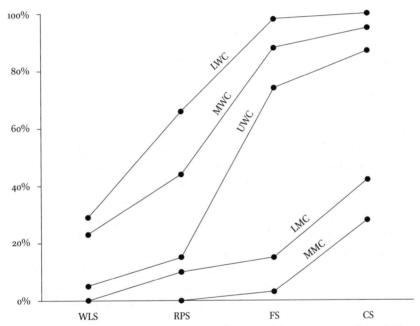

Source: Trudgill, *Social Differentiation of English*, 92. Used by permission of Cambridge University Press.

Figure 1. The use of *-in'* in Norwich by class and style (percentages)

Two observations may be made. First, all the subjects used a higher proportion of the *-in'* style as the context became more informal. Second, any given social group consistently used a higher proportion of the *-in'* style than another group of a socially higher class.[17]

---

[17] Trask, *Historical Linguistics*, 277–78.

The variation that seemed arbitrary as raw data reveals its linguistic and social significance when it is properly analyzed. In the above example, the probability of the speaker's choosing one style over another may be estimated if we know the speaker's social class and the degree of formality of the situation. Or, conversely, the percentage of the speaker's use of one style over the other hints at the speaker's social class and the context in which the speaker is speaking.

4. EBH, LBH, and the Variationist Approach: The Purpose and Outline of the Present Study

As we have seen briefly (and will see more extensively in the next chapter), at the center of the debate over the linguistic dating of biblical texts are the data that typically show variation between Early and Late Biblical Hebrew. This situation, I am convinced, fully warrants the employing of the variationist approach in the study of EBH and LBH. I believe that the linguistic variables in BH will be most adequately explained by the method that has been developed to explain linguistic variation in general.[18]

As far as I know, the present study is the first effort to apply the variationist approach to the study of BH. Thus, as a pilot study, its primary objective is not to evaluate *all* of the relevant data and announce a final verdict; rather, it is to establish a method, which may be employed by other scholars or refined further by them. Accordingly, in tackling the problem, I consider it more important to adhere strictly to the proposed procedure than to treat the subject extensively.[19] This does not mean, however, that I do not have anything to put forth for the present debate. The variationist approach I will use provides us with not only a fresh look but also an important potential solution to the seemingly irreconcilable debate.

The present study will proceed as follows.

The following chapter (ch. 2) is a survey of scholarship, which comprises three sections. In the first section, I will treat the work of the scholars before Hurvitz who looked at BH from a diachronic perspective.

---

[18] This point will be elaborated in chapter 3.

[19] An extensive discussion, and critique, of the issue of linguistic dating was helpfully done by Young, Rezetko, and Ehrensvärd, *Linguistic Dating* (above, n. 5). Cf. my survey of this work in chapter 2.

They should appropriately be understood to have laid the foundations for Hurvitz's enterprise of the linguistic dating of biblical texts. The middle section treats Hurvitz's establishment of his method and his own use of it in dating several biblical books and texts. This section also discusses the younger scholars who employed Hurvitz's method in their own work. In the last section, I will survey the challenges raised against Hurvitz. The challengers have objected both to the presuppositions upon which Hurvitz's method is based and to the method itself. We will also have an opportunity to survey Hurvitz's own responses to the challengers' arguments.

Chapter 3 establishes the method of the present study. This chapter is divided into three sections. The first section reviews the work of those Hebraists who have used sociolinguistic insights and methods in their study of Classical Hebrew. The second section discusses and expounds important sociolinguistic concepts that are foundational for the present study. These concepts include *linguistic variation, variation analysis* (or *the variationist approach*), and the discipline of *historical sociolinguistics*. This section also defends the application of the variationist approach to the Hebrew Bible corpus. In the third, last section, I will explain in detail how I will use the variationist approach in the analysis of the BH data. I will discuss what kind of data we will collect, how we will collect them, and how we will interpret them.

Upon the methodological foundations laid in chapter 3, chapters 4 and 5 attempt to make theoretical and empirical assessments of the two opposing views on the linguistic dating of biblical texts. Chapter 4 is a theoretical assessment, in which I will argue that the variationist understanding of linguistic change provides a tool with which to explain the biblical evidence that is not categorical (i.e., ambiguous). I will also argue that this understanding further provides a theoretical framework that can embrace the two seemingly irreconcilable opinions propounded by Hurvitz and by his challengers. Chapter 5 is an empirical assessment of the two opposing views. Here, I will do a sociolinguistic analysis of eight linguistic variables from the Hebrew Bible. For all of these linguistic variables, Hurvitz and his followers maintain that they are markers of the chronological shift from EBH to LBH, whereas the challengers argue that they are merely stylistic options. In each analysis, the data that are observed will be used to adjudicate between the two opposing arguments regarding the linguistic dating of BH texts.

The last chapter is a summary and conclusion of the present study.

CHAPTER TWO

LINGUISTIC DATING OF BIBLICAL HEBREW TEXTS:
A SURVEY OF SCHOLARSHIP

This chapter surveys scholarship on the diachronic approach to BH, with attention to the linguistic dating of BH texts. It will roughly follow a chronological scheme, with the discussion of Avi Hurvitz at the center. Hurvitz is the most important figure to consider on this subject, since he is thought to have perfected the method for the linguistic dating of BH texts. The main body of this chapter comprises three sections. The first section discusses the scholars whose works laid the foundations for Hurvitz's project. The second section treats Hurvitz, his method, and those who follow him. The third section surveys the recent challenges raised against Hurvitz and Hurvitz's responses to them. I will conclude the chapter by highlighting some basic issues in the current debate.

1. *Toward the Method: Scholarship before Avi Hurvitz*

Among those whose findings and achievements became foundational for Hurvitz, four scholars are important: Wilhelm Gesenius, S. R. Driver, Arno Kropat, and E. Y. Kutscher.

1.1. *Wilhelm Gesenius*

Wilhelm Gesenius is noted for freeing the study of Hebrew from theological considerations.[1] His works pioneered the diachronic study of BH, and so paved the way for the linguistic dating of BH texts. For example, Gesenius surveys the history of the Hebrew language in his *Geschichte der hebräischen Sprache und Schrift* (1815), which Mark F. Rooker considers to be the beginning of a diachronic approach to BH.[2]

---

[1] Irene Garbell, "Gesenius, Heinrich Friedrich Wilhelm," *EncJud*² 7: 562.

[2] Wilhelm Gesenius, *Geschichte der hebräischen Sprache und Schrift: Eine philologisch-historische Einleitung in die Sprachlehren und Wörterbücher der hebräischen Sprache* (Leipzig: F. C. W. Vogel, 1815; repr., New York: G. Olms, 1973). See also Mark F. Rooker, *Biblical Hebrew in Transition: The Language of the Book of Ezekiel* (JSOTSup 90; Sheffield: JSOT Press, 1990), 27.

   In this work, two points are important to our discussion. First, Gesenius
notes in BH two distinct layers, which fall into two successive periods: one
used before the exile, the other during and after the exile.[3] He believes
that BH changed through time and that late Hebrew differed from early
Hebrew in grammar, vocabulary, orthography, and style. Thus, in analyzing
the language of the later books in the Hebrew Bible, Gesenius points out
the linguistic features that he believes to be late. Second, as for method,
Gesenius emphasizes the importance of parallel passages in observing the
late features of BH. For example, he believes that one might find the characteristics of late Hebrew by analyzing the passages in Chronicles that
are parallel to the ones in Samuel–Kings, because the Chronicler replaced
earlier expressions and spellings in Samuel–Kings, which had become difficult and rare in his own day, with more commonly used later forms.[4]

   To the eye of today's student, it is clear how Gesenius's contribution
has stood the test of time. Not only did the above two points become
foundational for the studies that soon followed Gesenius's, but they are
still so for many of today's studies.

1.2. *S. R. Driver*

By the beginning of the twentieth century, a few scholars continued Gesenius's research and studied BH from a diachronic perspective.[5] Representative is an extensive study by S. R. Driver. In his *Introduction* (first edition
in 1891), Driver pays close attention to the language of each book in the
Hebrew Bible.[6] He notes that the style of earlier books is contrasted with
the style of postexilic books such as Ezra, Nehemiah, Malachi, Chronicles,
Esther, Daniel, and Ecclesiastes:

> The purest and best Hebrew prose style is that of JE and the earlier narra-
> tives incorporated in Jud. Sam. Kings: Dt. (though of a different style) is also
> thoroughly classical: Jer., the *latter* part of Kings, Ezekiel, II Isaiah, Haggai,
> show (though not all in the same respects or in the same degree) *slight* signs
> of being later than the writings first mentioned; but in the "memoirs" of Ezra
> and Nehemiah (*i.e.* the parts of Ezra and Neh. which are the work of these
> reformers themselves) and (in a less degree) in the contemporary prophecy

---

[3] Gesenius, *Geschichte*, 21.
[4] Gesenius, *Geschichte*, 37–40.
[5] See a brief survey in Rooker, *Biblical Hebrew in Transition*, 28.
[6] S. R. Driver, *An Introduction to the Literature of the Old Testament*. My citations are
from Driver, *An Introduction to the Literature of the Old Testament* (new edition revised
1913; New York: Charles Scribner's Sons, 1914).

of Malachi, a more marked change is beginning to show itself, which is still more palpable in the Chronicles (c. 300 B.C.), Esther, and Ecclesiastes. The change is visible in both vocabulary and syntax.[7]

Driver observes the following changes in vocabulary and syntax. In vocabulary, new words infiltrated, "often of Aramaic origin, occasionally Persian," and some existing words acquired new meanings or applications. In syntax, "the ease and grace and fluency of the earlier writers (down to at least Zech. 12–14) has passed away," and "the style is often laboured and inelegant," with "new and uncouth constructions."[8]

Driver explicitly locates the point of division between the two types of BH in the age of Nehemiah. The basis for this argument is the language of Zechariah, an early postexilic book, whose style is "singularly pure." He notes that the diction of Zechariah 12–14 very much resembles that of Amos.[9]

In short, Driver corroborates Gesenius's chronological division of two types of BH by making an extensive analysis of the language of each book in the Hebrew Bible. At the same time, he argues that the divide between the early style and the late one falls in the fifth century B.C.E.

1.3. Arno Kropat

Although Gesenius and Driver studied biblical language and literature with an interest in linguistic diachrony and thus frequently pointed out differences between what we may call Early Biblical Hebrew (= EBH) and Late Biblical Hebrew (= LBH), their purpose was not to present a systematic description of EBH or of LBH. Such a description, however, is necessary for the linguistic dating of BH texts, because only a fuller picture of either EBH or LBH (or both) may provide us with reliable criteria against which to date a chronologically problematic text. In this sense, Arno Kropat's study of the Chronicler's syntax in 1909 moved scholarship a step forward.[10] The purpose of Kropat's study is to analyze the syntax of the books of Chronicles, Ezra, and Nehemiah and to compare it with the

---

[7] Driver, *Introduction*, 505. Emphasis original.

[8] Driver, *Introduction*, 505.

[9] Driver, *Introduction*, 505 n.

[10] Arno Kropat, *Die Syntax des Autors der Chronik verglichen mit der seiner Quellen: Ein Beitrag zur historischen Syntax des Hebräischen* (BZAW 16; Giessen: Alfred Töpelmann, 1909).

earlier books in the Hebrew Bible.[11] As a result, Kropat is able to specify the features that would indicate LBH.

We should note two characteristics in Kropat's treatment of the Chronicler's language. On the one hand, when he analyzes it, Kropat uses both synoptic and non-synoptic passages. This will become a matter of disagreement among later scholars.[12] On the other, Kropat believes that the Chronicler's *Vorlage* was the proto-Masoretic text of Samuel–Kings, which was more or less the same as the Masoretic Text (= MT) of Samuel–Kings. Today, this belief may be problematic because we now have evidence that the text of Samuel–Kings that the Chronicler used was not the same as the present MT of Samuel–Kings.[13]

1.4. *E. Y. Kutscher*

The great discovery of the Dead Sea Scrolls (= DSS) in 1947 radically changed the diachronic study of Hebrew in general and the study of LBH in particular. The discovery filled what was once a gap in the history of the Hebrew language: a period between BH and Mishnaic Hebrew (= MH), which extends from the middle of the second half of the first century B.C.E. to the end of the second century C.E.[14] The most important scholar in the early study of Qumran Hebrew (= QH) was E. Y. Kutscher. His works that are relevant to our discussion include a study of the Isaiah Scroll (Hebrew original, 1959; English translation, 1974), an article on the language of the DSS (1972), and a posthumously published monograph on the history of the Hebrew language (1982).[15]

Kutscher's contribution to our subject may be summarized in two points. First, the main thesis of his monograph on the Isaiah Scroll is

---

[11] Kropat, *Syntax der Chronik*, v.

[12] For example, Robert Polzin excludes synoptic passages in examining the Chronicler's language, whereas Hurvitz uses them. See further below.

[13] For example, Sara Japhet argues that "as far as the 'textual variants' go, Chronicles may reflect a better reading than the MT of its source, implying that the corruption or redactions of Samuel–Kings attested by the MT occurred either later than the Chronicler's use of his *Vorlage*, or in a different textual tradition" (Japhet, *I and II Chronicles: A Commentary* [OTL; Louisville, Ky.: Westminster/John Knox, 1993], 28). See further Japhet, *Chronicles*, 28–29.

[14] E. Y. Kutscher, "Hebrew Language, the Dead Sea Scrolls," *EncJud²* 8:635.

[15] Kutscher, *The Language and Linguistic Background of the Isaiah Scroll (1QIsaᵃ)* (STDJ 6; Leiden: Brill, 1974; Hebrew original published in 1959); idem, "Hebrew Language, the Dead Sea Scrolls," *EncJud²* 8:634–49 (the article originally published in the first edition in 1972); and idem, *A History of the Hebrew Language* (ed. Raphael Kutscher; Jerusalem: Magnes, 1982).

that the language of 1QIsa[a], which more or less represents QH, reflects the contemporary Hebrew and Aramaic spoken in the region.[16] In other words, Kutscher argues that, although it functioned as a literary vehicle, the language of the Isaiah scroll (and thus QH) was not an artificial language but rather included aspects of the living language. This leads to our second point, which concerns the elements that constituted QH. Kutscher discerns three major elements in QH: (1) BH (including both "Basic" BH, found mainly in the Pentateuch, and LBH); (2) Imperial Aramaic, which had become the lingua franca of the Near East and also the vernacular of the whole of Syria-Palestine and which influenced the development of Hebrew; and (3) vernacular Hebrew, which later became MH and which increasingly infiltrated literary Hebrew.[17] By saying that BH is one element of QH, Kutscher suggests continuity between the two.[18]

2. *The Method Established:*
Robert Polzin, Avi Hurvitz, and the Followers

The 1970s mark a new phase in the diachronic study of BH: Robert Polzin published a revision of his dissertation on the typology of the language of P,[19] and Avi Hurvitz embarked on the project to which he would dedicate his entire career, that is, the diachronic study of BH.[20] Their works are pioneering for the following two reasons. First, the primary purpose of their studies was, for the first time, to date biblical material on the basis of linguistic data. Second, as they sought to achieve this goal, they worked on establishing rigorous methods. Indeed, the methods developed by these two scholars have since been employed by a younger generation. Here I discuss Polzin first and then Hurvitz.[21]

---

[16] Kutscher, *Isaiah Scroll*, 3.

[17] Kutscher, "Hebrew Language," 8:635; idem, *Isaiah Scroll*, 23–44.

[18] The continuity between BH and QH is the grounds for one of the three criteria of Hurvitz's method (i.e., the criterion of *extrabiblical sources*). See below for Hurvitz's method.

[19] Robert Polzin, *Late Biblical Hebrew: Toward an Historical Typology of Biblical Hebrew Prose* (HSM 12; Missoula, Mont.: Scholars, 1976).

[20] See below for his works.

[21] This is despite the fact that Hurvitz's earliest publications in our subject predate Polzin's monograph. Discussing Hurvitz after Polzin is more convenient because Hurvitz has extended the diachronic method and continues to contribute to the discussion.

2.1. *Robert Polzin and His Influence*

The purpose of Polzin's *Late Biblical Hebrew* is "to characterize the typological nature of P's language" in terms of its relationship to Classical
Biblical Hebrew (= CBH), on the one hand, and to LBH, on the other.[22]
To accomplish this purpose, Polzin proceeds in two stages: he identifies
the features of LBH and then compares P's language with them. To make
a list of LBH features, Polzin analyzes the Chronicler's language, which
he believes is representative of LBH, in comparison with samples of CBH
that he has taken from JE (from Exodus and Numbers), the Court History
(2 Sam 13–20; 1 Kgs 1), and Deuteronomy.[23] As a result, Polzin proposes 19
features that are typical of LBH, of which six are attributable to the influence of Aramaic.[24] Having the 19 features as standards, Polzin examines
the language of P. He concludes that the language of P, in its typology, is
located between CBH and LBH. This suggests that P should be dated to
the transitional period between CBH and LBH, that is, the exilic period.[25]

---

[22] Polzin, *Late Biblical Hebrew*, 1. For most scholars, the term 'Classical Biblical Hebrew'
(= CBH) is interchangeable with EBH and Standard BH. See below, p. 19 n. 36.

[23] Polzin, *Late Biblical Hebrew*, 91; for the complete list of passages taken from the
above sources, see Polzin, *Late Biblical Hebrew*, 117–18 nn. 10–13.

[24] The following are the LBH grammatical features that Polzin has identified on the
basis of the Chronicler's language. First, the features that are not attributable to Aramaic
influence: A.1. the radically reduced use of אֵת with pronominal suffix; A.2. the increased
use of אֶת before noun in the nominative case (i.e., אֶת emphatic); A.3. the expression of
possession by prospective pronominal suffix with a following noun, or לְ + noun, or שֶׁל +
noun; A.4. collective nouns construed as plurals; A.5. a preference for plural forms of
words and phrases which the earlier language uses in the singular; A.6. the rare use of
an infinitive absolute in conjunction with the finite form of the same verb and the non-
use of the infinitive absolute as a command; A.7. the reduced use of בְּ/כְּ + the infinitive
construct (and even when it is used, it shows a different usage from the earlier language);
A.8. the repetition of a singular word (i.e., Latin *quivis*); A.9. the use of the third-person
masculine plural suffix for the third-person feminine plural; A.10. almost no use of the
first-person singular imperfect with הָ◌- (the lengthened imperfect or cohortative); A.11.
the reduced use of וַיְהִי; A.12. a substantive placed before a numeral and used in the plural;
and A.13. the increased use of the infinitive construct with לְ. Second, the features that
were caused by Aramaic influence: B.1. the word order of material measured + its measure
(+ number); B.2. לְ used as mark of the accusative; B.3. the non-assimilation of נ in מִן before
a noun without an article; B.4. the use of לְ emphatic before the last element of a list; B.5.
the attributive use of רַבִּים before the substantive; and B.6. the use of עַד לְ. Polzin, *Late
Biblical Hebrew*, 28–69.

[25] Polzin, *Late Biblical Hebrew*, 112. In his work, Polzin distinguishes two layers in P,
following the consensus. The earlier layer, Pᵍ, is the groundwork of P, and the later layer,
Pˢ, is secondary additions or extensions to Pᵍ (Polzin, *Late Biblical Hebrew*, 87–88).
The following is a summary of Polzin's typology of the Hebrew prose (adapted from
Polzin, *Late Biblical Hebrew*, 112):

For the present discussion, I highlight the following in Polzin's approach. First, although Polzin agrees with Kropat that the Chronicler's language is representative of LBH, he disagrees with him with regard to the value of the synoptic passages and thus excludes them from his analysis. By doing so, Polzin believed he could penetrate to the Chronicler's actual language and avoid studying the language of the Chronicler's "sources."[26] Second, Polzin excludes lexical data from his analysis and uses only grammatical-syntactical ones, because he thinks the latter are more reliable and efficient than the former.[27]

Several scholars have subsequently criticized some details of Polzin's method and results.[28] Nevertheless, Polzin's typology of BH was a significant advance in the diachronic study of BH and a major breakthrough in the linguistic dating of BH texts. Indeed, it provided foundations for scholars such as Allen R. Guenther, Andrew E. Hill, and Mark F. Rooker. Guenther's dissertation analyzes and compares the syntax of the prose in Jeremiah 37–45 and Esther 1–10.[29] While he innovatively incorporates linguistic theories in his study, Guenther also juxtaposes the results of his analysis of the language of Jeremiah and Esther with Polzin's typology of BH prose. Hill uses Polzin's method and results more actively in his dissertation and short studies.[30] Hill employs Polzin's LBH features to decide whether the language of Haggai, Zechariah, and Malachi is closer to EBH

JE		no	the EBH corpus.
The Court History		no	the EBH corpus.
Deuteronomy	*shows*	no	*LBH features,*	the EBH corpus.
Pg		4	*so it belongs to*	the transitional phase.
Ps		8		the transitional phase.
Chronicles		13		the LBH corpus.

[26] Polzin, *Late Biblical Hebrew*, 12.

[27] Polzin, *Late Biblical Hebrew*, 15–16, 124. Although this is his belief, Polzin appreciates the value of a serious lexical study such as Hurvitz's. He himself offers a list of the Chronicler's lexical features in a separate chapter. See Polzin, *Late Biblical Hebrew*, 123–58.

[28] For reviews and critiques of Polzin, *Late Biblical Hebrew*, see Gary A. Rendsburg, "Late Biblical Hebrew and the Date of 'P'" (review of Polzin, *Late Biblical Hebrew*), *JANESCU* 12 (1980): 65–80; Ziony Zevit, "Converging Lines of Evidence Bearing on the Date of P," *ZAW* 94 (1982): 493–501; Hurvitz, *A Linguistic Study of the Relationship between the Priestly Source and the Book of Ezekiel: A New Approach to an Old Problem* (CahRB 20; Paris: J. Gabalda, 1982), 163–70; and Rooker, *Biblical Hebrew in Transition*, 35–53.

[29] Allen R. Guenther, "A Diachronic Study of Biblical Hebrew Prose Syntax: An Analysis of the Verbal Clause in Jeremiah 37–45 and Esther 1–10" (Ph.D. diss., University of Toronto, 1977).

[30] Andrew E. Hill, "The Book of Malachi: Its Place in Post-Exilic Chronology Linguistically Reconsidered" (Ph.D. diss., University of Michigan, 1981); idem, "Dating the Book of Malachi: A Linguistic Reexamination," in *The Word of the Lord Shall Go Forth: Essays in Honor of David Noel Freedman in Celebration of His Sixtieth Birthday* (ed. Carol L. Meyers

or to LBH. On the basis of his linguistic analysis that has been modeled after Polzin's typology, Hill concludes that Haggai, Zechariah, and Malachi chronologically come close to the earlier layer of P.[31] Rooker also employs Polzin's results as his starting point.[32] Rooker's work will be treated after the following section since it is also under Hurvitz's influence.

2.2. *Avi Hurvitz and His Method*

Avi Hurvitz is the most prominent and influential figure in the subject of the linguistic dating of BH texts on account of the amount, scope, and depth of his works. A student of Kutscher, Hurvitz started publishing his works in the 1960s.[33] Since the completion and publication of his doctoral dissertation in 1972, he has devoted himself exclusively to the diachronic study of BH.[34] Hurvitz's contribution to our subject is unique, different from both his predecessors' and Polzin's. This is because Hurvitz's most significant contribution lies not in providing data and results but in establishing methods, which are productive and replicable, of defining LBH features and texts. We will discuss his method below; before we do so, however, we should first note the presuppositions on which Hurvitz bases his method. Four will be treated, three of which Hurvitz inherited from his predecessors.

The presuppositions. First, Hurvitz, following Gesenius, Driver, Kutscher, and others, recognizes *linguistic heterogeneity* within BH. Thus Hurvitz accepts that the main body of BH falls into two types: the first type, which comprises the greater part of the Hebrew Bible, is defined mainly with the prose of the Pentateuch and the Deuteronomistic History (= DtrH); the other type is defined mainly with the prose sections of the books composed during the Second Temple period (importantly, Esther, Daniel, Ezra, Nehemiah, and Chronicles).[35]

---

and M. O'Connor; Winona Lake, Ind.: Eisenbrauns, 1983), 77–89; and idem, "Dating Second Zechariah: A Linguistic Reexamination," *HAR* 6 (1982): 105–34.

[31] Hill, "Dating Malachi," 82–83. For Polzin's division of P's layers, see above, p. 16 n. 25. For a brief discussion of Guenther's and Hill's studies, see Ian Young, Robert Rezetko, and Martin Ehrensvärd, *Linguistic Dating of Biblical Texts* (2 vols.; London: Equinox, 2008), 1:27–29.

[32] Rooker, *Biblical Hebrew in Transition* (above, n. 2).

[33] One of Hurvitz's earliest works is "The Usage of שש and בוץ in the Bible and Its Implications for the Date of P," *HTR* 60 (1967): 117–21.

[34] Rooker, *Biblical Hebrew in Transition*, 30. Hurvitz's dissertation has been published as *The Transition Period in Biblical Hebrew: A Study in Post-Exilic Hebrew and Its Implications for the Dating of Psalms* (Jerusalem: Bialik, 1972; in Hebrew).

[35] This is in accord with Kutscher's division of BH. See Kutscher, *History*, 12. See also Hurvitz, *Priestly Source and Ezekiel*, 157–59; idem, "Continuity and Innovation in Biblical

Second, Hurvitz, like his predecessors, believes that the typological division of BH reflects the *chronological development* of BH: hence the name EBH for the style of the Pentateuch and DtrH, and LBH for the style of some postexilic books.[36] This is supported by biblical and extrabiblical evidence. As we have seen, scholars have defined EBH mainly on the basis of the earlier books (e.g., the Pentateuch and DtrH) and LBH mainly with postexilic books (e.g., Esther–Chronicles). Also, Hurvitz argues that extrabiblical sources serve as an external control for the periodization of BH. Regarding EBH, Hurvitz maintains that, "by and large, there is a far-reaching linguistic uniformity underlying both the pre-exilic inscriptions and the literary biblical texts written in classical BH."[37] For LBH, Hurvitz holds that it has continuity with Hebrew and Aramaic sources such as the DSS, the fragments of Ben Sira, the letters of Bar Kokhba, the corpus in MH, and the literature in Imperial Aramaic in the Persian period.[38]

Hebrew: The Case of 'Semantic Change' in Post-Exilic Writing," in *Studies in Ancient Hebrew Semantics* (ed. T. Muraoka; AbrNSup 4; Leuven: Peeters, 1995), 2–4; Susan Anne Groom, *Linguistic Analysis of Biblical Hebrew* (Carlisle, Cumbria: Paternoster, 2003), 31–35; and Young, Rezetko, and Ehrensvärd, *Linguistic Dating*, 1:7–8.

As is well known, there is yet a third linguistic layer, which is distinct from both these styles. Archaic Biblical Hebrew (= ABH) is the Hebrew of a few poems preserved in the Pentateuch and DtrH (e.g., Gen 49; Exod 15; Deut 32; and Judg 5). Archaic BH is not our immediate concern because the corpus's small size limits its usefulness for the purpose of dating. For the definition of ABH, see Kutscher, *History*, 79–80, and cf. Angel Sáenz-Badillos, *A History of the Hebrew Language* (trans. John Elwolde; Cambridge: Cambridge University Press, 1993), 56–62; Groom, *Linguistic Analysis*, 31–33. A new work came out most recently on the dating of ABH poetry. See Robyn C. Vern, *Dating Archaic Biblical Hebrew Poetry: A Critique of the Linguistic Arguments* (Perspectives on Hebrew Scriptures and Its Contexts 10; Piscataway, N.J.: Gorgias, 2011), who argues that linguistic data may not be considered to be reliable criteria for the dating of ABH poetry. I thank Christl M. Maier for bringing this work to my attention.

[36] Originally, Kutscher calls the Hebrew of preexilic prose Standard Biblical Hebrew (= SBH), instead of EBH. Thus his tripartite division of BH presents ABH (above, n. 35), SBH, and LBH (Kutscher, *History*, 12). Standard Biblical Hebrew is also called Classical Biblical Hebrew (= CBH; Hurvitz, *Priestly Source and Ezekiel*, 157). According to this scheme, EBH should cover both ABH, the Hebrew of some preexilic poems, and SBH (or CBH), the Hebrew of the prose in the Pentateuch and DtrH (Ian Young, "Introduction: The Origin of the Problem," in *Biblical Hebrew: Studies in Chronology and Typology* [ed. Ian Young; JSOTSup 369; London: T&T Clark, 2003], 3–4). In this study, however, I consider EBH generally interchangeable with SBH and CBH, first, because ABH comprises a very small portion of the BH material and the great bulk of EBH is SBH (or CBH), and, second, because our primary concern in this study does not lie in the archaic poems written in ABH but in the distinction between preexilic Hebrew and postexilic Hebrew.

[37] Hurvitz, "The Historical Quest for 'Ancient Israel' and the Linguistic Evidence of the Hebrew Bible: Some Methodological Observations," *VT* 47 (1997): 308.

[38] Hurvitz, "Historical Quest," 310–11. Likewise, Hurvitz, "Continuity and Innovation," 2–3.

Third, Hurvitz, following his predecessors, believes that the watershed moment in the development of BH falls in *the exilic period*.[39] So Hurvitz writes as follows:

> Since it is precisely the biblical compositions undisputedly dated to the post-exilic era (like Ezra, Nehemiah, Daniel, Esther, Chronicles) which exhibit the greatest departures from Standard BH, it was only natural to associate this linguistic change with the particular historical circumstances of that time: i.e., the impact of the disaster ensuing on the fall of Jerusalem in 586 B.C.E. The far-reaching consequences of this disaster affected every aspect of Jewish life in post-exilic times—political, social, cultural, and religious. The linguistic transition discernible within the classical tradition of BH, specifically in the later parts of the Old Testament, has therefore been regarded as part and parcel of that general comprehensive transformation.[40]

Thus Hurvitz offers a sociohistorical explanation for the change from EBH to LBH. In linguistic terms, Hurvitz understands the change as an example of "languages in contact."[41] During the exile, EBH was exposed to Aramaic, which had become the lingua franca of the region and which was ever expanding its influence. After the exile, the Hebrew language entered a new phase, that is, LBH, whose difference from EBH is "recognizable" with "innovative elements" or "neologisms," which "betray deviations from the classical forms" of EBH.[42]

---

[39] See, for example, Gesenius, *Geschichte*, 21; Kutscher, *History*, 71–73, 81. So Sáenz-Badillos, *History*, 112–16. Cf., however, Driver's opinion on this (above, p. 13).

[40] Hurvitz, "The Relevance of Biblical Hebrew Linguistics for the Historical Study of Ancient Israel," in *Proceedings of the Twelfth World Congress of Jewish Studies, Jerusalem, July 29–August 5, 1997: Division A: The Bible and Its World* (ed. Ron Margolin; Jerusalem: World Union of Jewish Studies, 1999), 26*.

[41] Hurvitz, "Relevance of BH Linguistics," 28*.

[42] Hurvitz, "Continuity and Innovation," 3. See also, idem, "Hebrew and Aramaic in the Biblical Period: The Problem of 'Aramaisms' in Linguistic Research on the Hebrew Bible," in Young (ed.), *Biblical Hebrew*, 33–34. Consequently, LBH is defined by "neologisms" more than anything else—regardless of the obvious diversity within the LBH corpus. Hurvitz writes, "Yet, Late Biblical Hebrew is by no means a uniform linguistic entity or a consistent 'dialect.' Rather, it ought to be viewed as a *repertoire of post-classical neologisms* of which late biblical writers availed themselves—although the way in which those late elements were used and the degree to which they appear vary from one composition to another." Hurvitz, "The Recent Debate on Late Biblical Hebrew: Solid Data, Experts' Opinions, and Inconclusive Arguments," *HS* 47 (2006): 209. Emphasis original.

Hurvitz's dual explanation (i.e., linguistic and sociopolitical) for the change from EBH to LBH may be supported with comparative evidence. For example, in the history of English, the divide between Old English and Middle English is explained by the Norman conquest in 1066 C.E., which was followed by the influential influx of the French language. See, for example, Elly van Gelderen, *A History of the English Language* (Amsterdam: John Benjamins, 2006), 10.

Further, according to Hurvitz, the contact between preexilic Hebrew and Aramaic during the exilic period brought *irreversible change* to the former. After the exile, the speakers of Hebrew were no longer able to speak preexilic Hebrew, and the biblical authors were not able to "accurately reproduce the outdated style of Classical/Standard BH." They may have tried to do so, but they always betray "their own linguistic background," that is, the diction of LBH.[43] The linguistic dating of biblical texts thus becomes possible.

Last, the fourth presupposition of Hurvitz's method is his insistence on *the use of the* MT as the ground on which the study of BH must properly take place. By working exclusively from the MT without emendation, he argues, one avoids conjectures and speculations. Hurvitz is of course aware that the MT is subject to corruptions in its transmission. Nevertheless, as a methodological principle, Hurvitz believes that a linguistic study should be based on "*actual* texts" rather than on "*reconstructed* texts." As Hurvitz notes, the latter may be easier to work with, but we do not know whether or not they ever existed.[44]

The method. Now we turn to Hurvitz's method of defining an LBH feature.[45] A linguistic feature is defined as belonging to LBH if it meets the following three criteria: *linguistic distribution, linguistic contrast,* and *extrabiblical sources.*

The first criterion, *linguistic distribution,* requires that the linguistic feature in question should occur exclusively or mainly in undisputed postexilic books such as Esther, Daniel, Ezra, Nehemiah, and Chronicles. If the feature occurs in only one book, we cannot rule out the possibility that it belongs to the diction of the individual author. If the feature is distributed through all or most of these books, we may understand that it was used by postexilic writers in general.

Meeting the above criterion, however, does not prove that the feature was newly invented in the postexilic period. Possibly the preexilic writers

---

[43] Hurvitz, "Can Biblical Texts Be Dated Linguistically? Chronological Perspectives in the Historical Study of Biblical Hebrew," in *Congress Volume, Oslo 1998* (ed. André Lemaire and Magne Saebø; VTSup 80; Leiden: Brill, 2000), 154.

[44] Hurvitz, *Priestly Source and Ezekiel,* 19. Emphasis original. Hurvitz's presuppositions are more extensively treated in Young, Rezetko, and Ehrensvärd, *Linguistic Dating,* 1:12–18.

[45] Hurvitz's own discussion of his method is found in Hurvitz, "Linguistic Criteria for Dating Problematic Biblical Texts," *HA* 14 (1973): 74–79. See also the treatment by Young, Rezetko, and Ehrensvärd in their *Linguistic Dating,* 1:20–23.

just did not have an occasion to use this item. To rule out such a possibility, one needs the second criterion, *linguistic contrast* (or *opposition*). That is, the feature in question should be contrasted with an EBH counterpart that has a similar meaning and is used in a similar context.

The third criterion, although logically not necessary, strengthens the case. It stipulates that the word, expression, or structure in question should also be found in contemporary or later *extrabiblical sources*, which include the corpora from the DSS, MH, and contemporary Imperial Aramaic, the last of which, although not a Hebrew dialect, had a great influence on many of the innovations that occurred in LBH.

Let us take an example from the book of Ezekiel. In Ezek 13:9, there is the lexeme כְּתָב "writing, record." Is the word an LBH item? First, the lexeme meets the criterion of linguistic distribution, since it is found in Esther, Daniel, Ezra, Nehemiah, and Chronicles. Second, it satisfies the criterion of linguistic contrast, since in earlier books, the same or a similar meaning is expressed by סֵפֶר or מִכְתָּב. Third, כְּתָב is found in the DSS (1Q34 3 III, 7), Ben Sira (e.g., 39:32; 44:5), and MH (*m. Šabb.* 12:5), thus meeting the criterion of extrabiblical sources. Therefore, the lexeme כְּתָב in Ezekiel may safely be identified as an LBH feature.[46]

Working with the above three criteria, then, one is able to argue that a word, expression, or structure is a marker of LBH. This does not, however, prove that the book or text that contains this feature is an LBH text. In order to argue that a *book* or *text* is written in LBH, Hurvitz adds a fourth criterion, that the text should demonstrate an *accumulation* of LBH features.

Before we end our discussion of Hurvitz's method, we should note two points in his method that are contrasted with Polzin's approach. First, whereas Polzin's analysis of the Chronicler's language excludes the synoptic passages, Hurvitz includes them in collecting the features of LBH.[47] Second, Hurvitz does not hold that grammatical-syntactical data are more

---

[46] Rooker, *Biblical Hebrew in Transition*, 139–40. One might object that the EBH writers knew the form כְּתָב but just did not have a chance to use it, especially since the root כתב was well-known through the entire biblical period. This situation is theoretically possible, but is practically excluded with the criterion of linguistic contrast: that is, the evidence suggests that the EBH writers used סֵפֶר or מִכְתָּב *instead of* כְּתָב, when expressing the same or a similar concept.

[47] It is important to note, however, that the two scholars' modi operandi do not in principle contradict each other. Polzin tries to *describe* LBH; so for him, an ideal text would be one without any possible interference from the language of his sources. On the other hand, Hurvitz tries to *collect* and *identify* linguistic contrasts that may reflect a possible change in postexilic Hebrew. If a difference is found between the Chronicler's wording

objective and reliable than lexical data. In fact, much of Hurvitz's important evidence is lexical.[48]

2.3. *Studies That Employ Hurvitz's Method*

Following the establishment of Hurvitz's method, many studies have been produced that attempt to date biblical texts on linguistic grounds. Hurvitz himself has been productive, and many younger scholars have followed him.

Hurvitz has published monographs and essays that analyze the language of P, Ezekiel, Psalms, Job, and Ecclesiastes. Regarding P and Ezekiel, which are related thematically, he demonstrates that when the two have linguistically contrasted forms, Ezekiel always uses a postexilic form while P always uses a preexilic form. This enables Hurvitz to argue that P is linguistically earlier than Ezekiel and therefore preexilic.[49] Regarding the Psalter, Hurvitz argues that some psalms are very likely to be postexilic and that some others are possibly so.[50] As for Job, its prose sections betray

---

and that of his biblical sources, it is likely to have resulted from the Chronicler's use of his own diction.

[48] Rezetko, one of Hurvitz's challengers, has criticized Hurvitz's heavy use of lexical data; Hurvitz later responds to him. See further below.

[49] Hurvitz, *Priestly Source and Ezekiel*, 170. Dating P on linguistic grounds is a hotly debated subject that calls for a separate study. See the various works by Hurvitz in the bibliography. Against Hurvitz's preexilic dating of P, see Joseph Blenkinsopp, "An Assessment of the Alleged Pre-Exilic Date of the Priestly Material in the Pentateuch," *ZAW* 108 (1996): 495–518; Frank H. Polak, "Parameters for Stylistic Analysis of Biblical Hebrew Prose Texts," in *Bible and Computer: The Stellenbosch AIBI-6 Conference: Proceedings of the Association Internationale Bible et Informatique "From Alpha to Byte": University of Stellenbosch, 17–21 July, 2000* (ed. Johann Cook; Leiden: Brill, 2002), 277–79 (esp. 279). Cf. Baruch A. Levine, who, though not addressing Hurvitz directly, also argues for the Persian provenance of some of P's terms: Levine, "Late Language in the Priestly Source: Some Literary and Historical Observations," in *Proceedings of the Eighth World Congress of Jewish Studies, Jerusalem, August 16–21, 1981: Panel Sessions: Bible Studies and Hebrew Language* (Jerusalem: World Union of Jewish Studies, 1983), 69–82. Advocating P's antiquity on linguistic grounds, some scholars have responded to Blenkinsopp's aforementioned article: Jacob Milgrom, "The Antiquity of the Priestly Source: A Reply to Joseph Blenkinsopp," *ZAW* 111 (1999): 10–22; Hurvitz, "Once Again: The Linguistic Profile of the Priestly Material in the Pentateuch and Its Historical Age: A Response to J. Blenkinsopp," *ZAW* 112 (2000): 180–91; and Rendsburg, "Once More the Dual: With Replies to J. Blau and J. Blenkinsopp," *ANES* 38 (2001): 35–39. Milgrom argues for P's antiquity also in his commentary on Leviticus. For his discussion of linguistic evidence, see Milgrom, *Leviticus 1–16: A New Translation with Introduction and Commentary* (AB 3; New York: Doubleday, 1991), 3–8.

[50] The following psalms are very likely to be postexilic: Ps 103; 117; 119; 124–125; 133; 145. The psalms that are possible, though not certain, to be postexilic include Ps 19; 28; 33; 40; 45; 63; 75; 104; 106–107; 109; 111–113; 116; 126; 128; 135; 137; 143; 146–148. Hurvitz, *Transition Period*, 70–176.

a late date.[51] As for Ecclesiastes, although it shows many peculiarities that may not be explained in chronological terms, its final form shows "distinctive isoglosses" with the texts from the Second Temple period.[52]

Ronald L. Bergey uses Hurvitz's method faithfully in his dissertation on Esther.[53] Bergey presents "a diachronic analysis of selected grammatical and lexical features" of the book of Esther, which he designates as "a post-exilic Hebrew prose composition."[54] After analyzing 22 grammatical and 36 lexical features in Esther, Bergey concludes that "the Book of Esther's place in the linguistic milieu of post-exilic BH prose appears to be closer to the latter part of the post-exilic literary spectrum than to the earlier."[55]

Mark F. Rooker's dissertation on the language of Ezekiel is important for its position on the scholarly spectrum.[56] In this work, Rooker critically synthesizes his two important predecessors, Polzin and Hurvitz. Rooker starts with Polzin's study of the language of P.[57] Discussing Polzin's 19 grammatical features of LBH, however, Rooker accepts only 15 as valid.[58] The revised list of 15 LBH features leads him to reject Polzin's conclusion that P represents the transitional status of BH. Instead, he maintains that the transitional status should be assigned to the book of Ezekiel. Rooker supplements this preliminary thesis by rigorously employing Hurvitz's method. With Hurvitz's method of defining LBH features, Rooker demonstrates that as many as 20 grammatical items and 17 lexical items in Ezekiel belong to LBH.[59] He also shows that the same book contains 31 EBH counterparts that are contrasted with the LBH features used in

---

[51] Hurvitz, "The Date of the Prose-Tale of Job Linguistically Reconsidered," *HTR* 67 (1974): 17–34. Cf. Young's recent critique: Young, "Is the Prose Tale of Job in Late Biblical Hebrew?" *VT* 59 (2009): 606–29.

[52] Hurvitz, "The Language of Qoheleth and Its Historical Setting within Biblical Hebrew," in *The Language of Qohelet in Its Context: Essays in Honour of Prof. A. Schoors on the Occasion of His Seventieth Birthday* (ed. Angelika Berlejung and Pierre Van Hecke; OLA 164; Leuven: Peeters, 2007), 23–34 (quotation from p. 34).

[53] Ronald L. Bergey, "The Book of Esther: Its Place in the Linguistic Milieu of Post-Exilic Biblical Hebrew Prose: A Study in Late Biblical Hebrew" (Ph.D. diss., Dropsie College for Hebrew and Cognate Learning, 1983).

[54] Bergey, "Book of Esther," 1.

[55] Bergey, "Book of Esther," 185. For his analysis of the 22 grammatical and 36 lexical features, see pp. 27–167.

[56] Published as *Biblical Hebrew in Transition* (above, n. 2).

[57] Polzin, *Late Biblical Hebrew* (above, n. 19).

[58] For Polzin's 19 LBH grammatical features, see above, p. 16 n. 24. From Polzin's list, Rooker excludes the following: from the features not attributable to Aramaic influence, A.3, A.10, and A.13; from the features caused by Aramaic influence, B.4. Rooker, *Biblical Hebrew in Transition*, 52.

[59] Rooker, *Biblical Hebrew in Transition*, 65–176.

the book.[60] Rooker concludes, accordingly, that Ezekiel is "the exemplar of Biblical Hebrew in Transition."[61]

Hurvitz's influence is also notable in the work of Gary A. Rendsburg and his student Richard M. Wright.

A published version of Wright's dissertation dates the J source by closely following the three criteria of Hurvitz's method (i.e., linguistic distribution, linguistic contrast, and extrabiblical sources).[62] Wright analyzes morphological, syntactical, phraseological, and lexical features from J and shows that they are contrasted with the corresponding LBH features. He also notes that Persian loanwords are absent from J. His conclusion is, first, that "the strongest contrast is [seen] between the language background of 'J' and that of the late post-exilic period" and, second, that in several instances "'J' does not display characteristics of LBH that occur in exilic and early post-exilic texts."[63]

Although Hurvitz's method was designed for a diachronic analysis of BH, Rendsburg attempts to show that it can also be useful for a synchronic description of BH. In several monographs and essays, Rendsburg argues for the existence of regional dialects of BH, especially "Israelian Hebrew," or the northern dialect, in the Hebrew Bible.[64] In isolating the features of this northern dialect, Rendsburg models his method on Hurvitz's method of defining LBH features. In order to define a linguistic item as characteristically northern, the linguistic item should, first, appear either exclusively or primarily in the texts that most scholars consider northern or non-Judahite (linguistic distribution). Second, the proposed Israelian Hebrew feature should be contrasted with a feature within Judahite Hebrew

---

[60] Rooker, *Biblical Hebrew in Transition*, 183–84.

[61] Rooker, *Biblical Hebrew in Transition*, 186. For a critical review essay, see Jacobus A. Naudé, "The Language of the Book of Ezekiel: Biblical Hebrew in Transition?" *OTE* 13 (2000): 46–71.

[62] Richard M. Wright, *Linguistic Evidence for the Pre-Exilic Date of the Yahwistic Source* (Library of Hebrew Bible/Old Testament Studies 419; London: T&T Clark, 2005).

[63] Wright, *Yahwistic Source*, 161. Whenever he speaks of J, Wright uses quotation marks since he is "not convinced personally of the existence of a 'J' source" (Wright, *Yahwistic Source*, 4).

Wright is criticized mainly on two grounds. First, many scholars note that Wright's argument is circular, as J belongs to the corpora that Hurvitz and others presupposed as preexilic material with which they contrasted the undisputed postexilic literature in identifying LBH features. Second, some scholars hold that Wright's argument is an argument from silence. That is, Wright does not show that J *uses* EBH features but only that J *does not use* LBH features. See, for example, Christoph Levin, review of Wright, *Yahwistic Source*, *RBL* 8 (2006). Online: http://bookreviews.org/pdf/4860_5055.pdf.

[64] See the bibliography.

(linguistic contrast). Third, that same item should have a cognate in one of the languages neighboring the northern kingdom (such as Aramaic, Ugaritic, Phoenician, or one of the Transjordanian dialects) (extrabiblical sources). Fourth, a text is considered northern only when there is a concentration of northern features (accumulation). In addition, Rendsburg uses the final form of the MT for his linguistic analysis of BH.[65]

3. *The Method Challenged*

In recent years, several scholars have challenged Hurvitz's enterprise, both its presuppositions and methods. In summarizing the challengers' arguments, we may conveniently start from the four publications published during the last several years, which are mentioned in the previous chapter. To repeat, they are an essay collection edited by Ian Young entitled *Biblical Hebrew: Studies in Chronology and Typology* (2003), sections of two consecutive volumes of *Hebrew Studies* (vols. 46–47 [2005–2006]), and a two-volume collaborative work by Ian Young, Robert Rezetko, and Martin Ehrensvärd entitled *Linguistic Dating of Biblical Texts* (2008).[66] The first three works (the essay collection and the sections of *HS* 46–47) contain contributions by both those who advocate linguistic dating and those who object to it. All of the authors of *Linguistic Dating* are challengers of Hurvitz. This last work is particularly important to our discussion for a few reasons.

First, the three authors, Young, Rezetko, and Ehrensvärd, who are the most productive and prominent of the challengers, offer in a single work a unified voice that critiques Hurvitz's methods. They maintain that "the scholarly use of language in dating biblical texts, and even the traditional standpoint on the chronological development of BH, are in need of thorough re-evaluation."[67] At the same time, they argue that "EBH" and "LBH"[68]

---

[65] Rendsburg, *Linguistic Evidence for the Northern Origin of Selected Psalms* (SBLMS 43; Atlanta: Scholars, 1990), 15–17; idem, *Diglossia in Ancient Hebrew* (AOS 72; New Haven, Conn.: American Oriental Society, 1990), 31–33; and idem, *Israelian Hebrew in the Book of Kings* (Bethesda, Md.: CDL Press, 2002), 18–19.

[66] Young (ed.), *Biblical Hebrew* (above, n. 36); *HS* 46 (2005): 321–76; *HS* 47 (2006): 83–210; Young, Rezetko, and Ehrensvärd, *Linguistic Dating* (above, n. 31).

[67] Young, Rezetko, and Ehrensvärd, *Linguistic Dating*, 1:4.

[68] Young, Rezetko, and Ehrensvärd use quotation marks for these terms when they express disapproval of the terms' chronological connotation.

should be considered "co-existing styles of literary Hebrew throughout the biblical period."[69]

Second, spanning more than seven hundred pages, the work is an encyclopedic resource for the subject of the linguistic dating of BH texts. The authors provide a useful summary of work by Hurvitz and others who have followed him. In a chapter surveying scholarship on the linguistic dating of biblical books, they exhaust scholarly opinions about each book of the Hebrew Bible. Beyond the thoroughness of the bibliography, they even provide a complete list of the 460 grammatical and lexical items that scholars from Kropat (1909) to Wright (2005) have suggested to be characteristics of LBH.[70]

Third, this book gathers and categorizes by subject the earlier arguments and assertions of each of the three authors, who developed and described their theories over the course of many years' work. Thus, one may survey the three challengers' arguments by following the different subject headings such as critique of principles (ch. 3 of vol. 1), critique of methods (ch. 4 of vol. 1), preexilic inscriptions (ch. 6 of vol. 1), dialects and diglossia (ch. 7 of vol. 1), Aramaic (ch. 8 of vol. 1), Mishnaic Hebrew (ch. 9 of vol. 1), Qumran Hebrew and Ben Sira (ch. 10 of vol. 1), loanwords (ch. 11 of vol. 1) and textual criticism (ch. 13 of vol. 1).

For these reasons, it is more fitting to discuss the challengers' arguments by subject rather than by scholar, as it will help us to have an

---

[69] Young, Rezetko, and Ehrensvärd, *Linguistic Dating*, 2:72. I believe it is helpful to quote similar statements made by the three authors throughout their book: "EBH and LBH would thus turn out to be two styles of postexilic Hebrew, conservative and non-conservative" (2:88); "Thus, LBH is not simply postexilic Hebrew. It is *one* sort of BH in the postexilic period alongside EBH. Both EBH and LBH use the same linguistic forms, just to different degrees, and the use of either EBH or LBH is a stylistic choice, not a consequence of chronology" (2:89; emphasis original); "Thus, it is a reasonable suggestion that even in the preexilic period LBH could have been a style of Hebrew that co-existed with EBH" (2:91); "Rather, again, we have different stylistic choice made by different authors of the biblical period" (2:91).

At this point, I would like to express my gratitude to Robert Rezetko for correcting some of my earlier statements about his and Young, Rezetko, and Ehrensvärd's positions. While the proof of the present book was being made, Rezetko kindly contacted me via email after he had read my dissertation (the earlier version of the present book). One important correction, which he gave me and which I have been able to incorporate in the present book, is that the challengers' position—that linguistic dating is not possible—does not entail that there were no authentic linguistic shifts in BH. They think that BH changed over time. Their main argument, however, is that when it comes to the issue of linguistic dating (or the distinction between EBH and LBH), EBH and LBH should largely (not in every or many details) be regarded as contemporaneous writing styles.

[70] Young, Rezetko, and Ehrensvärd, *Linguistic Dating*, 2:160–214.

overview of the issues and questions in the current debate. The following discussion owes much to Young, Rezetko, and Ehrensvärd's *Linguistic Dating* and their earlier works. Important arguments by other scholars will also be mentioned.

3.1. *Challenges to the Presuppositions*

We have seen above the four presuppositions for Hurvitz's method of the linguistic dating of BH texts (pp. 18–21). Below I will summarize the challengers' arguments raised against these presuppositions.

Against linguistic heterogeneity in BH. This is the least challenged of the presuppositions. Frederick H. Cryer, nonetheless, argues for the homogeneity of BH. His argument is based on comparative data. If the use of BH stretches over a thousand years, Cryer argues, it should show a high degree of internal heterogeneity, just as the period between today and the writing of the English epic *Beowulf* (ca. 8th century C.E.) or of the German epic the *Nibelungenlied* (13th century C.E.) has rendered both works unintelligible to most modern readers.[71] Cryer claims that this sort of heterogeneity does not exist in BH and concludes therefore that "the OT was *written* more or less at one go, or at least over a relatively short period of time."[72]

Ehrensvärd's critique of Cryer is helpful.[73] Ehrensvärd notes that it is methodologically sounder to compare BH with other classical Semitic languages than with modern European languages. Standard Arabic, for example, has changed remarkably little through the last millennium and a half.[74] Ehrensvärd further argues that within BH "we cannot expect to find diversity on the scale Cryer is looking for." Like the case of Standard Arabic, "being the standard literary language, it [BH] was in many respects the same throughout the entire Biblical period and developed relatively little." Thus, there exists "no 'sharp distinction'" but "only rela-

---

[71] Frederick H. Cryer, "The Problem of Dating Biblical Hebrew and the Hebrew of Daniel," in *In the Last Days: On Jewish and Christian Apocalyptic and Its Period* (ed. Knud Jeppesen, Kirsten Nielsen, and Bent Rosendal; Aarhus: Aarhus University Press, 1994), 186–87.

[72] Cryer, "Problem," 192. Emphasis original.

[73] Ehrensvärd, "Once Again: The Problem of Dating Biblical Hebrew," *SJOT* 11 (1997): 29–40. This is a review article of Cryer, "Problem," where Ehrensvärd supports the traditional chronological understanding of BH. As we have seen, however, he no longer subscribes to the position espoused in this article.

[74] Ehrensvärd, "Once Again," 31–32.

tively subtle—but recognizable!—differences" between the two types of BH, and "it takes the utmost care and stringency of method to distinguish them." Only some neologisms that deviate from the EBH usage will reveal that the language of some late books is LBH.[75]

Cryer's provocative essay did not win many followers, and Ehrensvärd's article represents the majority. The diversity in BH may not be as dramatic as in the European languages Cryer takes as an example, but it is still recognizable. Even Hurvitz's challengers acknowledge that the main body of BH shows two dissimilar styles, although they explain them differently.

Against the chronological explanation. The second presupposition for Hurvitz's method is that the typological division of BH corresponds to its chronological development. The challenges against this presupposition will be treated in this and the next subsections. In this subsection, I will survey the challengers' arguments that deal with more general issues; in the following subsection, I will focus on the specific issue of the book of Chronicles, which, according to the advocates of linguistic dating, best represents LBH.

Philip R. Davies, who is well known for his assertion that the entire Hebrew Bible is a creation of the postexilic community in Yehud, raises the possibility that EBH and LBH could have coexisted during the postexilic period.[76] Early Biblical Hebrew, according to Davies, could have been a literary language of the postexilic period, which would have imitated and descended from the spoken language of preexilic Judah. LBH, on the other hand, would have been the language that was close to the spoken language of postexilic Yehud.

For his case, Davies discusses several significant points, two of which should be noted here. First, he points out the persisting character of literary languages. For example, languages such as Akkadian, Greek, Latin, and Arabic survived or do survive long after they ceased to be vernacular. Davies takes the example of Standard Babylonian, a literary dialect of Akkadian, which started to be used in the middle of the second

---

[75] Ehrensvärd, "Once Again," 35.
[76] Davies, "Biblical Hebrew and the History of Ancient Judah: Typology, Chronology and Common Sense," in Young (ed.), *Biblical Hebrew*, 150–63. For his case for the postexilic provenance of the entire Hebrew Bible, see, for example, Davies, *In Search of 'Ancient Israel'* (2nd ed.; London: Sheffield Academic Press, 1995).

millennium B.C.E. and changed little for over a thousand years.[77] Second, Davies pays attention to scribal practice. He asks: "Did Judaean scribes really forget, within two generations [i.e., from Haggai to Nehemiah], how to write CBH?" He further states, "These scribes did, after all, continue to copy, and even to edit *and expand*, texts in CBH up to the time in which the Qumran biblical manuscripts were copied."[78] In other words, scribal practice, Davies maintains, makes it likely that the postexilic scribes were competent in writing flawless EBH. Therefore, Davies argues, the possibility should not be ruled out that EBH and LBH were two stylistic options for postexilic writers, one being a literary language modeled on preexilic Hebrew and the other a vernacular of the period.[79]

Davies's argument that EBH could have been a literary language during the postexilic period would be seriously weakened if EBH could be shown to be *identical* to the vernacular of the preexilic period.[80] The natural language of the preexilic period has been fossilized in the inscriptions from the period. And, as we have seen, Hurvitz indeed uses these inscriptions as an external control to support the absolute dating of EBH.

Young disagrees with Hurvitz on this, however. In his essay discussing Hebrew inscriptions, Young studies the relationship of the Hebrew of the preexilic inscriptions to EBH and to LBH by discussing more than one hundred lexemes and structures of the inscriptions.[81] Young notes that the Hebrew of the preexilic inscriptions is indeed closer to EBH than to LBH. He argues, however, that it is not identical to EBH.[82] According to Young, the Hebrew of the inscriptions should be considered an independent dialect within Hebrew.[83] It therefore cannot be used to prove that some biblical books must have been written in the preexilic period or that EBH could not have been written in the postexilic period.[84] In relation to LBH, a further point is discussed. In the preexilic inscriptions, Young finds 27 linguistic features that are characteristic of LBH. Young acknowledges that the tie between the inscriptions and LBH is not as strong as the tie

---

[77] Davies, "Typology, Chronology," 156–57, 159.

[78] Davies, "Typology, Chronology," 155. Emphasis original.

[79] Davies, "Typology, Chronology," 156.

[80] That is, only if the two are *identical*. If the two had been *similar*, Davies's argument would still stand, since it postulates that there was continuity between preexilic spoken Hebrew and the EBH of biblical literature.

[81] Young, "Late Biblical Hebrew and Hebrew Inscriptions," in Young (ed.), *Biblical Hebrew*, 276–311.

[82] Young, "Hebrew Inscriptions," 308.

[83] Young, "Hebrew Inscriptions," 308.

[84] Young, "Hebrew Inscriptions," 280, 309.

between the inscriptions and EBH. Still, the adherents of the traditional approach should explain how LBH features made their way into preexilic documents.[85] Young, therefore, refuses to view the preexilic inscriptions as an external control for EBH. If Young is correct, the evidence from the preexilic inscriptions cannot rule out the possibility that EBH was used during the postexilic period.[86]

Against the chronological explanation: the lateness of Chronicles. Among the five core postexilic books (i.e., Esther, Daniel, Ezra, Nehemiah, and Chronicles), Chronicles has been considered pivotal. Thus, although there have been disagreements concerning the use of synoptic passages, scholars have almost unanimously agreed that the language of Chronicles, when compared with the language of Samuel–Kings, reveals the diction of postexilic Hebrew. We have seen that many scholars, when they attempt to describe LBH, start by analyzing the language of Chronicles.

This understanding is being challenged, however. I will note two scholars in this regard: A. Graeme Auld and Robert Rezetko. I will spend more space on Rezetko because, whereas Auld's studies are literary and source-critical, Rezetko's studies treat linguistic data and are hence more directly relevant to our present discussion.

Auld maintains that the books of Samuel–Kings are as late as Chronicles.[87] He proposes a theory that there was a common source which

---

[85] Young, "Hebrew Inscriptions," 292–99. Young further notes that this is in harmony with the biblical evidence: that is, preexilic biblical books contain LBH features. This is, Young notes, the reason that Hurvitz proposed the fourth criterion in evaluating a text or a book: only the accumulation of LBH features will mark a work as LBH. Young, "Hebrew Inscriptions," 299.

[86] The challengers' argument against the preexilic inscriptions as an external control is presented also in Young, Rezetko, and Ehrensvärd, *Linguistic Dating*, 1:143–72, where the authors reach the same conclusion as Young's and discuss some aspects of the situation not treated in Young, "Hebrew Inscriptions."

[87] A. Graeme Auld, *Kings without Privilege: David and Moses in the Story of the Bible's Kings* (Edinburgh: T&T Clark, 1994). Since the publication of this monograph, many have examined and critiqued Auld's hypothesis proposed in it. See, for example, Steven L. McKenzie, "The Chronicler as Redactor," in *The Chronicler as Author: Studies in Text and Texture* (ed. M. Patrick Graham and Steven L. McKenzie; JSOTSup 263; Sheffield: Sheffield Academic Press, 1999), 70–90; Zipora Talshir, "The Reign of Solomon in the Making: Pseudo-Connections between 3 Kingdoms and Chronicles," *VT* 50 (2000): 233–49. One of Auld's students has supported the teacher's idea in his study of 1 Sam 31:1–13 and 1 Chr 10:1–12: Craig Y. S. Ho, "Conjectures and Refutations: Is 1 Samuel XXXI 1–13 Really the Source of 1 Chronicles X 1–12?" *VT* 45 (1995): 82–106. Auld himself has replied to his critics through many subsequent essays. See the convenient reprint of his essays: Auld, *Samuel at the Threshold: Selected Works of Graeme Auld* (SOTSMS; Aldershot, England: Ashgate, 2004).

both the author of Samuel–Kings and the author of Chronicles shared and which originated no earlier than the exile. Accordingly, Samuel–Kings as well as Chronicles must be dated later than the exile. If Samuel–Kings is postexilic, the studies by Hurvitz, his predecessors, and his followers cannot stand, because their arguments are based on the assumption that the language of Samuel–Kings is earlier than that of Chronicles.

In his essay that criticizes Hurvitz's method, Rezetko evaluates 16 features in Chronicles that scholars generally consider "late."[88] Examining these 16 features, Rezetko maintains that the argument for the lateness of the Chronicler's language is tentative. Instead, he holds, "Many distinctive linguistic features of Chronicles and other 'late' BH compositions are stylistic idiosyncrasies devoid of any diachronic value or are explicable by (strictly speaking) non-chronological factors such as dialect, diglossia, and editorial and scribal activity."[89]

The above assertion leads Rezetko to suggest further that "the study of the language of Samuel–Kings and Chronicles *should be liberated from assumptions concerning the literary composition and development of these books*," that is, "the assumptions that Chronicles *post-dates* (by a substantial lapse in time), *utilized* and *changed* Samuel–Kings."[90] According to Rezetko, this is the fallacy of "literary-linguistic circularity."[91]

---

[88] Rezetko, "Dating Biblical Hebrew: Evidence from Samuel–Kings and Chronicles," in Young (ed.), *Biblical Hebrew*, 215–50. Rezetko uses quotation marks to show his doubt regarding the (relative) lateness of the Chronicler's language.

The 16 features Rezetko evaluates are the following: (1) defective and full spelling; (2) the noun affirmative וּת-; (3) אֲנִי and אָנֹכִי; (4) בְּ + the third-person masculine plural suffix; (5) theophoric names ending with יָה- and יָהוּ-; (6) the paragogic ה (הֹ-); (7) the syntax of numerals; (8) the word order of the name and the title (e.g., הַמֶּלֶךְ שְׁלֹמֹה vs. שְׁלֹמֹה הַמֶּלֶךְ); (9) assimilation and non-assimilation of נ in מִן; (10) אֵין negating the infinitive; (11) collective nouns construed as plurals; (12) and (13) the *quivis* construction and the double plural construct-chain formation; (14) *wayyiqtol* and past *weqatal*; (15) וַיְהִי and temporal sequences; and (16) the vocabulary of Chronicles. Rezetko, "Dating Biblical Hebrew," 223–38.

I thank Robert Rezetko for his correction on my dissertation (the earlier version of the present book; see above, n. 69). Unlike Auld, Rezetko does not think that there was an exilic common source that both Samuel–Kings and Chronicles followed. Instead, he holds that Chronicles was based on earlier editions of Samuel–Kings. At the same time, however, he believes that Samuel–Kings continued to develop literarily, editorially, and textually through the exilic and the postexilic periods and therefore one cannot reduce Samuel–Kings to preexilic, exilic, or postexilic period. See his *Source and Revision in the Narratives of David's Transfer of the Ark: Text, Language, and Story in 2 Samuel 6 and 1 Chronicles 13, 15–16* (Library of Hebrew Bible/Old Testament Studies 470; London: T&T Clark, 2007).

[89] Rezetko, "Dating Biblical Hebrew," 222.

[90] Rezetko, "Dating Biblical Hebrew," 239. Emphasis original.

[91] Rezetko, "Dating Biblical Hebrew," 240. Rezetko, "Dating Biblical Hebrew" is criticized by Hurvitz in his "Recent Debate" (above, n. 42). Some points in this article are discussed below.

Rezetko's first essay is supplemented by his next one. In his essay examining "late" common nouns in the book of Chronicles, Rezetko examines 124 common noun lexemes in Chronicles that may be considered late.[92] His conclusion includes the following: First, regarding the distribution of "common nouns, [which are] the most productive part of speech in BH, Chronicles is mostly EBH with some LBH lexical elements sprinkled here and there.[93] Second, "Chronicles' 'late' common nouns are habitually explainable by recourse to *non-chronological interpretations.*" That is, with text-critical evidence and literary analysis, one may interpret many occurrences of "late" words in Chronicles as the postexilic author's "purposeful" choice.[94] Therefore, Rezetko raises the possibility that EBH and LBH were coexistent styles.

Against the exile as the watershed of BH. As we have seen above, Hurvitz, along with other scholars, believes that a categorical change occurred in BH during the exilic period. Accordingly, postexilic writers were unable to write flawless EBH, a fact which enables us to date biblical texts on linguistic grounds.

As we have seen in chapter 1, however, in his essay that attacks many aspects of Hurvitz's methods and principles, Ehrensvärd argues for the existence of "postexilic EBH."[95] To repeat, the language of Isaiah 40–66, Joel, Haggai, Zechariah, and Malachi is not just close to EBH but is itself EBH. The support for this claim consists of two points. First, "no clear LBH features are shown to occur in these books, and the limited number of LBH features that scholars point to in the books can at best only tentatively be ascribed to LBH." Second, even if we accept that there is a limited number of LBH features in these postexilic prophets, the texts should still be considered EBH texts because "EBH texts contain LBH features, occasionally even clear LBH features."[96]

To argue the first point, Ehrensvärd discusses the linguistic items that Hurvitz and Hill have identified as characteristics of LBH and dismisses

---

[92] Rezetko, "'Late' Common Nouns in the Book of Chronicles," in *Reflection and Refraction: Studies in Biblical Historiography in Honour of A. Graeme Auld* (ed. Robert Rezetko, Timothy H. Lim, and W. Brian Aucker; VTSup 113; Leiden: Brill, 2007), 379–417. Again, Rezetko uses quotation marks to show his doubt about the lateness of Chronicles.

[93] Rezetko, "'Late' Common Nouns," 417.

[94] Rezetko, "'Late' Common Nouns," 379. Emphasis original.

[95] Ehrensvärd, "Linguistic Dating of Biblical Texts," in Young (ed.), *Biblical Hebrew*, 164–88.

[96] Ehrensvärd, "Linguistic Dating," 176.

most of them as inconclusive.[97] Ehrensvärd also cites Rooker, who has argued that the language of Isaiah 40–66 supports its preexilic dating.[98] Obviously, if we accept the majority opinion about the date of Isaiah 40–66 (which is late exilic and postexilic), the author(s) of Isaiah 40–66 used EBH during the late exilic and postexilic periods.

For the second point, Ehrensvärd conducts an experiment and looks for LBH features in 1 Samuel 1–3. Although Ehrensvärd finds no LBH words in chs. 1–3 and no LBH grammatical features in ch. 3, he finds in chs. 1 and 2 six grammatical features of LBH.[99] Ehrensvärd notes that "this is a remarkable frequency of LBH grammatical features" and that "it goes to show that EBH texts can contain a number of LBH features and still count as EBH texts." He concludes that "it seems fair, then, to regard Isaiah 40–66, Joel, Haggai, Zechariah, and Malachi as EBH texts: they have their (expected) share of features that *may* belong to LBH, and no clear LBH features."[100]

Provocatively, Ehrensvärd goes further and raises the possibility that all of the books written in EBH may have come from the postexilic period (more specifically, during the time of Haggai and Zechariah 1–8). This is a corollary of accepting his position. In the corpus defined by the use of EBH, Haggai and Zechariah 1–8 are the only texts that are explicitly dated. Therefore, if one wants to adhere strictly to linguistic methods, all the texts using EBH, "with due caution," should be dated to the early postexilic period, the period when Haggai and Zechariah 1–8 were written.[101]

Therefore, the case of postexilic EBH raises a serious challenge for Hurvitz and those who take the exile as the divide between EBH and LBH. At best, it shifts the divide to a period after the building of the second

---

[97] Ehrensvärd, "Linguistic Dating," 177–83.

[98] Ehrensvärd, "Linguistic Dating," 181. The conclusion of Rooker's article is that "Ezekiel, from the exilic period as well as post-exilic Hebrew literature, always indicates later linguistic features than those we find in Isaiah 40–66." Rooker, "Dating Isaiah 40–66: What Does the Linguistic Evidence Say?" *WTJ* 58 (1996): 312; repr. in *Studies in Hebrew Language, Intertextuality, and Theology* (Texts and Studies in Religion 98; Lewiston, N.Y.: Edwin Mellen, 2003).

[99] The six LBH grammatical features that Ehrensvärd has identified in 1 Samuel 1–2 are the following: (1) the use of the preposition עַל instead of אֶל (3 occurrences [1:10, 13; 2:11]); (2) a preference for verbal suffixes over אֵת + suffix (17 verbal suffixes against no nonforced instances of אֵת + suffix); (3) the use of the periphrastic construction הָיָה + participle to express cursivity (1 occurrence [2:11]); (4) the non-use of apodotic ו in front of verbs (2 occurrences [2:16, 36]); (5) the וְאָקְטְלָה pattern (1 occurrence [2:28]); and (6) peculiar uses of verb forms (3 occurrences of frequentative *wayyiqtol* [1:7; 2:16] and non-past *wayyiqtol* [2:29]). Ehrensvärd, "Linguistic Dating," 183–85.

[100] Ehrensvärd, "Linguistic Dating," 185. Emphasis original.

[101] Ehrensvärd, "Linguistic Dating," 187.

temple, with the result that the postexilic prophets are counted among the EBH texts;[102] at worst, it demands that *all* EBH texts be dated to the postexilic period.[103]

Against the use of the MT *in its present form.* The use of the final form of the MT is one of the founding principles of the linguistic dating of BH texts, not only for Hurvitz but also for those who employ his methods. The challengers criticize this principle and emphasize that "the relevance of textual criticism has regularly been minimized or disregarded in diachronic linguistic research on BH."[104] Citing Eugene Ulrich, they remark that the text of the Hebrew Bible was fluid and pluriform until the first century C.E. and that the development of the biblical text proceeded "*from* textual variety *to* textual uniformity."[105]

As evidence, they make the following comparisons: between synoptic texts within the MT; between multiple copies of biblical books or passages among the DSS; and between the received text of the Hebrew Bible, on the one hand, and other Hebrew witnesses (the DSS and the Samaritan Pentateuch) and ancient translations (into Greek, Latin, Aramaic, and

---

[102] This is Driver's position, as we have seen. See also Levin, review of Wright, 2.

[103] Ehrensvärd's "Linguistic Dating" is supplemented by his subsequent article, "Why Biblical Texts Cannot Be Dated Linguistically," *HS* 47 (2006): 177–89. Here, his thesis is that "texts in Early Biblical Hebrew could have been composed after the exile" and that "a mastery of what is called Classical or Standard or Early Biblical Hebrew" was "present" in this period. Ehrensvärd, "Why Biblical Texts," 177, 188.

From a different perspective, Jacobus A. Naudé argues that although BH clearly changed over time, there was no divide of any sort in its development. Naudé's argument rests on his redefining of the notion 'linguistic change'. According to Naudé, the term linguistic change, in general usage, is a conflation of two discrete processes: the *change of grammar* and the *diffusion* of the change. First, linguistic change takes place when the parent's grammar is inaccurately transmitted to the child. It is an instantaneous event, because it occurs at the level of individual. Once a change occurs, the next step is a spread of the specific change from one speaker to another. This is *diffusion*, a process which takes time and occurs at the level of society. Accordingly, Naudé maintains, each grammar (i.e., the language of one specific period) diffuses the changes that have already occurred in its mother grammar while at the same time initiating its own changes that its mother grammar did not show. With this understanding, Naudé asserts that there was not one critical moment in the history of BH. Each stage of BH introduced to its own grammar a few changes that its immediate parent grammar did not show, and not one stage shows a picture radically different from its immediate parent. See further Naudé, "Language of Ezekiel" (above, n. 61) and idem, "The Transitions of Biblical Hebrew in the Perspective of Language Change and Diffusion," in Young (ed.), *Biblical Hebrew*, 189–214.

[104] Young, Rezetko, and Ehrensvärd, *Linguistic Dating*, 1:341.

[105] Young, Rezetko, and Ehrensvärd, *Linguistic Dating*, 1:343. Emphasis original. Cf. Eugene Ulrich, *The Dead Sea Scrolls and the Origins of the Bible* (Studies in the Dead Sea Scrolls and Related Literature; Grand Rapids, Mich.: Eerdmans, 1999), 31.

Syriac), on the other.[106] Young, Rezetko, and Ehrensvärd argue that the above comparisons would seriously undermine the argument for the stability of biblical texts, which is essential to the linguistic dating of biblical texts.[107] They note that "if the text of any given biblical book was fluid then the language of that book was also fluid." Thus, there is "no *a priori* reason to assume…that the language of the MT equates to the original language of biblical books." That is, "the linguistic characteristics of the extant texts of the Hebrew Bible could be due to authorial, editorial and/ or scribal activity."[108]

Hurvitz earlier refuted an argument similar to the one proposed by Young, Rezetko, and Ehrensvärd. Responding to Thomas L. Thompson, Hurvitz argued that the editorial activity carried out by the Masoretes "did not mutilate the original wording" and that it is "a gross methodological error to interpret the *literary 'editing'* of the Hebrew Bible in terms of *linguistic 'revision'*, and to argue 'that this revision of tradition substantially affects access to earlier strata of the tradition.'"[109] Hurvitz further asserted, "Had the texts of the Hebrew Bible undergone an extensive process of language leveling and re-formulation, … we would have expected to find a linguistically homogeneous, uniform type of BH—which, as we have seen, is absolutely not the case presented by the extant Hebrew version of the OT."[110]

Young, Rezetko, and Ehrensvärd do not think that Hurvitz is wrong: they do not suppose that there was a comprehensive linguistic revision of the Hebrew Bible text. Yet, they believe that "scribes modified individual linguistic elements *occasionally* and *unsystematically*."[111] "This view," the

---

[106] Young, Rezetko, and Ehrensvärd, *Linguistic Dating*, 1:343–44. Another piece of evidence treated importantly by Young is the transmission of the Gilgamesh epic. Studying the Standard Babylonian manuscripts, Young argues that "the scribal transmission of Gilgamesh" strengthens "the case that the transmission of Biblical Hebrew was subject to high fluidity." Young continues, "This is yet one more piece of evidence that we must be very sceptical that the details of the language of the MT exhibit the language of the original authors. Hence we must be even more sceptical of conclusions about, for example, dating biblical books, drawn from linguistic evidence." Young, "Textual Stability in Gilgamesh and the Dead Sea Scrolls," in *Gilgameš and the World of Assyria: Proceedings of the Conference Held at Mandelbaum House, The University of Sydney, 21–23 July 2004* (ed. Joseph Azize and Noel Weeks; ANESSup 21; Leuven: Peeters, 2007), 183.

[107] Young, Rezetko, and Ehrensvärd, *Linguistic Dating*, 1:344.

[108] Young, Rezetko, and Ehrensvärd, *Linguistic Dating*, 1:345.

[109] Hurvitz, "Relevance of BH Linguistics," 31*. Emphasis original. Hurvitz quotes from Thomas L. Thompson, "The Intellectual Matrix of Early Biblical Narrative: Inclusive Monotheism in Persian Period Palestine," in *The Triumph of Elohim: From Yahwism to Judaism* (ed. Diana V. Edelman; CBET 13; Kampen: Kok Pharos, 1995), 110.

[110] Hurvitz, "Relevance of BH Linguistics," 31*.

[111] Young, Rezetko, and Ehrensvärd, *Linguistic Dating*, 1:346–47. Emphasis added.

authors maintain, "accounts best for the variety of spelling in the Hebrew Bible and it is one possible explanation for many typically LBH features in EBH texts."[112] According to Young, Rezetko, and Ehrensvärd, changing a biblical text from EBH to LBH or vice versa does not require "*a substantial amount of linguistic modification.*"[113] In other words, even though the later linguistic revision had been only occasional and unsystematic, it would make it impossible to date a biblical text on linguistic grounds.

Last, there is a debate about the question of whether or not scribal activity affected different aspects of BH to a different degree. For example, Hurvitz believes that although scribal activity may have affected the vocalization of BH to a great degree, the consonantal text remained for the most part intact.[114] It is thus generally noted that unlike in the areas of orthography and phonology, linguistic study is viable in the areas of vocabulary and syntax. Young, Rezetko, and Ehrensvärd agree that the degrees of alteration were different among the different aspects of language. Nevertheless, they argue that "there is evidence that editors and scribes did not leave vocabulary and syntax untouched."[115] Obviously, their belief is that editors and scribes retouched the vocabulary and syntax to the degree that would make it difficult for us to study the original language.

3.2. Challenges to Hurvitz's Method

Young, Rezetko, and Ehrensvärd criticize each of the four criteria of Hurvitz's method.[116]

Regarding the first criterion (linguistic distribution), they first note that the contrast between EBH and LBH is rarely a matter of exclusive choice, but rather one of frequency.[117] In other words, purported LBH features are not entirely absent from EBH texts, although they occur more often in the LBH corpus than in the EBH corpus. Likewise, purported EBH features, which the EBH corpus uses more frequently than the LBH corpus, are found many times in the LBH corpus. Young, Rezetko, and Ehrensvärd illustrate the situation with Rooker's study of Ezekiel's language.[118]

---

[112] Young, Rezetko, and Ehrensvärd, *Linguistic Dating*, 1:347.
[113] Young, Rezetko, and Ehrensvärd, *Linguistic Dating*, 1:348. Emphasis original.
[114] Hurvitz, "Relevance of BH Linguistics," 31* n. 31.
[115] Young, Rezetko, and Ehrensvärd, *Linguistic Dating*, 1:346.
[116] The criteria of Hurvitz's method of defining LBH features and texts are discussed above, on pp. 21–22.
[117] Young, Rezetko, and Ehrensvärd, *Linguistic Dating*, 1:83, 86.
[118] Rooker, *Biblical Hebrew in Transition*.

There, among the 37 linguistic oppositions between EBH and LBH that Rooker discusses, only 2 cases show an exclusive distribution, that is, an EBH feature not used in the LBH corpus and an LBH feature not used in the EBH corpus. In 9 cases, an LBH feature does not appear in the EBH corpus, but the corresponding EBH feature occurs in the LBH corpus. In 26 cases, an LBH feature is used in the EBH corpus, and the corresponding EBH feature occurs in the LBH corpus.[119] Additionally, Young, Rezetko, and Ehrensvärd observe that only very few LBH features are attested in *all* of the LBH texts. Thus, they say, "It is often difficult to determine which feature in which book would represent truly late language." On these grounds, they argue that the choice between EBH and LBH was a "matter of style, not chronology."[120]

The challengers' argument against the second criterion (linguistic contrast) derives from their disapproval of the first (linguistic distribution). That is, "opposition between EBH and LBH is undermined to the extent that we find any given EBH feature in LBH texts and LBH feature in EBH texts." Consequently, Young, Rezetko, and Ehrensvärd argue that "many linguistic features traditionally characterised as late or early actually fail, upon closer scrutiny, to meet the criteria of linguistic distribution and opposition."[121]

Regarding the third criterion (extrabiblical sources), Young, Rezetko, and Ehrensvärd raise three issues. First, they maintain that the extrabiblical sources that are used to supplement Hurvitz's method are not "adequate." For example, they note the fact that there is no extant extrabiblical Hebrew material from the sixth to the third century B.C.E., the period to which many scholars would date the composition or editing of much of the Hebrew Bible.[122] Second, extrabiblical sources are different in genre and quality from the BH material. They ask, "Is it reasonable, for example, to compare inscriptional and literary Hebrew?"[123] Young, Rezetko, and Ehrensvärd devote several chapters to discussing the evidence drawn from the preexilic inscriptions, Aramaic, MH, QH, and Ben Sira (chs. 6, 8–10 of vol. 1), arguing that none of these corpora may serve as an external control for the divisions of BH. That is, inscriptional Hebrew is a different kind of Hebrew from EBH; postbiblical Hebrew and Aramaic texts are independent of the literature of LBH. Third, Young, Rezetko, and

---

[119] Young, Rezetko, and Ehrensvärd, *Linguistic Dating*, 1:84.
[120] Young, Rezetko, and Ehrensvärd, *Linguistic Dating*, 1:86, 87.
[121] Young, Rezetko, and Ehrensvärd, *Linguistic Dating*, 1:88, 89.
[122] Young, Rezetko, and Ehrensvärd, *Linguistic Dating*, 1:90.
[123] Young, Rezetko, and Ehrensvärd, *Linguistic Dating*, 1:91.

Ehrensvärd maintain that some relevant data in extrabiblical sources have not been adequately discussed. For example, מלכות occurs in an Old Aramaic source, a fact which will weaken the argument of Hurvitz and his followers that this word is a characteristic of LBH.[124]

As we have seen, a fourth criterion should be met if a text is to be declared LBH: that of accumulation. Young, Rezetko, and Ehrensvärd criticize this criterion mainly on two grounds. They hold that the criterion is dependent on a subjective judgment by an individual scholar. For example, how many LBH features make a text an LBH text? Hurvitz and his followers do not have an established standard, as Young, Rezetko, and Ehrensvärd state.[125] Also, Young, Rezetko, and Ehrensvärd criticize the criterion's validity. The point of departure for the linguistic dating of BH texts is "the late phase of BH, the undisputed postexilic corpus and unmistakable late features attested in it," and one observes the lack of symmetry here.[126] Whereas "certain linguistic features can be declared late because they are found" in undisputed LBH books, "there is no argument for an accumulation of presence of early features since there are few if any early features." "Thus," Young, Rezetko, and Ehrensvärd conclude, "it is impossible to argue the antiquity of, say, the Pentateuch, on the basis of early language."[127]

Last, we should note the challengers' critique of Hurvitz's use of lexical data. In many of Hurvitz's works, lexical data play a decisive role in determining whether or not a text belongs to LBH. In *Linguistic Dating*, on the other hand, the authors note three problems with using lexical data in studying linguistic change in BH: instability, randomness, and correspondence. That is, lexical data are unstable in comparison with grammar, which is more complex and invariable (instability); the occurrence of an individual word depends on randomness because the Hebrew Bible contains only a limited selection of the total ancient Hebrew vocabulary (randomness); and the lexicon of LBH is virtually identical with that of EBH (correspondence).[128] Therefore, Young, Rezetko, and Ehrensvärd argue that "the main focus in linguistic dating of biblical texts should be

---

[124] Young, Rezetko, and Ehrensvärd, *Linguistic Dating*, 1:91.
[125] Young, Rezetko, and Ehrensvärd, *Linguistic Dating*, 1:94.
[126] Young, Rezetko, and Ehrensvärd, *Linguistic Dating*, 1:92.
[127] Young, Rezetko, and Ehrensvärd, *Linguistic Dating*, 1:93. For a more exhaustive critique of the criterion of accumulation, see idem, *Linguistic Dating*, vol. 1, chapter 5, "Early vs. Late Biblical Hebrew: Linguistic Features and Rates of Accumulation."
[128] Young, Rezetko, and Ehrensvärd, *Linguistic Dating*, 1:115–16.

grammar, which provides a more reliable and efficient basis for chronological analysis than does vocabulary."[129]

3.3. *Hurvitz's Responses*

My discussion in the previous sections of the challengers' arguments owes
greatly to Young, Rezetko, and Ehrensvärd's *Linguistic Dating*. This work
was published in 2008 and is currently one of the last published words in
the debate. However, it is still possible to glean Hurvitz's responses to the
challenges surveyed above, partly because many important ideas of the
challengers became available with the publication of Young (ed.), *Biblical
Hebrew* in 2003, and also because Hurvitz previously published articles
responding to Thomas L. Thompson and Philip R. Davies, who had earlier
argued that the Hebrew Bible is a product of postexilic Yehud.[130]

---

[129] Young, Rezetko, and Ehrensvärd, *Linguistic Dating*, 1:118. Cf. Rezetko, "Dating Biblical Hebrew," 237–38, 245–49.

In this regard, Mats Eskhult's presentation of the peculiarities in late BH prose syntax,
for example, must be a welcome challenge to Young, Rezetko, and Ehrensvärd (Eskhult,
"Traces of Linguistic Development in Biblical Hebrew," *HS* 46 [2005]: 353–70). The three
authors actually cite the following comment by Eskhult in full agreement: "Old-fashioned
words, phrases, and forms are well-known devices in the art of archaizing; but a writer
cannot possibly archaize his syntax beyond the horizon of his own understanding of the
language as system" (Eskhult, "Traces of Linguistic Development," 369; cf. Young, Rezetko,
and Ehrensvärd, *Linguistic Dating*, 1:118). On the other hand, Eskhult presents the following
syntactical features of the late BH narrative prose that are contrasted with the classical BH
narrative prose: (1) the increase of indirect speech in comparison to classical BH's preference for direct speech; (2) the discontinued use of the *qatal* form in performative utter-
ances; (3) the decrease of *wĕqatalti*; (4) the vanishing of the infinitival paronomasia (e.g.,
זָכֹר תִּזְכֹּר); (5) the use of participle for the iterative aspect, which was earlier expressed by
yiqtol; (6) the decrease of the presentative הִנֵּה(וְ); (7) the increase of the periphrastic form
(הָיָה + participle); (8) the use of the article before a finite verb as a relative; (9) the incon-
sistent use of the introductory וַיְהִי; and (10) a new way of providing anterior information
for the narrative proper (e.g., וְלִפְנֵי מִזֶּה "Now before this…" [Neh 13:4–5] instead of classical וְ + subject + *qatal*, i.e., …וֶאֱלִישָׁע חָלָה "Now Elisha had fallen sick…" [2 Kgs 13:14]).
Eskhult concludes, "Authors of late books had to take pains to understand the complicated
system of tense, aspect, and modality in the earlier literature," and therefore, "the authors
of the late biblical prose, though confident in their own competence, definitely produced
a Hebrew that displays traces of late linguistic development so far as the verbal syntax is
concerned" (Eskhult, "Traces of Linguistic Development," 370).

[130] For example, Davies, *In Search of 'Ancient Israel'*; Thompson, "Intellectual Matrix."

Hurvitz's responses to the challengers are found in the following works: "Continuity and
Innovation" (1995); "Historical Quest" (1997); "Historical Linguistics and the Hebrew Bible:
The Formation and Emergence of Late Biblical Hebrew," in *Hebrew through the Ages: In
Memory of Shoshanna Bahat* (ed. Moshe Bar-Asher; Studies in Language 2; Jerusalem: The
Academy of the Hebrew Language, 1997; in Hebrew), 15–28; "Relevance of BH Linguistics"
(1999); "Can Biblical Texts Be Dated?" (2000); and "Recent Debate" (2006).

Hurvitz's responses may be summarized in four points. First, as a response to the argument that BH, as a literary language, was stable and changed minimally (above, pp. 29–30), Hurvitz remarks that the assumption that BH was largely literary in nature "by no means allows us to reject *a priori* the possibility that it was subject to a process of linguistic change during the biblical period," because "the phenomenon that a literary language betrays—in written records—traces of historical development is by no means rare or exceptional and is well attested in various literatures."[131]

Second, Hurvitz affirms the lateness of Chronicles spending a substantial portion of his article "Recent Debate." As we have seen, the lateness of the book and its language had been the foundation of the diachronic study of BH, but Auld and Rezetko challenged it (above, pp. 31–33). Hurvitz maintains that the lateness of Chronicles, which is supported by the literary evidence of the book, is "fully confirmed by the linguistic profile of the Hebrew employed in the book."[132] Hurvitz writes the following:

> In both the synoptic and non-synoptic passages, Chronicles makes wide use of grammatical forms, lexical items, and syntactical constructions unattested in Standard Biblical Hebrew but well-documented in post-exilic times—both in late biblical compositions and late extra-biblical sources.[133]

As a test case, Hurvitz discusses the two biblical forms of the place name 'Damascus'. The opposition between דַּמֶּשֶׂק in Samuel–Kings and דַּרְמֶשֶׂק in Chronicles, Hurvitz remarks, is best explained by chronological difference, because the longer form is used also in QH, the Peshitta, and rabbinic literature, but not in texts in Egyptian, Akkadian, and Old Aramaic of the First Temple period.[134] With the evidence mustered, Hurvitz argues that Rezetko's suggestion for "non-chronological explanations [for the two

---

Indeed we see a change of tone in Hurvitz's works after 1995, in which Hurvitz makes efforts to defend his principles and methods, something that had been unnecessary while his method remained to be the consensus.

[131] Hurvitz, "Historical Quest," 303.

[132] Hurvitz, "Recent Debate," 195.

[133] Hurvitz, "Recent Debate," 195.

[134] Hurvitz, "Recent Debate," 197–99. Hurvitz adds four additional lexical neologisms in Chronicles. They are אִגֶּרֶת (2 Chr 30:1, 6; against preexilic סֵפֶר), גִּנְזַךְ (1 Chr 28:11; against the SBH root אצר), אֲדַרְכֹּנִים (1 Chr 29:7; a new term in the postexilic period), and מִדְרָשׁ (2 Chr 13:22; 24:27; a new technical term, found also in rabbinic literature and the DSS). Hurvitz, "Recent Debate," 200–201.

types of BH] such as dialect, diglossia, and editorial and scribal activities"[135] is "in *this specific case* ... beside the point and irrelevant."[136]

The third point of Hurvitz's responses pertains to the challengers' argument for "postexilic EBH" or the coexistence of EBH and LBH during the postexilic period (above, pp. 33–35). Hurvitz unequivocally states that Standard BH (i.e., EBH) did not coexist with LBH. He says that although "the style and diction of indisputably late biblical compositions may create the illusion of being an integral part of Standard Biblical Hebrew," "when properly examined, the misleading 'classical' appearance turns out to be nothing more than an external façade."[137] Thus, Hurvitz argues that Haggai, Zechariah, and Malachi, whose language Ehrensvärd argues to be an example of postexilic EBH, "*do* contain unmistakable imprints of Late Biblical Hebrew."[138] Hurvitz explains that the sparseness of the evidence is due to the books' dates, which are "*the beginning* of the Persian period, when Late Biblical Hebrew was just making its debut on the biblical scene and had not yet acquired a defined habitat in the newly developing linguistic landscape."[139] Accordingly, the critical point in the history of BH for Hurvitz is obviously the exile or "somewhere after the destruction of Jerusalem and the fall of Judah."[140] He asserts, "The challengers' suggestion to prolong the life of Standard Biblical Hebrew beyond this point rests upon an inadequate evidential basis."[141]

The fourth point I want to note in Hurvitz's responses concerns his use of lexical evidence. As we have seen, the challengers often argue that lexical data are not as reliable or objective as grammatical or syntactical data (above, pp. 39–40). Hurvitz argues, however, that "in principle, such generalized assertions are highly questionable, since each and every element—whether lexical or syntactical—ought to be evaluated on its own terms." Hurvitz continues, "If the syntactical evidence confirms ... the post-classical nature of the Late Biblical Hebrew corpus and thus allows a correlation to be established between the testimony of the (late) syntax

---

[135] Rezetko, "Dating Biblical Hebrew," 249.

[136] Hurvitz, "Recent Debate," 199. Emphasis original. Zipora Talshir calls Hurvitz's response to Rezetko "solid" (Talshir, "Synchronic and Diachronic Approaches in the Study of the Hebrew Bible: Text Criticism within the Frame of Biblical Philology," *Text* 23 [2007]: 8 n. 21). Cf., however, Rezetko's latest rejoinder: Rezetko, "The Spelling of 'Damascus' and the Linguistic Dating of Biblical Texts," *SJOT* 24 (2010): 110–28.

[137] Hurvitz, "Recent Debate," 204–5.

[138] Hurvitz, "Recent Debate," 206. Emphasis original.

[139] Hurvitz, "Recent Debate," 206. Emphasis original.

[140] Hurvitz, "Recent Debate," 207.

[141] Hurvitz, "Recent Debate," 208.

and the (late) lexicon, there is no justification to disregard or dismiss the evidence gained from the lexical data."[142]

4. *Summary: Issues in the Current Debate*

We have briefly surveyed scholarship on the diachronic approach to BH with special attention to the subject of the linguistic dating of biblical texts. For a long time after Hurvitz established the method of dating linguistic features and biblical texts, a consensus existed. What was once a consensus, however, is now being rigorously challenged. To summarize basic issues in the current debate:

First, we may say, with due caution, that the challengers agree with the advocates of linguistic dating that two different styles are discerned in BH. The challengers, on the other hand, disagree with the advocates in understanding the implication of this difference. Hurvitz and his followers explain the difference as stemming from the chronological development of BH, whereas the challengers believe that the difference may be explained by non-chronological factors such as dialect, diglossia, and editorial and scribal activity.

Second, the challengers, at least implicitly, acknowledge the validity of Hurvitz's criteria for identifying LBH features. That is, in ideal situations— if there were an exclusive distribution and a categorical opposition—we could securely identify an LBH feature by following Hurvitz's three criteria (i.e., linguistic distribution, linguistic contrast, and extrabiblical sources). The problem, however, is that situations are seldom ideal. In most cases, the data are not neatly distributed, and the distinction between EBH and LBH features has to depend on frequency. This is the reason that Hurvitz and his followers have to use a fourth criterion (accumulation). That is, an LBH text may be identified as such by a *sufficient accumulation* of LBH features, and an EBH text, even with a few LBH features, may still be identified as EBH if those LBH features show *negligible* accumulation. But the challengers would ask, *how much accumulation is to be sufficient and how little accumulation is to be negligible?*

Third, consequently, there is the issue of LBH in preexilic literature, that is, LBH features that are found in preexilic biblical texts and inscriptions. The advocates of linguistic dating might ascribe the LBH features

---

[142] Hurvitz, "Recent Debate," 202–3.

in early biblical literature to scribal activity of a later period. However, LBH in preexilic inscriptions is difficult to explain. The challengers would ask, if LBH existed during the preexilic period, how can we date a text on the basis of the contrast between EBH and LBH? This returns to the previous issue, that is, that EBH and LBH texts can be distinguished only by frequency or tendency.

Fourth, the challengers argue for "postexilic EBH." They maintain that some postexilic prophets (such as Isaiah 40–66, Joel, Haggai, Zechariah, and Malachi) employ impeccable EBH. On the other hand, the advocates of linguistic dating argue that postexilic literature always betrays the diction of LBH.

Fifth, there is disagreement about the validity of using extrabiblical sources. Whereas Hurvitz believes that extrabiblical sources can serve as an external control both for EBH and LBH, the challengers argue that they should be viewed as independent corpora.

Sixth, Hurvitz and the challengers disagree about studying the Hebrew language exclusively of the MT. Hurvitz argues that studying the language only of the MT is possible for at least vocabulary and syntax. The challengers argue that although there might not have been a comprehensive linguistic revision of the text, "unsystematic" and "occasional" scribal interferences will likely make it impossible for us to date the text on linguistic grounds.

Seventh, the two groups disagree about the validity of lexical data. The challengers argue that lexical data are unstable and random and that the lexicon of EBH is practically the same as that of LBH. Hurvitz, however, argues that as long as lexical data complement or are complemented by the data of other subfields of linguistics, they constitute valid criteria.

These issues are at the heart of today's debate between the traditional chronological understanding of BH and the challengers' alternative view. In most cases, the two groups' understandings of the biblical data seem difficult to reconcile. In order to break an apparent impasse, therefore, we may have to use a new kind of approach that can embrace the two seemingly irreconcilable positions.

CHAPTER THREE

THE VARIATION ANALYSIS OF THE HEBREW BIBLE CORPUS: THE METHOD

The present project is motivated by the question of whether we can date biblical texts solely on the basis of linguistic evidence. This question may properly be discussed with a method that is able to embrace and deal empirically with as many facets of the biblical data as possible. Such, I believe, is *the variationist approach* (or *variation analysis*) of sociolinguistics, which I have chosen as the method of the present study. In this chapter I will discuss this method and argue that it is valid, necessary, and profitable in investigating the question of the linguistic dating of BH texts. The chapter comprises three sections. In the first section, I survey a few Hebraists who have studied BH using sociolinguistic methods. Sociolinguistics is the matrix for the variationist approach, and these scholars have offered important insights for doing the variation analysis of the BH corpus. In the second section, I set a methodological framework. I describe the characteristics of linguistic variation and of variation analysis, and then justify the application of the variationist approach to the BH corpus. The discipline of *historical sociolinguistics* is introduced, which provides a basis for conducting the variation analysis of the BH data. In the third section, I discuss extensively how I will practice the method, that is, how I will use the variationist approach with the BH corpus in the following chapters.

1. *Sociolinguistics and the Study of Biblical Hebrew: The Precursors*

Sociolinguistics is based on the assumption that language and society are intricately related. Specifically, it seeks to understand the sociological implications of language use. Its interests include language change, language choice, language and class, language and gender, and speech style.[1] Since sociolinguistics is a young discipline which emerged only in

---

[1] Florian Coulmas, "Sociolinguistics," in *The Handbook of Linguistics* (ed. Mark Aronoff and Janie Rees-Miller; Malden, Mass.: Blackwell, 2001), 563–64; William M. Schniedewind,

the 1960s, its insights and methods have been used in the study of BH only by a few Hebraists.[2] I will survey three scholars: William M. Schniedewind, Agustinus Gianto, and Frank H. Polak.

In his "Prolegomena," William M. Schniedewind points out that the current study of Classical Hebrew is flawed because it has been dominated by formalist approaches and paid little attention to the society that spoke it.[3] This is a serious disadvantage, as Schniedewind states, because "language choice and language change can be socially loaded"[4] and the "disconnect between Hebrew language and its speakers...takes the study of language out of context."[5] Schniedewind therefore argues that "the study of historical Hebrew linguistics must begin with social changes in ancient Palestine"[6] because "social history provides clues for identifying periods when we might expect seminal changes in the Hebrew language," while "language change points to changes in the social life of ancient Israel and early Judaism."[7]

Illustrative are his studies on Qumran Hebrew (= QH).[8] Schniedewind notes that the well-known idiosyncrasies of QH are not adequately explained by traditional formal approaches, which employ the methods of historical, comparative, structural, and generative linguistics. He then argues that when the idiosyncrasies of QH are seen from a sociolinguistic perspective, that is, against the backdrop of the society that spoke it, they are understood as the outcome of ideological manipulation of linguistic forms with which the speakers of QH tried to differentiate them-

---

"Prolegomena for the Sociolinguistics of Classical Hebrew," *JHS* 5 (2004–2005): §1.4. Online: http://www.jhsonline.org/Articles/article_36.pdf.

[2] The earliest sociolinguistic studies include, for example, William Labov, "The Social Motivation of a Sound Change," *Word* 19 (1963): 273–309; idem, *The Social Stratification of English in New York City* (Urban Language Series; Washington, D.C.: Center for Applied Linguistics, 1966); and Peter Trudgill, *The Social Differentiation of English in Norwich* (Cambridge Studies in Linguistics 13; Cambridge: Cambridge University Press, 1974).

[3] Schniedewind, "Prolegomena" (above, n. 1), §1.

[4] Schniedewind, "Prolegomena," §2.9.

[5] Schniedewind, "Prolegomena," §1.3.

[6] Schniedewind, "Prolegomena," §5.3.

[7] Schniedewind, "Prolegomena," §5.5. In addition to sociolinguistics, Schniedewind maintains that the study of Classical Hebrew should also incorporate anthropological linguistics, which is related to but different from sociolinguistics. Whereas sociolinguistics addresses "issues like language change, language choice, language and gender, and speech register," anthropological linguistics "incorporates theories of culture into the study of language" (Schniedewind, "Prolegomena," §1.4).

[8] Schniedewind, "Qumran Hebrew as an Antilanguage," *JBL* 118 (1999): 235–52; idem, "Linguistic Ideology in Qumran Hebrew," in *Diggers at the Well: Proceedings of a Third International Symposium on the Hebrew of the Dead Sea Scrolls and Ben Sira* (ed. T. Muraoka and J. F. Elwolde; STDJ 36; Leiden: Brill, 2000), 245–55.

selves from others. In this sense, Schniedewind calls QH "antilanguage."[9] Schniedewind's case study constitutes a convincing argument regarding QH's well-known idiosyncrasies; thus it confirms the theoretical foundation of sociolinguistics: that understanding language requires apprehending society.

In his "Variations in Biblical Hebrew," Agustinus Gianto examines grammatical and lexical variations in BH in light of the sociolinguistic understanding of dialectology.[10] He introduces two sociolinguistic concepts: *social markers* and *social registers*. Social markers, Gianto explains, are "variants that agree with the social status of the speakers and their awareness of the significance of such variants." Social registers, on the other hand, are variants that correlate to various social circumstances independent of the social identification of the speakers.[11] By surveying some variations in the Hebrew Bible and their significance in context, Gianto argues that the Hebrew Bible provides useful examples of both phenomena. He groups the examples of social markers in BH into three categories: (1) examples reflecting certain group-awareness and attitudes toward outsiders (e.g., שִׁבֹּלֶת vs. סִבֹּלֶת in Judg 12:6; Nehemiah's complaint about the lack of knowledge of Hebrew among the Jewish children [Neh 13:24]; a preference for the hypercorrect pronunciation such as בְּאֹר over בּוֹר); (2) the alternate forms of address or self-reference (e.g., אַתָּה vs. אֲדֹנִי); and (3) the diversity in theophoric elements in proper names. Likewise, Gianto discusses four kinds of social registers: (1) the diglossia of spoken and written language; (2) code-switching (e.g., the switch from Hebrew to Aramaic in Gen 31:47 and Jer 10:11; the form of III-ה with paragogic נ and without נ); (3) various types of discourse, such as exhortatory speech, narrative, and expository discourse, that determine the meaning and use of verbal forms; and (4) interpretation of *yiqtol* in archaizing poetry depending on the semantic context.[12] Gianto concludes that the social markers and registers that he has examined are "part of the mechanism which shaped the language of the Hebrew Bible and which also produced elements of diversity of Hebrew."[13]

Gianto's study is a pilot one in that it discusses only some of the relevant data. Frank H. Polak, on the other hand, provides a more exhaustive statistical treatment.

---

9   Schniedewind, "Antilanguage," 235–36.
10 Agustinus Gianto, "Variations in Biblical Hebrew," *Bib* 77 (1996): 493–508.
11 Gianto, "Variations," 497–98.
12 Gianto, "Variations," 498–508.
13 Gianto, "Variations," 508.

Polak's starting point is the sociolinguistic understanding of the difference between oral and written language and literature.[14] Following this
understanding, Polak maintains with regard to the BH style that "the more
a text is rooted in the scribal context, the more complicated its language,
in terms of hypotaxis, length of the noun string, and the number of explicit
sentence constituents" and that "the closer a text is to spoken language
and oral literature, the simpler it is, in terms of syntactic structure, refer-
ence, and clause length."[15]

Polak attempts to place various BH narratives onto the above continuum of oral and written literature. Of importance is his use of statistics.
He counts the number of clauses in each pericope and the number of
arguments in each clause.[16] He then calculates the percentages of different
types of clauses.[17] Polak's statistics group BH narratives into three corpora.
The first corpus, which includes the Elijah–Elisha tales, the Samuel–Saul–
David narrative, the Abraham–Jacob cycle, and many narrative sections
from Exodus, Numbers, and Judges, uses a "classical" style which is rooted
in "spontaneous spoken language" and which uses shorter clauses and simpler structures with fewer references.[18] The second corpus, which includes
texts from the late Judean monarchy and the first stages of the Babylonian
period (Deuteronomy, the redaction of Kings, the Jeremiah history, and
part of the priestly writings), represents the late preexilic and exilic style,
which is rooted in written language and which uses complex syntactic

---

[14] Polak cites, for example, Jack Goody, *The Interface between the Written and the Oral*
(Cambridge: Cambridge University Press, 1987), 262–72; Wallace L. Chafe, "Linguistic Dif-
ferences Produced by Differences between Speaking and Writing," in *Literacy, Language,
and Learning: The Nature and Consequences of Reading and Writing* (ed. David R. Olson,
Nancy Torrance, and Angela Hildyard; Cambridge: Cambridge University Press, 1985),
105–23. See Polak, "The Oral and the Written: Syntax, Stylistics and the Development of
Biblical Prose," *JANES* 26 (1998): 60–61 n. 9. See also the works cited in Polak, "Oral and
Written," 101–2 nn. 57–62.

[15] Polak, "Oral and Written," 59. Polak calls the former the "complex-nominal" style
and the latter the "rhythmic-verbal" style. See Polak, "Oral and Written," 75; idem, "Style
Is More Than the Person: Sociolinguistics, Literary Culture and the Distinction between
Written and Oral Narrative," in Young (ed.), *Biblical Hebrew*, 44–45.

[16] An *argument* is an element required by a predicate without which a clause is grammatically incomplete. A noun, adjective, or independent pronoun can be an argument
when it is a subject, object, or complement of a clause. See further Polak, "Sociolinguistics:
A Key to the Typology and the Social Background of Biblical Hebrew," *HS* 47 (2006): 130–31
n. 64.

[17] For Polak's statistics, see his "Key to Typology," 135–36, 145–48; also idem, "Oral and
Written," 69–71. In addition to narratives, Polak uses the same method in analyzing dif-
ferent styles of quoted speech and the narrator's discourse. See Polak, "The Style of the
Dialogue in Biblical Prose Narrative," *JANES* 28 (2001): 53–95.

[18] Polak, "Key to Typology," 141–48; idem, "Oral and Written," 78–87.

structures with embedded clauses and more references.[19] Polak's third corpus consists of texts from the Persian era: Ezra, Nehemiah, Esther, the parts of the Chronicler's history not paralleled by his biblical sources, and part of the priestly writings, especially in Numbers. This last group uses a style that shows traits similar to the second corpus, with the additional feature of Aramaisms.[20]

Two aspects of Polak's studies should be noted. First, Polak's categorization of BH narrative styles may provide further support for the validity of the linguistic dating of biblical texts. As we can see, Polak's three corpora, which he divides first and foremost on the basis of formal criteria, also correspond to the chronological strata of BH. So, if one considers Polak's methods and results to be valid, one may examine a narrative text with regard to the complexity of its clauses, categorize the narrative into one of Polak's three styles, and date the narrative to the period that provides the matrix for the particular style. For example, if a text is dominated by the syntactic structure that is simple with fewer references, it belongs to the oldest layer of BH; if a style mainly shows complex structures, with embedded clauses and more references, it belongs to either late preexilic to exilic BH or postexilic BH.[21] The second, and for us more important, contribution by Polak is his use of statistics. Polak's statistical analyses help us to see patterns and tendencies in different BH narrative styles that were not previously obvious when they were examined individually. Moreover, to our advantage, statistical studies such as Polak's allow us to carry out similar experiments so that we may further verify, revise, or disprove previous theories.[22]

Schniedewind, Gianto, and Polak are important precursors to the present study. Schniedewind has demonstrated the importance of a sociolinguistic framework in the study of BH. Gianto has introduced the concept of variation, which deserves further attention. Polak has provided examples of exhaustive studies that use statistical analysis. The present

---

[19] Polak, "Key to Typology," 119, 136–40; idem, "Oral and Written," 92–96.

[20] Polak, "Key to Typology," 119, 127–36; idem, "Oral and Written," 96–100; and idem, "Sociolinguistics and the Judean Speech Community in the Achaemenid Empire," in *Judah and the Judeans in the Persian Period* (ed. Oded Lipschits and Manfred Oeming; Winona Lake, Ind.: Eisenbrauns, 2006), 602–6.

[21] See Polak's theory on the development of the Hebrew narrative style in his "Key to Typology," 160–62. See also Polak, "Oral and Written," 69, 100–101.

[22] Polak's studies are detailed and exhaustive, and a thorough review is beyond the scope of the present discussion. Young, Rezetko, and Ehrensvärd provide a helpful summary and evaluation in their *Linguistic Dating*, 1:32–37, 95–102.

study starts from the foundations laid by these scholars, then attempts to broaden the horizon by exploring some less trodden territory.

2. *Linguistic Variation, Variation Analysis, Historical Sociolinguistics, and the Biblical Hebrew Corpus*

We have seen in chapter 1 an illustration of sociolinguistic variation analysis, in the form of Peter Trudgill's study of the variation of the present participle ending (e.g., *running* vs. *runnin'*). I avoided using technical terms there, but this is the right place to define some key terms in the study of linguistic variation.[23] *Linguistic* (or *language*) *variation* refers to the phenomenon in which a linguistic item has alternate realizations that are linguistically, or grammatically, equivalent.[24] For example, in Trudgill's study, the variation was the vacillation between *-ing* and *-in'* in pronouncing the verbal ending *-ing*. The item of variation is called a *linguistic variable*; the realizations are called *variants* or *variant forms*. Again in Trudgill's example, the underlying linguistic variable (ing) was realized as two variants or variant forms, which were *-ing* and *-in'*.[25] A linguistic variable is also called a *dependent variable*, since it is conditioned by (but does not condition) such factors as social class, gender, age, and style (i.e., the degree of being formal or informal). The conditioning factors are called *independent variables*. (This designation, of course, calls for caution in our understanding of the term 'variable'.) As we have seen, Trudgill incorporated two independent variables: style (i.e., word-list speech, reading-passage speech, formal speech, and casual speech) and social class (i.e., middle middle class, lower middle class, upper working class, middle working class, and lower working class).

---

[23] For the sociolinguistic terms to be defined here, one may consult Joan Swann et al., *A Dictionary of Sociolinguistics* (Edinburgh: Edinburgh University Press, 2004), esp. s.v. "language variation," "linguistic variable," "variant," "dependent variable," and "independent variable."

[24] In Trudgill's study, the two pronunciations of *-ing* and *-in'* are identical *linguistically* (i.e., grammatically), but different *non-linguistically* (i.e., socially or stylistically). This distinction between linguistic (or grammatical) meaning and social meaning is important for variationist sociolinguistics. For example, see the following sentences:

He doesn't know anything.
He don't know nothing.

The two sentences express the same grammatical meaning, but each conveys a very different social meaning, in this case, possibly with regard to the speaker's social status.

[25] In sociolinguistics, parentheses are used to designate the underlying form of a linguistic variable.

2.1. *Linguistic Variation and Variation Analysis*

Below I discuss linguistic variation and the study of it, highlighting four important aspects.

Variation is an essential component of language. As Robert Bayley observes, the central idea of variation analysis is "that an understanding of language requires an understanding of variable."[26] In other words, linguistic variables are an essential component of language. This idea is a latecomer in linguistics. Until the first sociolinguists embarked on their enterprise, linguists had regarded linguistic variables as mere anomalies and exceptions.[27] Variables had been considered meaningless and insignificant and had to be cleared so that linguists could penetrate to what they considered the proper object of linguistic study, that is, categorical processes such as phonological, morphological, and syntactical rules, which belong to, say, the 'langue' of Saussure or the 'linguistic competence' of the Chomskyan tradition. The first sociolinguists, however, were decisively different from their predecessors and colleagues in their embracing of linguistic variables as the central subject of their studies. Their researches began to demonstrate that variables are as constituent of language as the categorical rules of grammar and that a proper understanding of language requires a study not only of categorical processes but also of variations.[28]

Variation has "structured heterogeneity." Following the earliest variationist linguists, Bayley further notes that linguistic variation is characterized by "orderly or 'structured heterogeneity.'"[29] Linguistic variables are not *free* in the sense that they occur at random. Rather, they occur in statistically predictable patterns because the speaker's choice between variants is "systematically constrained by multiple linguistic and social factors."[30]

---

[26] Robert Bayley, "The Quantitative Paradigm," in *The Handbook of Language Variation and Change* (ed. J. K. Chambers, Peter Trudgill, and Natalie Schilling-Estes; Malden, Mass.: Blackwell, 2002), 117. See my fuller quotation of Bayley in chapter 1, p. 5.

[27] For some of the earliest sociolinguistic studies, see above, n. 2.

[28] J. K. Chambers, *Sociolinguistic Theory: Linguistic Variation and Its Social Significance* (2nd ed.; Language in Society 22; Oxford: Blackwell, 2003), 13–14, 26–27.

[29] Bayley, "Quantitative Paradigm," 117. The idea of "orderly heterogeneity" comes from Uriel Weinreich, William Labov, and Marvin I. Herzog, "Empirical Foundations for a Theory of Language Change," in *Directions for Historical Linguistics: A Symposium* (ed. W. P. Lehmann and Yakov Malkiel; Austin, Tex.: University of Texas Press, 1968), 99–100.

[30] Bayley, "Quantitative Paradigm," 117. Linguistic factors include specific phonetical, phonological, morphological, or syntactical contexts that are favorable to a particular variant. For example, in English, the optional deletion of word-final /t/ after a consonant is influenced by the sound that follows. Word-final /t/ is deleted more frequently when it

Of course, it should be remembered that these factors do not *dictate* the outcome of the choice. The study of linguistic variation treats probability, but not rules or mechanical processes, which are properly the realm of grammar.

Variation is the mechanism of language change. A very important discovery by variationist sociolinguists is that linguistic variation is the mechanism of linguistic change. Gregory R. Guy explains it:

> The structural view of linguistic organization that has dominated theoretical thought in linguistics for most of this century makes change appear puzzling and dysfunctional. If the elements of language are defined by their place in a finely articulated categorical mental grammar, then how and why do they change at all? How does a system based on discretely opposed categories sustain the ultimate indiscretion of mergers, splits, and other transmutations of the categories? Why does change not act like grit in the gears of a machine, producing catastrophic failure rather than organic adaptation? Yet seen in light of the fact that all speech-communities and all speakers regularly and easily use and manipulate linguistic variables and variable processes, the puzzle disappears. The linguistic processes that yield change are diachronic extensions of variable processes that are extant in synchronic usage and synchronic grammar.[31]

In short, a change in progress, say, from rule A to rule B, does not disrupt the linguistic system, because the speakers possess both rules in their linguistic competence and know how to negotiate them jointly. Conversely, changes do not occur without variation, that is, "without passing through a period where what will turn out to be the 'old' form and the 'new' form are both simultaneously present in the community."[32]

This concept of *change through variation* is illustrated by the following table, which proposes several stages of a linguistic change from the exclusive use of one variant to the exclusive use of another. In Table 2, X is the form before change; Y is the form after change. E_i is the linguistic or social

---

is followed by an obstruent and less frequently when it is followed by a vowel (e.g., *wes' side* vs. *west end*). Gregory R. Guy, "Variationist Approaches to Phonological Change," in *The Handbook of Historical Linguistics* (ed. Brian D. Joseph and Richard D. Janda; Malden, Mass.: Blackwell, 2004), 375.

As social factors, sociolinguists emphasize social class, sex, and age. Styles, or different degrees of formality, are also an important context that induces the choice of a particular variant. Sociolinguists may use the following styles: word-list style, reading-passage style, interview style, and casual style. See Chambers, *Sociolinguistic Theory*, 4–8.

[31] Guy, "Variationist Approaches," 370. See also James Milroy, *Linguistic Variation and Change: On the Historical Sociolinguistics of English* (Language in Society 19; Oxford: Blackwell, 1992), 2–3.

[32] Guy, "Variationist Approaches," 370.

environment that would initiate change and is favorable to the new form Y; E_2 is the environment that is favorable to the old form X. X/Y indicates the use of both forms, that is, the state of variation.

Table 2. Variation model of change

Stage of change		E1	E2
1	Categorical status, before undergoing change	X	X
2	Early stage begins variably in restricted environment	X/Y	X
3	Change in full progress, greater use of new form in E1 where change first initiated	X/Y	X/Y
4	Change progresses toward completion with movement toward categoricality first in E1 where change initiated	Y	X/Y
5	Completed change, new variant	Y	Y

Source: Walt Wolfram and Natalie Schilling-Estes, "Dialectology and Linguistic Diffusion," in Joseph and Janda (ed.), *Handbook of Historical Linguistics*, 716, who have simplified the models presented by Charles-James N. Bailey, *Variation and Linguistic Theory* (Washington, D.C.: Center for Applied Linguistics, 1973). Used by permission of John Wiley & Sons Limited.

Therefore, as Guy puts it, linguistic variation and linguistic change are "two faces of the same coin." Linguistic variation is "the inevitable synchronic face" of linguistic change, and linguistic change is always a diachronic extension of linguistic variation. In other words, a linguistic change, which can be discerned only in retrospect (i.e., from a diachronic perspective), presents itself as a linguistic variation across different social groups or contexts, when it is observed at a specific point in time.[33]

Variation has social significance. Variationist linguists attempt to illuminate the *social* significance of language variation, which is represented as "the *correlation* of dependent linguistic variables with independent social

---

[33] Guy, "Variationist Approaches," 370. It is important to note, however, that linguistic variation does not always result in linguistic change. There are cases where the variation is stable for a prolonged time. An example is the English alternation between *-ing* and *-in'*, which has been stable for over six centuries. Guy, "Variationist Approaches," 371.

From its inception, the goal of variationist linguistics has been to understand and illuminate linguistic change. Indeed, the phrase *variation and change* seems like a fixed expression in the discipline. For example, one of the leading journals in the discipline is entitled *Language Variation and Change*; an encyclopedic textbook on linguistic variation is entitled *The Handbook of Language Variation and Change* (above, n. 26); and James Milroy's pioneering work is entitled *Linguistic Variation and Change* (above, n. 31).

variables."[34] The social variables to which sociolinguists pay attention include such factors as style, gender, age, and social class. In the example of the variation *-ing* vs. *-in'* of Norwich, England, the speaker's choice correlated with his or her social class and the degree of formality (i.e., the style he or she adopts). In his 1966 study of the New York speakers' pronunciation (and non-pronunciation) of the intervocalic /r/, Labov discovered that as the speaker's social class became higher and the style more formal, she or he became more likely to pronounce the sound.[35]

Accordingly, variationist sociolinguistics is also called *correlational* sociolinguistics. Indeed, correlation is so important that it is a prerequisite to the study of linguistic variation. If a correlation is not observed between a linguistic variable and independent variables, the study cannot stand.[36]

2.2. *The Variation Analysis of Written Data: The First Case*

With the foregoing understanding of the characteristics of linguistic variation and variation analysis, we should now ask a question that is central to this chapter: is it legitimate to use the variationist approach in the study of BH variables? Before we address this question, however, we should first discuss a prerequisite question: is it legitimate to use the variationist approach on written data? Only when we are able to answer the latter question affirmatively can we rightfully address the legitimacy of the variation analysis of the BH corpus. In this and the following subsections, I will answer the second, prerequisite question.

To begin with, it should be noted that variation analysis was from the outset designed for the study of spoken language. Thus, it is the *speaker's* choice, not the writer's, to which the sociolinguist pays attention.[37] Trudgill and Labov studied the *speakers* of Norwich and of New York (see above). The best data for variationist sociolinguists are sociolinguistic interviews, tape recordings, and acoustic analysis.[38] All this may raise suspicion as to the legitimacy of the variationist approach in studying written documents. In some cases, however, scholars apply the variationist approach to written data.

---

[34] Chambers, *Sociolinguistic Theory*, xix. Emphasis added.

[35] Labov, *Social Stratification of English*, 237–43. See R. L. Trask's convenient summary of both Trudgill's and Labov's studies in his *Historical Linguistics* (London: Arnold, 1996), 277–79.

[36] Chambers, *Sociolinguistic Theory*, 26.

[37] E.g., Bayley, "Quantitative Paradigm," 117.

[38] Edgar W. Schneider, "Investigating Variation and Change in Written Documents," in Chambers et al. (ed.), *Handbook of Language Variation and Change*, 67.

On the one hand, scholars conduct the variation analysis of written data in order to examine the spoken language of the past. In this case, the variationist linguist's goal is not to study the language of the document but to study the spoken language *represented* in it. Accordingly, the document becomes a pathway to the variation and change of spoken language, and a primary task for the variationist linguist is to evaluate the character of the text at hand, to examine how close it is to the vernacular, and to determine whether or not to use it.[39]

In this situation, the Hebrew Bible corpus does not prove to be a very good resource for the study of BH variables. First, it is very difficult, if not impossible, to argue from the available evidence that BH represents, reflects, or even is based on the language that was spoken in Palestine from the Iron Age to the Hellenistic period. Some even put forth an argument that BH is strictly a literary language, a "scholarly construct" of the postexilic period.[40] Second, even if we accept that BH was at least *based* on spoken language, and thus we can possibly reach spoken Hebrew *through* biblical literature, we still have to evaluate different types of biblical texts to see whether they constitute a good pathway. And in this process, we would end up losing a substantial part of the biblical data, since not many texts would have been speech-based.[41] This is a serious disadvantage for

---

[39] Schneider, "Variation and Change in Written Documents," 67–68. Schneider observes that only a relatively small amount of historical texts may be used for variation analysis. He discusses four requirements that the text should meet to qualify as valid data. First, "texts should be as close to speech, and especially vernacular styles, as possible." Second, "to facilitate correlations with extralinguistic parameters, the texts should be of different origins, i.e. stem from several authors from different social classes, possibly also age groups, and both sexes, and should represent varying stylistic levels." Third, "texts must display variability of the phenomenon under investigation, i.e. the use of functionally equivalent variants of a linguistic variable." Fourth, "with quantification being the staple methodology of variationism, texts must fulfill certain size requirements. There is no figure specifying any precise minimum number of words required—but usable texts must provide reasonably large token frequencies of individual variants, and they should (though need not) allow quantitative analyses of several phenomena, i.e. display variation in a wider range of linguistic phenomena." Schneider, "Variation and Change in Written Documents," 71.

[40] See Philip R. Davies, *In Search of 'Ancient Israel'* (2nd ed.; London: Sheffield Academic Press, 1995), 100. Davies follows Ernst Axel Knauf, "War 'Biblisch-Hebräisch' eine Sprache? Empirische Gesichtspunkte zur linguistischen Annäherung an die Sprache der althebräischen Literatur," *ZAH* 3 (1990): 11–23, who argues on the basis of the preexilic inscriptions that BH was never a spoken language but an artificial literary construct in the postexilic period. See also Edward Ullendorff, "Is Biblical Hebrew a Language?" *BSOAS* 34 (1971): 241–55; repr. in *Is Biblical Hebrew a Language? Studies in Semitic Languages and Civilizations* (Wiesbaden: Otto Harrassowitz, 1977), 3–17.

[41] Of course, we do have dialogues and quotations, but they are not the majority of the biblical material. Also, apart from the problem of whether they are records of actual speeches, it should be noted that most speeches in the Bible were put in writing at a time

a student of BH who wants to exploit every bit of the small corpus that
has been handed down.

2.3. *The Variation Analysis of Written Data: The Case of Historical Sociolinguistics*

Fortunately, however, scholars employ the variationist approach on written documents for another purpose—in this case, for studying written
language itself, not for excavating speech *from* it. When they do so, they
work in the discipline of *historical sociolinguistics.* Historical sociolinguistics was once a subdiscipline of sociolinguistics but has now become
independent. The name is apt because the two words designate the discipline's subject matter and method. That is, historical sociolinguistics
studies *historical* documents (i.e., documents of the past) with the *sociolinguistic* method of variation analysis.

The use of a sociolinguistic method (i.e., the variationist approach)
with documents of the past stands on two principles. The first is the
uniformitarian principle. A concept formulated in modern geology, this
principle, as employed in linguistics, dictates that the linguistic variations
and changes of the past should be no different from the linguistic variations and changes of today and that one may infer knowledge of the linguistic variations and changes of the past by comprehending the same
of today. This is the basis on which the sociolinguistic method used for
present-day speech (i.e., the variationist approach) may also be used for
the language of the past.[42]

The second but equally important principle pertains to one major dis-
juncture between historical sociolinguistics and its mother discipline: that
is, whereas sociolinguistics investigates *spoken* language, historical sociolinguistics examines *written* language. One may rightfully ask whether
or not written data of any kind are a legitimate object of sociolinguistic
study. To be more specific, does written language show linguistic variations that can be analyzed like the variations of spoken language? As an

---

and a place far removed from the original time and place. This situation renders written
data a not good pathway. Cf. Schneider, "Variation and Change in Written Documents,"
70–81.

[42] Labov, *Principles of Linguistic Change*, vol. 1, *Internal Factors* (Language in Society
20; Oxford: Blackwell, 1994), 21–23. Cf. Terttu Nevalainen and Helena Raumolin-Brunberg,
Historical Sociolinguistics: Language Change in Tudor and Stuart England (Longman Linguistics Library; London: Longman, 2003), 22; Alexander Bergs, *Social Networks and Historical Sociolinguistics: Studies in Morphosyntactic Variation in the Paston Letters (1421–1503)*
(Topics in English Linguistics 51; Berlin: M. de Gruyter, 2005), 43–45.

answer to this question, I quote the historical sociolinguist Alexander Bergs: "The written language mode...forms an independent linguistic system, a mode of expression that is neither totally dependent on nor prerequisite to any other mode of expression."[43] Like spoken language, written language experiences language change; it may show "as great a deal of variation as spoken language, on all levels of language, from orthography to discourse." And for the historical sociolinguist, *"any kind of variation will do."*[44] In other words, in historical sociolinguistics, written documents of any kind may come under examination; in this discipline—unlike the situation in which written data are a pathway to the spoken language of the past—written data do not have to be close to spoken language, nor do they necessarily have to represent it.[45]

This understanding of written language is greatly helpful to our study of the BH corpus. To begin with, it is no longer required that the data for analysis be close to spoken language. Accordingly, the amount of data increases considerably. It becomes possible to study all of the BH texts, not just the texts that are considered to reflect the vernacular, and thus our statistical study will obtain more validity. Hence Bergs's confident statement: historical sociolinguistics "does not *suffer* from a lack of natural, spoken linguistic data...Instead, historical sociolinguistics must be bold enough to loosen its ties with present-day sociolinguistics and traditional historical linguistics, and to develop its own methodologies, aims, and theories."[46]

The foregoing two principles—the uniformitarian principle and the principle of understanding written language as an independent linguistic system—are the foundation on which the sociolinguistic method may properly be used with the written data of the past. Accordingly, it should

---

[43] Bergs, *Social Networks*, 20. Cf. Douglas Biber, *Variation across Speech and Writing* (Cambridge: Cambridge University Press, 1988), who has demonstrated that the stylistic diversity of different genres of English writing can be as dynamic as that of English speeches, and that this diversity makes it impossible for us to discover a single parameter with which to dichotomize speech and writing.

[44] Bergs, *Social Networks*, 18. Emphasis original. Note also Merja Kytö's statement: "Historical data can be valid in their own right for the study of the relation between spoken and written language, regardless of the extent to which the data are removed from the productions of native speakers." Kytö, *Variation and Diachrony, with Early American English in Focus: Studies on Can/May and Will/Shall* (Bamberger Beiträge zur englischen Sprachwissenschaft 28; Frankfurt am Main: Peter Lang, 1991), 36–37.

[45] Hence historical sociolinguists' understanding of written language shores up Hurvitz's claim that even if it is a literary language, BH can be a proper object of diachronic linguistic study. See above chapter 2.

[46] Bergs, *Social Networks*, 21.

be emphasized that the method of historical sociolinguistics is in essence the method of present-day sociolinguistics. With regard to particulars, however, there are some differences between the method of the daughter discipline and that of the mother. To illustrate, I will survey a representative historical sociolinguistic study. By doing so, we will be able not only to see the important traits of historical sociolinguistics but also to appreciate its potential as an appropriate method for examining the BH data.

Helena Raumolin-Brunberg has examined the diffusion of the subject pronoun *you* in English during the late middle and early modern period (1350–1710).[47] As is known, the second-person pronoun *you* originally functioned only as an object, while the subject was expressed by the old form *ye*. From about 1480, the object form *you* was used as a subject alongside the old subject form *ye*, and in about 120 years, *you* ousted *ye*. Raumolin-Brunberg traces this development using two electronic corpora: the *Corpus of Early English Correspondence* (= *CEEC*) and the *Helsinki Corpus of English Texts* (= *HC*). The *CEEC* covers the time span from ca. 1410 to 1681, counting about 2.7 million words. It comprises over 6,000 letters written by 778 individuals, whose genders, periods, regions, and social statuses have been recorded as much as possible.[48] The *HC* covers Old and Middle English (ca. 750–1710), counting about 1.5 million words. It is a multigenre corpus. Like the *CEEC*, it incorporates non-linguistic variables such as the author's gender, social rank, period, region, etc.[49]

Raumolin-Brunberg's method is lucid. In the *CEEC* and the *HC*, she counts the occurrences of the two variants (*ye* and *you*), which amount to 17,982 (13,493 from the *CEEC* and 4,489 from the *HC*). Then, she correlates the use of *you* with the following independent variables: timing (periods of 40-year divisions), individual, genre, social class, gender, and region. First, when correlated with timing, the replacement of *ye* by *you* shows an S-curve which is typical of a linguistic change (with a slow start, a rapid acceleration, and a slow completion; see Figure 2). Second, when

---

[47] Helena Raumolin-Brunberg, "The Diffusion of Subject *You*: A Case Study in Historical Sociolinguistics," *Language Variation and Change* 17 (2005): 55–73.
[48] *Corpus of Early English Correspondence* (compiled by Terttu Nevalainen et al.; Helsinki: Department of English, University of Helsinki, 1998). For an overview, see Nevalainen and Raumolin-Brunberg, *Historical Sociolinguistics*, 43–52.
[49] *ki Corpus of English Texts* (compiled by the Helsinki Corpus project team; Helsinki: Department of English, University of Helsinki, 1991). See further Merja Kytö, *Manual ronic Part of the Helsinki Corpus of English Texts: Coding Conventions and Lists of texts* (3rd ed.; Helsinki: Department of English, University of Helsinki, 1996). ://icame.uib.no/hc/.

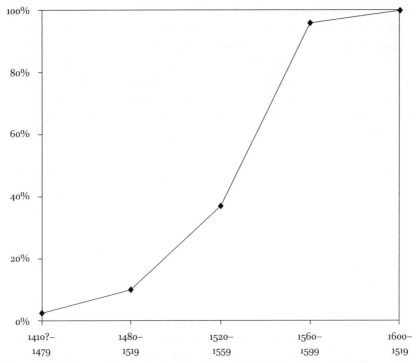

Source: Nevalainen and Raumolin-Brunberg, *Historical Sociolinguistics*, 60. Used by permission of Pearson Education Limited.

Figure 2. The replacement of subject *ye* by *you* in the *CEEC*: percentages of *you*

correlated with individuals, the use of *you* generally corresponds to the trend of the individual's time. Noteworthy is that during the period of rapid acceleration, about 60 percent of the individuals showed variability in their grammar by using both the old and the new forms. Third, for the multigenre *HC*, Raumolin-Brunberg correlates the use of *you* and *ye* with different genres. The occurrences of *you* and *ye* are uneven across various genres through different time periods, which makes her reluctant to draw a conclusion. So Raumolin-Brunberg minimizes her genre division and categorizes all the texts into two major genres: oral and literate.[50] As a result, she is able to show that *you* first spread through texts that

---

[50] For historical linguists, a 'literate' genre is synonymous with a typical written-based genre. To be more precise, 'oral' and 'literate' constitute the end points of a continuum of the two modes of expression, i.e., spoken language and written language. Nevalainen and Raumolin-Brunberg, *Historical Sociolinguistics*, 29.

were closer to spoken language and then only later permeated written language, on the basis of the fact that the difference in the first time period (1500–1570) between the two genre groups (68% vs. 58%) is statistically significant (see Table 3). Fourth, the correlation with social ranks suggests that the social origin of *you* was among the middle classes. Fifth, the correlation with gender suggests that women led the change. Sixth, concerning region, Raumolin-Brunberg could not find any specific place as the origin of the change.[51]

Table 3. Subject *ye* and *you* in the early modern section of the *HC*, 1500–1710 (oral and literate genres)

	Oral genres			Literate genres		
	ye	*you*	Use of *you*	*ye*	*you*	Use of *you*
1500–1570	193	410	68%	89	125	58%
1570–1640	11	513	98%	22	378	95%
1640–1710	17	658	97%	9	248	96%

Note: Numbers are occurrences in each period and genre. Literate genres: handbooks, science, educational treatises, philosophy, sermons, travelogue, biography, and letters non-private. Oral genres: fiction, drama, diary, trial proceedings, autobiography, and letters private.

Source: Raumolin-Brunberg, "Diffusion of *You*," 64. Adapted from the original. Used by permission of Cambridge University Press.

---

[51] Similar examples abound. In her pioneering work, Suzanne Romaine, the founder of historical sociolinguistics, investigates the development of the Middle Scots relative marker using standard sociolinguistic methods. Her corpus includes 6,300 relative clause tokens from seven verse and prose texts of various styles that were written in the Central Scots region between ca. 1530 and 1550 (Romaine, *Socio-Historical Linguistics: Its Status and Methodology* [Cambridge Studies in Linguistics 34; Cambridge: Cambridge University Press, 1982]). Merja Kytö, in her *Variation and Diachrony* (above, n. 44), examines the development of modals in Early American English within the framework of sociohistorical variation analysis. Kytö documents and analyzes the uses of *can, could, may, might, shall, should, will,* and *would* by using various digital corpora. In another article, Kytö elucidates the development of the third-person singular present indicative marker (-*s* and -*th*, as in *she says* and *she saith*) in Early Modern British and American English (Kytö, "Third-Person Present Singular Verb Inflection in Early British and American English," *Language Variation and Change* 5 [1993]: 113–39). Bergs, in his *Social Networks* (above, n. 42), attempts to trace the morphosyntactic variation and change in the late Middle English Paston letters by investigating the variations of the third-person plural pronouns, relativization patterns, and light verb constructions. In their *Historical Sociolinguistics: Language Change in Tudor and Stuart England* (above, n. 42), Nevalainen and Raumolin-Brunberg examine fourteen linguistic variables by correlating them with social variables such as gender, social stratification, and region.

Typical of historical sociolinguistics, Raumolin-Brunberg's study reveals some major methodological differences between present-day sociolinguistics and historical sociolinguistics. That is, whereas sociolinguistics focuses on *phonological* variations of the speakers of the *present*, historical sociolinguistics investigates mainly *morphological* or *syntactical* variations in documents of the *past*. These differences lead us to consider a few more aspects of the method of historical sociolinguistics.[52]

First, as historical sociolinguists treat the past, they most often encounter the problem of controlling data. Whereas sociolinguists, who study the language of their contemporaries, can always control, collect, and supplement their data, historical sociolinguists cannot do so.[53] One may legitimately ask whether we can accurately describe the language of the past only on the basis of what we have inherited, or whether our description would not be limited or even distorted by chance, which preserved some documents and lost others. Further, given that the purpose of historical sociolinguistics is, like that of sociolinguistics, a correlation between linguistic variables and social variables, we should also ask whether we can produce a sound correlation when we cannot gather further information about the author and the text. The problem of the limitedness of data, however, has been successfully remedied with the advent of the computerized database, examples of which are the *CEEC* and the *HC* discussed above. The coded database of documents, as we have seen in the example of Raumolin-Brunberg's study, enables the researcher to process the linguistic variables of almost all the surviving texts and correlate them freely with various non-linguistic variables (e.g., time period, genre, gender, social class, region, style, etc.), if they are known. The large amount of data, with the wide scope of analysis, can to a great degree complement the fragmentary nature of historical documents.[54]

---

[52] For other differences between historical sociolinguistics and present-day sociolinguistics, see Raumolin-Brunberg, "Historical Sociolinguistics," in *Sociolinguistics and Language History: Studies Based on the Corpus of Early English Correspondence* (ed. Nevalainen and Raumolin-Brunberg; Language and Computers: Studies in Practical Linguistics 15; Amsterdam: Rodopi, 1996), 16–19.

[53] Cf. Raumolin-Brunberg, "Historical Sociolinguistics," 17–19.

[54] Juan Camilo Conde-Silvestre, "Putting Sociolinguistics to the Test of Time" (review of Nevalainen and Raumolin-Brunberg, *Historical Sociolinguistics*), *International Journal of English Studies* 5 (2005): 212–13. Cf. Schneider, "Variation and Change in Written Documents," 70; Matti Rissanen et al., "Introduction," in *English in Transition: Corpus-Based Studies in Linguistic Variation and Genre Styles* (ed. Matti Rissanen, Merja Kytö, and Kirsi Heikkonen; Topics in English Linguistics 23; Berlin: M. de Gruyter, 1997), 3–5.

Second, since historical sociolinguists pay attention to *morphological* or *syntactical* variations—unlike sociolinguists who generally examine *phonological* variations—we may have difficulty in confirming that a certain pair of linguistic items constitute a linguistic variable. As we have seen, a linguistic variable should have two (or more) realizations that have the same linguistic (i.e., grammatical) meaning. In sociolinguistics, phonological variations are easy to establish, for the speaker will have no difficulty in knowing whether two (or more) different pronunciations express the same grammatical meaning. In historical sociolinguistics, however, the situation is somewhat different. Syntactical variations may often be difficult to establish because two expressions different in structure would seldom mean exactly the same thing. In practice, for this reason, we may have to be satisfied in finding near-synonymous structures. Morphological variables, on the other hand, are easier to establish. For example, it seems clear that in English 'thou' and 'you' are two variant forms for the second-person singular pronoun and that -*s* and -*th* (as in *he says* and *he saith*) are two variant forms for the third-person singular present verbal ending. The two items in each pair are grammatically equivalent.[55]

2.4. *The Variation Analysis of the Biblical Hebrew Corpus*

The legitimacy of historical sociolinguistics provides Hebraists with a framework for applying the variationist approach to the BH corpus. Some methodological problems should be addressed, however. When we remember the kind of data used in Raumolin-Brunberg's study, we note a few differences between them and the data from the Hebrew Bible.

First, whereas Raumolin-Brunberg had much information about the authors of her data, we have very little knowledge about biblical writers. Some biblical books seem to preserve the authors' names, but in some cases they are misleading, and in most cases they are not helpful, providing only limited amount of information about the authors' background. This means, consequently, that we cannot use such independent variables as the author's age, gender, social class, and geographical origin. Thus, our study of BH variables will be limited in scope when compared with other historical sociolinguistic studies. Nevertheless, this situation does

---

[55] For the difficulty of establishing syntactic equivalence, see Raumolin-Brunberg, "Prototype Categories and Variation Studies," in *English Historical Linguistics 1992: Papers from the 7th International Conference on English Historical Linguistics, Valencia, 22–26 September 1992* (ed. Francisco Fernández, Miguel Fuster, and Juan José Calvo; Current Issues in Linguistic Theory 133; Amsterdam: John Benjamins, 1994), 287–303.

not imply that the variation analysis of the BH corpus is impossible. There are other independent variables we can collect to correlate them with dependent linguistic variables. Genres or text types are in most cases evident.[56] Time periods can also be utilized for quite a few books, though surely not for all.[57]

Second, a major obstacle for any kind of linguistic study of biblical material is that we do not treat the original manuscripts, written by the original authors. This is a serious problem also for the historical sociolinguistic study of BH. Unlike the data used in most historical linguistic studies, the books and texts of the Hebrew Bible had been copied, transmitted, edited, and expanded for centuries until they were finalized by the Masoretes. Worse, the vowel signs in the MT began to be added between 600 and 750 C.E.[58] This is at least 760 years after Daniel, which is considered one of the latest books in the Hebrew Bible, probably written shortly before 164 B.C.E.[59] So we can never be sure whether the original author's diction is traceable in the present MT. As we have seen in chapter 2, this issue—the use of the MT for the study of BH—is hotly debated between Hurvitz and the challengers. It seems to me, however, to be unwise to give up even starting the analysis. To be in a safer side, I accept the generally supported assumption that morphology and syntax are more immune to revision than orthography and phonology.[60] My analysis will therefore not include orthography and phonology. In addition, I will avoid basing my argument on vocalizations.

With regard to the linguistic study of the Hebrew Bible corpus, there seem to be two valid choices. One may fully appreciate the problems and limitations of the study of language through the text of the Hebrew Bible and thus be discouraged from going further. Or one can be aware of its problems and limitations but proceed to do what one can do with what one has. I choose the latter, especially because what I do is a desideratum: as far as I know, the variationist historical sociolinguistic method has not

---

[56] 'Text type' is used differently from 'genre' in historical sociolinguistics. See below, p. 79 n. 104.

[57] Below I will discuss further the use of time periods as an independent variable and explicate why it is not circular to use them in evaluating the issue of the linguistic dating of biblical texts.

[58] Israel Yeivin, *Introduction to the Tiberian Masorah* (trans. and ed. E. J. Revell; SBL-MasS 5; Missoula, Mont.: Scholars, 1980), 164.

[59] John J. Collins, *Daniel: A Commentary on the Book of Daniel* (Hermeneia; Minneapolis, Minn.: Fortress, 1993), 61.

[60] Hurvitz, "Relevance of BH Linguistics," 31* n. 31. Cf. Young, Rezetko, and Ehrensvärd, *Linguistic Dating*, 1:346.

been applied to the Hebrew Bible corpus. Ultimately, a historical linguistic study is, as Labov says, "the art of making the best use of bad data."[61] Until we make the attempt, we will not know whether the data are *too* bad to show us something, or whether they, even with their deficiencies, can still reveal something.

3. *The Method*

In this section I outline my method, which will be applied to the Hebrew Bible corpus. I discuss the following: the corpus, the data, the dependent linguistic variable, and the independent variable.

3.1. *The Corpus*

Our corpus is the Hebrew portion of the Hebrew Bible (thus excluding the parts in Aramaic, i.e., Gen 31:47 [two words]; Jer 10:11; Dan 2:4–7:28; Ezra 4:8–6:18; 7:12–26). Our quantitative analysis will not include extrabiblical material such as Hebrew inscriptions, the DSS, and the corpus in MH, although they will be occasionally consulted when they illuminate some aspects of the biblical data. These are undeniably very important sources for the study of BH. Nevertheless, I exclude them mainly because our data from the Hebrew Bible are relatively well-defined in terms of time and genre. The entire Hebrew Bible is temporally distinct from the sources in MH (ca. 200 C.E.). The DSS, which are generally dated between 200 B.C.E. and 70 C.E., started to be written after the writing of most of the Hebrew Bible books.[62] Preexilic Hebrew inscriptions are contemporary with much of biblical material. However, they contrast with the Hebrew Bible corpus in terms of genre and purpose, the latter being a literary creation

---

[61] Labov, *Principles*, 1:11.

[62] Admittedly, the latest books or texts in the Hebrew Bible (e.g., Daniel) are thought to have been written in the second century B.C.E. This may challenge my decision to exclude the DSS from the following analysis. In practice, however, the inclusion of the DSS in the study of BH has some disadvantages: if our corpus would include the DSS, it would span over a thousand years. This would radically increase the degree of linguistic diversity within the corpus, and using one method with the entire corpus may not be appropriate. Of course, I am fully aware that analyzing more data will almost always be more beneficial. However, since this is a pilot study, it does not seem methodologically wise to cover too large an amount of data, and if we have to set a boundary, the one between the Hebrew Bible and the DSS seems to be a viable choice. Cf. Susan Anne Groom, *Linguistic Analysis of Biblical Hebrew* (Carlisle, Cumbria: Paternoster, 2003), 12, and her citation there of André Lemaire, "Response à J. H. Hospers," *ZAH* 6 (1993): 125.

filled with religious ideologies and intended for posterity, and the former mostly recorded in everyday life for ephemeral purpose.

Collecting data, I will use the MT, following Hurvitz and other scholars. We remember the challengers' pressing argument that the language of the MT may not be equated with the original language of biblical books.[63] However, I agree with Hurvitz that a linguistic study should be based on "*actual* texts" rather than "*reconstructed* texts."[64] Of course, caution is due in treating the data from the MT, especially where the reading is dubious or seems susceptible to corruption. As for Kethib and Qere attestations, I will consider both, since each form seems to have been preserved as part of legitimate traditions.[65]

3.2. *The Basic Unit for Collecting Data*

In collecting data from the Hebrew Bible corpus, we should ask an important question, one that a sociolinguist or a historical sociolinguist would not need to worry about: that is, what is the basic unit for collecting data? In present-day and historical sociolinguistics, it is always an individual— whether a speaker or a writer. The sociolinguist elicits data from each individual speaker, and the historical sociolinguist collects data from each individual writer. The individual is *the elemental independent variable*

---

[63] Young, Rezetko, and Ehrensvärd, *Linguistic Dating*, 1:345; also, chapter 2 of the present study.

[64] See Hurvitz, *Priestly Source and Ezekiel*, 19. Emphasis original. For the linguistic study of the Hebrew Bible, the MT seems to be the most apparent and sound choice. Hurvitz is followed by Gary A. Rendsburg, Cynthia L. Miller, and Susan Anne Groom: see Rendsburg, *Diglossia in Ancient Hebrew* (AOS 72; New Haven, Conn.: American Oriental Society, 1990), 31–33; Miller, *The Representation of Speech in Biblical Hebrew Narrative: A Linguistic Analysis* (HSM 55; Atlanta: Scholars, 1996), 17–19; and Groom, *Linguistic Analysis*, 19–22.

[65] Of course, the situation is not simple at all. Opinions vary greatly regarding the Kethib–Qere system. Emanuel Tov summarizes them into four options. The first opinion considers the Qere to be a correction of the Kethib. The traditions had the Kethib only; the Qere, which was previously not part of the traditions, was used to replace the existing reading. A second view maintains that the Qere and the Kethib both have been preserved because they are alternative readings. The Qere reflects the majority reading, whereas the Kethib reflects the minority. The third intermediate view embraces both of the foregoing views. That is, the Qere system was originally used as a marginal correction of the existing reading (i.e., the Kethib), but later the same system was used additionally to denote optional variants. The last option argues that the Qere tradition was only a reading tradition that dictated how the text should be read. Tov notes that most scholars accept the third position. See further Tov's discussion and bibliography in his *Textual Criticism of the Hebrew Bible* (2nd rev. ed.; Minneapolis, Minn.: Fortress, 2001), 58–63. Whatever option one chooses, it is not methodologically sound to choose only one reading tradition over the other.

in the sense that the collected data are first arranged (i.e., correlated) with the individual who has produced them.

The rationale behind this understanding is that an individual speaker/ writer is linguistically more or less *consistent* and *distinct*. Each individual is generally *consistent* in his or her choice of linguistic variables and at the same time relatively *distinct* in the same matter from others' choices of the same variables. Working with the Hebrew Bible corpus, then, we should expect a similar entity: a block of material which is linguistically consistent and distinct and thus resembles an individual speaker/writer of present-day or historical sociolinguistics. The unit of book seems to be an obvious choice, but the situation is not as simple as it first appears.

First, for most prophets, individual books will do. Each prophet is reasonably distinct and should be treated separately. On the other hand, we cannot expect from a prophetic book the same degree of consistency that we would find in an individual speaker/writer. It is generally understood that virtually all the prophetic books have been expanded secondarily. Nevertheless, with the exception of Isaiah and Zechariah, which I will discuss shortly, it does not seem necessary to separate each prophetic book into pieces. As test cases, we may briefly discuss Jeremiah and Ezekiel. The book of Jeremiah is thought to have been expanded with biographical material and then with Deuteronomic prose.[66] Also, Ezekiel 40–48, some think, may not have come from the same hand that was responsible for Ezekiel 1–39.[67] If we agree, however, that our analysis should be grounded in an actual text rather than in a hypothetical source, then only when additions and expansions are linguistically too disparate will we have to separate layers. Such is not the case for Jeremiah and Ezekiel. Ezekiel 40–48 are possibly from Ezekiel himself, and even if they are not, they are probably from the same tradition.[68] In the case of Jeremiah, the situation is more complex. Nevertheless, it still seems to be the best option to use the book as a whole, because the literary process was probably not so pro-

---

[66] For a convenient review of scholarship, see W. McKane, "Jeremiah, Book of (Twentieth-Century Interpretation)," *DBI* 1:570–74.

[67] E.g., Walther Zimmerli, *Ezekiel 1: A Commentary on the Book of the Prophet Ezekiel, Chapter 1–24* (trans. Ronald E. Clements; Hermeneia; Philadelphia: Fortress, 1979), 68–74. For a history of interpretation, see J. G. Galambush, "Ezekiel, Book of," *DBI* 1:372–75.

[68] For the argument that Ezekiel 40–48 are authentic to the prophet himself, see Moshe Greenberg, "The Design and Themes of Ezekiel's Program of Restoration," *Int* 38 (1984): 181–208; idem, *Ezekiel 1–20: A New Translation with Introduction and Commentary* (AB 22; Garden City, N.Y.: Doubleday, 1983), 14–15; and Daniel I. Block, *The Book of Ezekiel: Chapter 1–24* (NICOT; Grand Rapids, Mich.: Eerdmans, 1997), 17–23, esp. 20–21. For the position that Ezekiel 40–48 belong to the Ezekiel tradition, see Zimmerli, *Ezekiel 1*, 68–74.

longed as to make it necessary to separate later layers. That is, if we accept that the book's closing occurred shortly after the last event recorded in it (ca. 560 B.C.E.; Jer 52:31–34), the temporal distance between the prophet's last activities (ca. 585 B.C.E.) and the book's final layers are not so far as to demand us to isolate some materials.[69] We can reasonably assume that at least linguistically, the book of Jeremiah is relatively homogeneous (i.e., consistent), and it will thus be treated as one unit.[70] The other smaller prophetic books (again, except for Isaiah and Zechariah) will be treated in the same way: I consider that the linguistic profile of each of these prophetic books is more or less consistent.[71]

Zechariah and Isaiah, on the other hand, are not comparable to an individual speaker/writer in sociolinguistics. Almost all scholars consider Zechariah 9–14 to be fundamentally different from Zechariah 1–8, formally

---

[69] Admittedly, not all scholars would accept that the latest layers of Jeremiah belong to the early exilic period. Some scholars argue that the book was shaped or extensively expanded in the exilic or postexilic period. For examples, see Winfried Thiel, *Die deuteronomistische Redaktion von Jeremia 1–25* (WMANT 41; Neukirchen-Vluyn: Neukirchener Verlag, 1973); idem, *Die deuteronomistische Redaktion von Jeremia 26–45* (WMANT 52; Neukirchen-Vluyn: Neukirchener Verlag, 1981); and Robert P. Carroll, *Jeremiah: A Commentary* (OTL; Philadelphia: Westminster, 1986).

[70] "The language of the book is fundamentally EBH" (Young, Rezetko, and Ehrensvärd, *Linguistic Dating*, 2:36, and see their discussion there). Also, there is no consensus among scholars regarding what material is secondary and what is tertiary, and this renders it impossible to produce a solid list of the later passages.

[71] Certainly, many readers would find both the above and the following discussions about biblical books and texts, which do not consider fully the complex literary history of each biblical book, far too simple. For example, Hosea and Amos, the two books that address the northern kingdom, are well known for having been expanded by the Judean editors after the fall of Samaria. As for Micah, it is certain that a significant part came from the periods after the fall of Jerusalem (for these three books, see, for example, C. L. Seow, "Hosea, Book of," *ABD* 3:291–97; Bruce E. Willoughby, "Amos, Book of," *ABD* 1:203–12; and Delbert R. Hillers, "Micah, Book of," *ABD* 4:807–810). In a statistical study such as the present one, however, it is impracticable to detail all the possible layers of each book and take them into account. First, the more layers we identify in a certain book, the less linguistic data we obtain from each block of text, a situation which would diminish the validity of the study. Second, and more importantly, it is unlikely that scholars would reach an agreement regarding the extent of each expansion or addition in such books as Jeremiah, Hosea, Amos, Micah, and Isaiah. This is so because one must depend, at least in part, on conjectures in order to reconstruct a composition history of a certain biblical book. Hurvitz's maxim, which we have quoted earlier, again sounds apt here: the linguistic study of the Hebrew Bible corpus should be based on "*actual* texts" rather than "*reconstructed* texts" (Hurvitz, *Priestly Source and Ezekiel*, 19; emphasis original). Accordingly, the course I choose is to minimize the numbers of composition layers. Indeed—it should be emphasized—this strategy seems to be an accepted practice among those who participate in the debate over the linguistic dating of biblical texts. (See, for example, Wright, *Yahwistic Source*, 8–13 and Young, Rezetko, and Ehrensvärd's treatments of various data in their *Linguistic Dating*.)

and thematically.[72] I will accordingly divide Zechariah into two separate texts. The case is similar with Isaiah. A substantial portion of Isaiah 1–39 is rooted in the situation of the eighth century B.C.E. Isaiah 40–66, on the other hand, presuppose the situation after the exile. The time between the two blocks is nearly 200 years, and there is no way that we can consider the whole book to be a consistent unit for our collection of data.[73]

In the case of the Pentateuch, it is certain that each "book" should not be taken as a legitimate basic unit for collecting data, for, traditionally, Genesis through Deuteronomy has been considered one book written over five scrolls. At the same time, the Pentateuch should not be considered as one big block, either. Biblical scholarship has confirmed that the Pentateuch is not at all a unified work. Accordingly, in this case, we will use hypothetically reconstructed blocks of material, which are the sources of the Documentary Hypothesis.[74]

---

[72] See, for example, David L. Petersen, who argues for a close relationship between Zechariah 9–14 and Malachi and defends his treatment of the two in one volume. Petersen, *Zechariah 9–14 and Malachi: A Commentary* (OTL; Louisville, Ky.: Westminster John Knox, 1995), 1–6.

[73] As is well-known, the literary history of the book of Isaiah is very complex, and I will make below a further periodization of the book when I discuss the independent variable of time period.

[74] I am aware that the Documentary Hypothesis is no longer universally accepted in biblical scholarship. (Well-known challenges include, for example, Rolf Rendtorff, *The Problem of the Process of Transmission in the Pentateuch* [trans. John J. Scullion; JSOTSup 89; Sheffield: JSOT Press, 1990]; Erhard Blum, *Die Komposition der Vätergeschichte* [WMANT 57; Neukirchen-Vluyn: Neukirchener Verlag, 1984; and idem, *Studien zur Komposition des Pentateuch* [BZAW 189; Berlin: W. de Gruyter, 1990].) Nevertheless, a study such as the present one needs a working principle on which it may stand. The Documentary Hypothesis is still held by the majority of scholars. (For example, Joel S. Baden's recent monograph defends major claims of the classical form of the hypothesis, although he argues for the singularity of the redactor(s), that is, that J and E existed independently until they were combined with P. See Baden, *J, E, and the Redaction of the Pentateuch* [FAT 68; Tübingen: Mohr Siebeck, 2009]. In addition, Baden notes that "major introductions to the Old Testament or the Pentateuch continue to use the Documentary Hypothesis as the means of describing the formation of the Pentateuch" [p. 3]. The works he cites cover the ones written by scholars from the United States, Britain, Israel, and Europe [pp. 3–4]. To name some of them here: John J. Collins, *Introduction to the Hebrew Bible* [Minneapolis, Minn.: Fortress, 2004]; Michael D. Coogan, *The Old Testament: A Historical and Literary Introduction to the Hebrew Scriptures* [Oxford: Oxford University Press, 2006]; Ernest Nicholson, *The Pentateuch in the Twentieth Century: The Legacy of Julius Wellhausen* [Oxford: Oxford University Press, 1998]; Alexander Rofé, *Introduction to the Composition of the Pentateuch* [trans. Harvey N. Bock; Biblical Seminar 58; Sheffield: Sheffield Academic Press, 1999]; and Werner H. Schmidt, *Old Testament Introduction* [trans. Matthew J. O'Connell with David J. Reimer; 2nd ed.; Louisville, Ky.: Westminster John Knox, 1999].) Especially, the existence and extent of the priestly tradition and the Deuteronomic material is the least challenged aspect of the hypothesis, which I will use as the basis for my analysis (see below).

The division will be as follows: the Non-P material (or J/E) of Genesis through Numbers, the P source, and Deuteronomy (with P subtracted). I do not go further than this and divide the Non-P material in Genesis–Numbers into J and E, since this is the most disputed aspect of the pentateuchal source division. On the other hand, a high degree of consensus exists on the isolation of P from Genesis–Numbers and from Deuteronomy. Also, Deuteronomy, with a few P passages subtracted, can be considered linguistically more or less consistent, although one can surely discern different layers within the Deuteronomic tradition.[75] In preparing the lists of passages for P, Non-P, and Deuteronomy, I use the source ascriptions by the following scholars: S. R. Driver, J. Estlin Carpenter and G. Harford-Battersby, and Martin Noth.[76] The ascriptions of sources by these scholars are not identical. So, for the purpose of the present study, the units P, Non-P, and Deuteronomy will be defined minimally. That is, for P, I use a list which includes only the passages that all of the three works commonly identify as P.[77] For Deuteronomy, I subtract from the book the maximal list of P.[78] For Non-P, I subtract from Genesis–Numbers the maximal list

---

[75] For a review of scholarship, see S. D. McBride, "Deuteronomy," *DBI* 1:286–89. Admittedly, scholars discern a small amount of J and E in Deuteronomy. For the purpose of our study, however, I will not subtract them from Deuteronomy, since both J/E and Deuteronomy belong to the preexilic period and our analysis does not need a further periodization of preexilic texts (see below). Again, this is in order to minimize conjectures in our linguistic study.

[76] S. R. Driver, *An Introduction to the Literature of the Old Testament* (new ed. revised 1913; New York: Charles Scribner's Sons, 1914); J. Estlin Carpenter and G. Harford-Battersby, *The Hexateuch according to the Revised Version* (2 vols.; London: Longmans, Green, & Co., 1900); and Martin Noth, *A History of the Pentateuchal Traditions* (trans. Bernhard W. Anderson; Englewood Cliffs, N.J.: Prentice-Hall, 1972).

[77] The following is the minimal list of P: Gen 1:1–2:4a; 5:1–28*, 30–32; 6:9–22; 7:6, 11, 13–16a, 18–21, 24; 8:1–2a, 3b–5, 13a, 14–19; 9:1–17, 28–29; 10:1a, 2–7, 20, 22–23, 31–32; 11:10–27, 31–32; 12:4b–5; 13:6a, 11b–12a; 16:1a, 3, 15–16; 17:1–27; 19:29; 21:1b, 2b–5; 23:1–20; 25:7–11a, 12–17, 19–20, 26b; 26:34–35; 27:46; 28:1–9; 31:18b; 33:18a; 35:9–13, 15, 22b–29; 36:1–31, 40–43; 37:1, 2aα; 41:46a; 46:6–27; 47:27b–28; 48:3–6; 49:1a, 29–33; 50:12–13; Exod 1:1–5, 13, 14b; 2:23aβb–25; 6:2–30; 7:1–13, 19–20aα, 21b–22; 8:1–3, 11b–15; 11:9–10; 12:1–20, 28, 40–41, 43–51; 14:1–4, 8, 9b; 25:1–31:18a; 35:1–40:38; Lev 1:1–27:34; Num 1:1–10:28; 13:1–17a, 21b, 25–26a, 32a; 14:1a, 2, 5–7, 10, 26–30, 34–38; 15:1–41; 16:1a, 2b–11, 16–23, 24*, 27a*, 35; 17:1–19:22; 20:1aα, 2, 3b–4, 6–8aα, 8b–13, 22b–29; 21:4aα*; 22:1b; 25:6–31:54; 32:2–15, 17–32; 33:1–36:13; Deut 32:48–52*; 34:1aα, 5b, 7a, 8–9. It is not necessary for our purpose to treat differently what scholars have identified as older and younger layers of P. In our linguistic study, all materials in the priestly tradition will be treated as one single unit.

[78] Thus, the following passages will be subtracted from Deuteronomy: 1:3; 3:14; 4:41–43; 32:48–52; 34:1, 5b, 7–9.

of P.[79] By using the minimal lists, we will of course have less material to work with, but our analysis will be on firmer ground.

The Deuteronomistic History (= DtrH) presents a different case. We may reasonably consider that Joshua is rather distinct and consistent entity, especially with a clear beginning and ending. The boundaries of the other books, on the other hand, are not so clear as those of Joshua. So, for DtrH, it is difficult to maintain the canonical division into the four books. The simplest alternative is to take the four as one single block of material, since DtrH, as a whole, is distinct and rather consistent. Admittedly, there must have been many source materials that the Deuteronomist used, but, unlike the Pentateuch, it is impossible to generate a list of sources that scholarship will generally approve, because of the Deuteronomist's freer adaptation of his sources.

As for Chronicles and Ezra–Nehemiah, I will treat the two separately. The majority of scholars now believe that the Chronicler did not finalize the books of Ezra and Nehemiah.[80] On the other hand, Ezra and Nehe-

---

[79] Additionally, there are some non-P passages which are considered to be later than J/E and thus to be linguistically incompatible with both J/E and P. So I exclude the following from my analysis: Gen 22:15–18; Exod 13:1–16; 34:10–26. The secondary nature of Gen 22:15–18 has long been recognized; for an overview of scholarship, see Robert W. L. Moberly, "The Earliest Commentary on the Akedah," *VT* 38 (1988): 302–23. On the other hand, the argument for the lateness of the Exodus passages is recent; see Shimon Bar-On, "The Festival Calendars in Exodus XXIII 14–19 and XXXIV 18–26," *VT* 48 (1998): 161–95; Erhard Blum, "Das sog. 'Privilegrecht' in Exodus 34,11–26: Ein Fixpunkt der Komposition des Exodusbuches?" in *Studies in the Book of Exodus: Redaction, Reception, Interpretation* (ed. Marc Vervenne; BETL 126; Leuven: Leuven University Press, 1996), 347–66; and Bernard M. Levinson, "Goethe's Analysis of Exodus 34 and Its Influence on Wellhausen: The *Pfropfung* of the Documentary Hypothesis," *ZAW* 114 (2002): 212–23. I thank Joel S. Baden for the help he has given me on this issue. For his own treatment of Gen 22:15–18, see Baden, *J, E, and the Redaction*, 243–47.

The following is the minimal list of the non-P passages: Gen 2:4b–4:26; 5:29; 6:1–8; 7:1–5, 7–10, 12, 16b, 17b, 22–23; 8:2b–3a, 6, 8–12, 13b, 20–22; 9:18–27; 10:8–19, 21, 24–30; 11:1–9, 28–30; 12:1–4a, 6–20; 13:1–5, 7–11a, 12bβ–18; 15:1–21; 16:1b–2, 4–14; 18:1–33; 19:1–28, 30–38; 20:1–18; 21:1a, 6–34; 22:1–14, 19–24; 24:1–67; 25:1–6, 11b, 18, 21–26a, 27–34; 26:1–33; 27:1–45; 28:10–22; 29:1–23, 25–28a, 30–35; 30:1–20, 22b–43; 31:1–18aα, 19–54; 32:1–33; 33:1–17, 18b–20; 34:2b–3a, 3bβ, 5, 7, 11–12, 19, 26, 30–31; 35:1–4, 7–8, 14, 16–22a; 37:3–40:23; 41:1–45a, 47–57; 42:1–38; 43:1–45:28; 46:1–5, 28–34; 47:1–4, 6b, 12–27a, 29–31; 48:1–2, 8–22; 49:1b–17, 19–27; 50:1–11, 14–26; Exod 1:8–22, 15–22; 2:1–23aα; 3:1–6:1; 7:14–18, 20aβb–21a, 23–29; 8:4–11aα, 16–28; 9:1–7, 13–35; 10:1–11:8; 12:21–23, 25–27, 29–36, 37b–39; 13:17–19, 21–22; 14:5–7, 10bα, 11–14, 19–20, 21aβ, 24–25, 27aβb, 30–31; 15:1–18, 20–21, 22aβb–26; 16:4; 17:1bβ–18:27; 19:2b–25; 20:1–10, 12–26; 21:1–24:14; 32:1–15a, 16–35; 33:1–23; 34:1–9, 27–28; Num 10:29–33, 35–36; 11:1–12:16; 13:17b–20, 22–24, 27–31; 14:1b, 4, 11–25, 39b–45; 16:1b, 2aα, 12–15, 25, 26b, 27b–32a, 33abα, 34; 20:14–21; 21:1–3, 4aβ–9, 12–35; 22:2–25:5.

[80] A landmark study is Sara Japhet, "The Supposed Common Authorship of Chronicles and Ezra–Nehemiah Investigated Anew," *VT* 18 (1968): 330–71. See also H. G. M. Williamson, *1 and 2 Chronicles* (NCB; Grand Rapids, Mich.: Eerdmans, 1982), 5–11; Japhet, *I and II Chronicles: A Commentary* (OTL; Louisville, Ky.: Westminster/John Knox, 1993), 3–5; Gary

miah will be treated as one unit. It is understood that the separation of the two books is secondary, not attested in Jewish tradition until the Middle Ages. Modern critical scholarship conventionally regards the two as a single work.[81] As for Chronicles, I will use only the non-parallel passages, or, to be more precise, the portions in Chronicles wherever the book's reading is different from the MT of his supposed biblical sources (e.g., Samuel–Kings and the Pentateuch).[82] I understand that the Chronicler's sources must not have been identical to, for example, MT Samuel–Kings.[83] Also, it is obvious from the biblical account itself that the Chronicler had other sources than what have been preserved in the Hebrew Bible. Nevertheless, especially since our purpose includes examining the linguistic behavior of an individual book or text, it is methodologically important that we approach the Chronicler's own diction as much as possible. And insofar as the available evidence allows, we can do this by subtracting from Chronicles what we can know is extraneous, or what we may consider to resemble the Chronicler's actual sources (e.g., MT Samuel–Kings). I understand that this process can never be perfect, but I also believe that it is the best available methodological option.

In Job, the prose section (1:1–2:13; 42:7–17) is contrasted with the poetry section (3:1–42:6), though it is not impossible that one author could have written both sections. The two parts should be treated separately if we want to conduct a linguistic study of the book.[84] Psalms poses difficulty for us. Psalms is an anthology and cannot be considered homogeneous. Theoretically, it is best to analyze each psalm individually, but for this reason, the book is not very useful for a quantitative study such as the present one. Individual psalms present too few data from which a generalization may be made. As for Proverbs, it is also difficult to maintain its

N. Knoppers, *I Chronicles 1–9: A New Translation with Introduction and Commentary* (AB 12; New York: Doubleday, 2004), 73–89. Cf. Joseph Blenkinsopp, *Ezra–Nehemiah: A Commentary* (OTL; Philadelphia: Westminster, 1988), 47–54, who advocates the previous consensus that the Chronicler was responsible for both Chronicles and Ezra–Nehemiah. For a review of scholarship, see H. G. M. Williamson, "Ezra and Nehemiah, Books of," *DBI* 1:375–82.

[81] For the well accepted argument for the unity of Ezra and Nehemiah, see, for example, H. G. M. Williamson, *Ezra, Nehemiah* (WBC 16; Waco, Tex.: Word, 1985), xxi–xxii.

[82] For identifying the parallel and non-parallel passages of Chronicles, I will use Abba Bendavid, *Parallels in the Bible* (Jerusalem: Carta, 1972).

[83] See, for example, Japhet, *Chronicles*, 28–29.

[84] "The stylistic and theological incongruity of the prose narrative (1:1–2:13; 42:7–17) with the poetic dialogue led scholars to posit separate compositions" (C. A. Newsom and S. E. Schreiner, "Job, Book of," *DBI* 1:593). This is indeed how Hurvitz has conducted a linguistic study on Job. See Hurvitz, "The Date of the Prose-Tale of Job Linguistically Reconsidered," *HTR* 67 (1974): 17–34.

homogeneity, since it too is a collection. Thus, Psalms and Proverbs, for the reason discussed here and another to be mentioned below, will be excluded from our analysis.

The books in the Writings that have not been addressed in this subsection will be treated as one separate, independent unit. So, Song of Songs, Ruth, Lamentations, Ecclesiastes, Esther, and Daniel will each be considered a distinct and consistent unit for collecting data.

3.3. Dependent Variable

The linguistic variables I will analyze in this project are grammatical (i.e., morphological and syntactical), lexical, and phraseological ones. In selecting the variables for analysis, I will keep the following two criteria in mind. First, a linguistic item with two different realizations should be a true variable, that is, the two forms should be equivalent in their linguistic meaning, or, if such a situation is impossible, almost equivalent. Second, the variable should provide sufficient attestations across different text types so that we may correlate its occurrences with the independent variable of text type.[85] These two criteria prove to be quite exacting, and only several meet them of the many linguistic items that scholars have considered to indicate a shift from EBH to LBH. Since this is a pilot study, however, a strict adherence to the proposed method will be more important than an exhaustive treatment of the subject matter. In creating the list of variables, I have been greatly helped by my predecessors, especially, Young, Rezetko, and Ehrensvärd, who present a very long list of all of the linguistic items that various scholars have identified as contrasting features of EBH and LBH.[86]

A word is necessary about our decision to include lexical variables. As we have seen in chapter 2, not only Young, Rezetko, and Ehrensvärd, but also traditionalists such as Polzin are against using lexical data as conclusive evidence for the dating of a biblical text. Young, Rezetko, and Ehrensvärd criticize the use of lexical data for their instability (in comparison with morphology and syntax), randomness (with regard to occurrences of a particular word), and correspondence (between the lexicon of EBH and that of LBH; i.e., the two lexicons are virtually identical).[87] As we have seen, they argue that "the main focus in linguistic dating of biblical texts

---

[85] See below for the independent variable of text type.
[86] Young, Rezetko, and Ehrensvärd, *Linguistic Dating*, 2:160–214.
[87] Young, Rezetko, and Ehrensvärd, *Linguistic Dating*, 1:115–16.

should be grammar, which provides a more reliable and efficient basis for chronological analysis than does vocabulary."[88] I consider their challenge legitimate. Nevertheless, a closer look reveals that our two criteria for selecting linguistic variables can successfully remedy this disadvantage. First, if the proposed contrast between EBH and LBH proves to be a true variable, we can hardly say the datum is unstable. The opposite is what sociolinguistics has demonstrated repeatedly: the use of a variable is governed by structured heterogeneity, which is the reality behind what seems to be unstable. Second, when we use only those lexemes that occur quite frequently, the disadvantage of randomness is minimized. Third, the problem of correspondence is irrelevant to the present study, because variability already presupposes that the same two (or more) forms are used throughout the corpus.

3.4. *Independent Variable: Viable Options*

Dependent linguistic variables are to be correlated with independent social variables. In historical sociolinguistics, independent variables include the individual writer, the writer's age, gender, social class, and region, and the text's time period and genre (or text type). As we have seen above, many of these options are not usable for the Hebrew Bible corpus, because of the nature of biblical literature. We will use only three: individual book/text, time period, and text type.

As we have discussed above, an individual book or an isolated text or source will be the basic unit for collecting data. On the other hand, in the actual groupings of the data collected from individual books and texts, time period and text type will be used.

3.5. *The First Independent Variable: Time Period*

The independent variable of time period is critical to our question of whether the linguistic dating of biblical texts is possible. I expect to adjudicate between Hurvitz's chronological model and the challengers' stylistic model on the basis of the correlation between BH linguistic variables and the independent variable of time period. If we discern a correlation between a particular linguistic variable and time period, and if that correlation suggests that the choice between the different variant forms was constrained by chronology (i.e., time period), then this particular linguistic

---

[88] Young, Rezetko, and Ehrensvärd, *Linguistic Dating*, 1:118.

variable may support Hurvitz's chronological understanding of EBH and LBH. If the correlation does not support the diachronic model or if there is no meaningful correlation discerned, the particular linguistic item may not serve as the evidence for the chronological model.[89]

In collecting the time periods of different books, texts, and sources, the following should be borne in mind. First, dating should not be done on linguistic grounds. Needless to say, if it is, time period will no longer be *independent*, and the overall argument becomes circular. Second, the list of books and texts with agreed-upon dates should be minimized rather than maximized. This will of course reduce the amount of data in our tables and charts, but by avoiding the data of the books and texts whose dates are disputed, we will have more solid ground for our analysis.

I indeed understand the difficulty of dating biblical books and sources. Some scholars doubt the very existence of preexilic Israel and hence the production of any biblical literature during the preexilic period. Even in a conservative understanding, most biblical books were transmitted, edited, and expanded; each book is hardly a product of one particular point in time. Nevertheless, if one holds, along with the majority of biblical scholars, that references and allusions to historical events and entities constitute valid evidence, one can date some biblical texts and books rather solidly. In fact, certain historical events and entities were so crucial to the people who produced the Hebrew Bible that we may reasonably expect their references or allusions in a text or a book that postdates them. Such crucial events include, for example, Josiah's reform (ca. 628 B.C.E.), the capture of Nineveh by Neo-Babylonia and Media (612 B.C.E.), the capture and the fall of Jerusalem (597 and 586 B.C.E.), the return of the exiles following Cyrus's conquest of Babylonia (539 B.C.E.), the dedication of the second temple (515 B.C.E.), and the Maccabean revolt (167–164 B.C.E.). Also, the rise and fall of powerful empires such as Neo-Assyria, Neo-Babylonia, and Persia had a direct impact on Israel and Judah. References or allusions to the foregoing events and entities, and sometimes even a lack thereof, have provided scholars with useful criteria on the basis of which to date biblical texts and books.

Thus, the majority of biblical scholars would accept the following periodizations.[90]

---

[89] This is no doubt the most critical issue of the present study, which will be treated more fully through the remaining chapters.

[90] For the following periodizations, I have consulted three recent English *Introductions*: Schmidt, *Introduction* (above, n. 74); Collins, *Introduction* (above, n. 74); and Coogan, *Old Testament* (above, n. 74).

The following are thought to be preexilic: The *Non-P* (or *J/E*) material in the Pentateuch is dated between the tenth and eighth centuries by many scholars.[91] The great bulk of *Deuteronomy* is dated before Josiah's reform (ca. 628 B.C.E.).[92] *Isaiah 1–39*, except for chs. 13–14, 24–27, and 34–35 (see below), can probably be dated to the latter half of the eighth century B.C.E., since the last critical event recorded is Sennacherib's invasion of Palestine (701 B.C.E.). *Amos* and *Hosea* are internally dated to the middle of the eighth century B.C.E., and the core of *Micah* can be dated to the late eighth century B.C.E.[93] *Zephaniah*, who prophesied in the days of Josiah, does not seem to be aware of Josiah's reform (ca. 628 B.C.E.) or the rapid collapse of Assyrian power, so it can be dated around 630 B.C.E. *Nahum* prophesied and celebrated the fall of Nineveh (612 B.C.E.). Whether it is an authentic prophecy or a *vaticinum ex eventu*, the book seems to be chronologically closely tied to the event and should therefore be dated

---

Again, I must admit that the following discussion, which does not pay full attention to the literary history of each book, is far too simple. Nevertheless, as the majority opinion, it provides a reasonably solid working ground for us to proceed from in our sociolinguistic analysis of the BH variables. My purpose is to provide a fresh perspective from which to view a difficult problem in the study of BH. And for this purpose, I exploit what scholarship has achieved and agreed upon. The dating of a text or a book will each call for a separate study; it certainly exceeds what we can do here.

[91] In the case of the dating of J/E, the evidence is not so much references or allusions to verifiable historical events as D's dependence on them: what J/E pictures and suggests is presupposed or revised by D. I am aware that since the 1970s some scholars have attempted to redate the J/E material to the exilic or postexilic period (e.g., Hans Heinrich Schmid, *Der sogenannte Jahwist: Beobachtungen und Fragen zur Pentateuchforschung* [Zürich: Theologischer Verlag, 1976]; John Van Seters, *Abraham in History and Tradition* [New Haven: Yale University Press, 1975]; idem, *In Search of History: Historiography in the Ancient World and the Origins of Biblical History* [New Haven: Yale University Press, 1983]; idem, *Prologue to History: The Yahwist as Historian in Genesis* [Louisville, Ky.: Westminster/John Knox, 1992]; Hermann Vörlander, *Die Entstehungszeit des jehowistischen Geschichtswerkes* [Europäische Hochschulschriften: Reihe 23, Theologie 109; Frankfurt am Main: Lang, 1978]; Martin Rose, *Deuteronomist und Jahwist: Untersuchungen zu den Berührungspunkten beider Literaturwerke* [ATANT 67; Zürick: Theologischer Verlag, 1981]; Christoph Levin, *Der Jahwist* [FRLANT 157; Göttingen: Vandenhoeck & Ruprecht, 1993]). Nevertheless, the majority still accept the traditional date of J/E, which is before or around the fall of the northern kingdom (see the works cited above, n. 74). See a helpful summary of recent debates in Nicholson, *Pentateuch*, 132–95.

[92] Some scholars discern exilic materials in the book of Deuteronomy, but even if they are correct, the book was probably completed before or with the closing of DtrH, whose last recorded event occurred in ca. 560 B.C.E.

[93] It is certain that Hosea, Amos, and Micah have exilic and postexilic layers (above, n. 71). Nevertheless, for the reasons stated above (n. 71), it seems to be the best practical option to categorize them as preexilic literature. Again, this is not to ignore the complex literary history of these prophetic books, but to have a working ground from which to proceed.

close to 612 B.C.E.[94] *Habakkuk* may be dated to the end of the seventh century B.C.E., since it refers to the Chaldeans but does not seem to be aware of the capture of Jerusalem (597 B.C.E.).

A few books stretch from the late preexilic to the early exilic period. Thus, many scholars believe the great bulk of *DtrH* was completed during the reign of Josiah, while the history's last two chapters (2 Kgs 24–25) probably came from the early exilic period (with the last event recorded in 2 Kgs 25:27–30 occurring in ca. 560 B.C.E.).[95] *Jeremiah* may be dated to the preexilic to exilic period. The prophet was called in 627 B.C.E., according to the book's chronology, and his activity ceased shortly after the fall of Jerusalem (586 B.C.E.). On the other hand, the book has gone through a

---

[94] All the three *Introductions* I have consulted agree that the date should be close to 612 B.C.E. Collins and Coogan do not specify whether the prophecy is authentic or *ex eventu*, whereas Schmidt believes that it is authentic. Collins, *Introduction*, 324; Coogan, *Old Testament*, 357; and Schmidt, *Introduction*, 225. Note also J. J. M. Roberts: "A *terminus ad quem* is provided by the fall of Nineveh (612 B.C.), since Nahum's need to reassure his Judean audience that Yahweh really will destroy Assyria would hardly be necessary after that event" (idem, *Nahum, Habakkuk, and Zephaniah: A Commentary* [OTL; Louisville, Ky.: Westminster/John Knox, 1991], 38). For some scholars' opinion that the book was composed to celebrate the fall of Israel's enemy after the event, see D. L. Christensen, "Nahum, Book of," *DBI* 2:200.

[95] Again, one must establish a working ground for the subsequent discussions. I have chosen Frank Moore Cross's model of the double redaction of DtrH in the preexilic and the exilic periods over Noth's single exilic redaction or Rudolf Smend's and his students' multiple exilic and postexilic redactions (see Cross, "The Themes of the Book of Kings and the Structure of the Deuteronomistic History," in idem, *Canaanite Myth and Hebrew Epic: Essays in the History of the Religion of Israel* [Cambridge, Mass.: Harvard University Press, 1973], 274–89; Noth, *The Deuteronomistic History* [trans. David J. A. Clines et al.; JSOTSup 15; Sheffield: JSOT Press, 1981]; and Smend, "Das Gesetz und die Völker: Ein Beitrag zur deuteronomistischen Redaktionsgeschichte," in *Probleme biblischer Theologie: Gerhard von Rad zum 70. Geburtstag* [ed. Hans Walter Wolff; Munich: C. Kaiser, 1971], 494–509; the following are the work by Smend's students: Walter Dietrich, *Prophetie und Geschichte: Eine redaktionsgeschichtliche Untersuchung zum deuteronomistischen Geschichtswerk* [FRLANT 108; Göttingen: Vandenhoeck & Ruprecht, 1972]; Timo Veijola, *Die ewige Dynastie: David und die Entstehung seiner Dynastie nach der deuteronomistischen Darstellung* [STAT 193; Helsinki: Suomalainen Tiedeakatemia, 1975]; and idem, *Das Königtum in der Beurteilung der deuteronomistischen Historiographie: Eine redaktionsgeschichtliche Untersuchung* [STAT 198; Helsinki: Suomaleinen Tiedeakatemia, 1977]). Being aware of the complexities surrounding DtrH's composition, we, unfortunately, cannot discuss in the present study the strengths and weaknesses of the three models (as an introduction, see Steven L. McKenzie, "Deuteronomistic History," in *ABD* 2:160–68 and A. D. H. Mayes, "Deuteronomistic History," *DBI* 1:268–73). Notwithstanding, those who subscribe to Noth's model would agree that the date of DtrH is no later than the exile; those who follow Smend and his students would still accept that the major portion of the work came directly from preexilic sources. Additionally, it should be clear to the reader that, by choosing Cross's model, I also reject A. Graeme Auld's theory that there was an exilic common source shared by both the author of Samuel–Kings and the author of Chronicles and that Samuel–Kings is thus postexilic as is Chronicles (see my brief discussion of Auld in ch. 2 and the works cited there).

process of expansion during the exilic period. If we accept that the book of Jeremiah was related to the Deuteronomistic movement, Jeremiah was probably completed during the exilic period. To be sure, the ending of the present book is a verbatim quotation of 2 Kgs 25:27–30, and the book does not mention the return in 539 B.C.E.

Ezekiel and *Lamentations* are anchored in the catastrophic event of 586 B.C.E. A major part of Ezekiel's activity, according to the internal chronology, falls between 593 and 585 B.C.E.[96] Additionally, the vision of the new temple (chs. 40–48) is dated to 573 B.C.E., and a supplementary oracle against Egypt (29:17–20) is dated to 571 B.C.E. It is significant that the pronouncement against Egypt did not come true and thus hints at the closing of the book. Lamentations is believed to be composed shortly after the fall of Jerusalem, because of the vividness of its description of the event.

A significant part of *Isaiah*, that is, *chs. 13–14, 34–35, and 40–55*, is thought to have been added to the earlier edition of the prophet's work during the late exilic period. Isaiah 40–55, or Second Isaiah, explicitly mentions Cyrus, while chapters 13–14 and 34–35 seem to be thematically connected to it. A detailed discussion of the book's complex literary history is beyond our scope here.[97] We note, however, that scholars have a consensus that the above chapters can hardly have originated from the eighth-century prophet.[98]

The beginning of the Persian period certainly marks the terminus a quo of the following books and texts: *Isaiah 24–27, Isaiah 56–66, Haggai, Zechariah 1–8, Zechariah 9–14, Malachi, Esther, Daniel, Ezra, Nehemiah,* and *Chronicles*. Thus, Haggai and Zechariah 1–8 are situated at the beginning of the Persian period, internally dated to 520 B.C.E., and Isaiah 56–66, or Third Isaiah, seems to presuppose the situation of the same period. Ezra and Nehemiah are internally dated to the middle of the fifth century B.C.E., and their closings do not seem to be very far from this date.[99] Esther, Daniel, and Chronicles refer to or presuppose the events in the Persian period. It is difficult to pinpoint the dates of Zechariah 9–14,

---

[96] From "the fifth year of the exile of King Jehoiachin" (1:2) to "the twelfth year" (32:1; 33:21).

[97] For a review of scholarship, see Richard J. Clifford, "Isaiah, Book of: Second Isaiah," *ABD* 3:490–501; William R. Millar, "Isaiah, Book of: Isaiah 24–27 (Little Apocalypse)," *ABD* 3:488–90; and Christopher R. Seitz, "Isaiah, Book of: First Isaiah," *ABD* 3:472–88.

[98] Cf., however, Rooker, "Isaiah 40–66," who argues for the authenticity of all of Isaiah on linguistic grounds.

[99] That is, if we consider Artaxerxes in Ezra 7:1 to be Artaxerxes I. If this king is Artaxerxes II, Ezra's activity is set in the beginning of the fourth century.

Malachi, and Isaiah 24–27, but to many scholars, the contents of these texts seem to guarantee a date after the exile.

Last, the following books and texts present difficulty of varying degrees with regard to their dates. The *P* material in the Pentateuch is well-known for denying scholarly agreement. Wellhausen's dating of P to the postexilic period remained influential until the 1970s. Since Hurvitz's *Priestly Source and Ezekiel*, however, arguments based on linguistic data have presented a formidable challenge to Wellhausen's model. Now, for those who use Hurvitz's method, it has become a given that P is preexilic.[100] I will not, however, follow this convention. I identify P as a text of disputed dating. Although *Joel* is generally dated to the Persian period, the book lacks any historical references and thus should better be classified among those whose dates are not agreed upon. The writer of *Obadiah* is more or less believed to have witnessed the catastrophic events between 597 and 586 B.C.E. Nevertheless, evidence is scanty, and it is more cautious not to assign a specific date. *Jonah* is also difficult to date. The story is set in the period of Assyrian hegemony, but the book says Nineveh *was* a great city (3:3). It should then be placed after 612 B.C.E., the year of Nineveh's fall, but we do not know whether it is exilic or postexilic. *Psalms* and *Proverbs* are collections of songs and sayings, and it makes no sense to attempt to date each of the two compilations. Dating individual songs in Psalms might theoretically be valid, but for the present study, which uses statistics, it is practically not helpful. As for *Job*, we may probe into the book's philosophy and angelology, but they cannot constitute sure evidence for dating the book. *Song of Songs* too is difficult to date. The book does not provide us with any data that may be linked to historical events. *Ruth*, although it is narrative, is also difficult to date, since the story is set in the period of the judges and we do not know the book's lower limit.[101] *Ecclesiastes* is believed by the absolute majority to be late postexilic. Nevertheless, it is methodologically sounder to categorize the book with other books with disputed dates, since its postexilic dating is argued mainly from linguistic grounds.[102]

---

[100] For example, in his *Yahwistic Source*, Wright attempts to date J on the premise that P is preexilic.

[101] For example, Coogan observes that the book has been dated to anywhere between the tenth to the fourth centuries. Coogan, *Old Testament*, 226.

[102] Cf., especially, Young's preexilic dating of Ecclesiastes. Young argues that "Qoheleth's language … fits without strain as the unconventional writing style of an unconventional thinker of the late mornarchic era." Young, "Biblical Texts Cannot Be Dated Linguistically,"

The following summarizes our survey:

Preexilic:	Non-P; Deuteronomy; Isaiah 1–39 (excluding chs. 13–14, 24–27, and 34–35); Hosea; Amos; Micah; Nahum; Habakkuk; and Zephaniah
Late preexilic to early exilic:	DtrH and Jeremiah
Exilic:	Isaiah 13–14; 34–35; 40–55; Ezekiel; and Lamentations
Postexilic:	Isaiah 24–27; 56–66; Haggai; Zechariah 1–8; Zechariah 9–14; Malachi; Esther; Daniel; Ezra–Nehemiah; and Chronicles
Disputed or undecided:	P; Joel; Obadiah; Jonah; Psalms; Proverbs; Job; Song of Songs; Ruth; and Ecclesiastes

As we have discussed, we will not be able to use the data from the texts or books with disputed dates, when we attempt to correlate the BH variables with the independent variable of time period.

In closing the discussion of the independent variable of time period, an important note should be made. Accepting the existence of preexilic biblical literature does not preclude Young, Rezetko, and Ehrensvärd's understanding of BH. Young, Rezetko, and Ehrensvärd's position is, as we have seen, that the mixed attestations of the EBH and the LBH features lead to the understanding that EBH and LBH were "co-existing styles of literary Hebrew throughout the biblical period."[103] This claim does not entail that those texts written in EBH are therefore postexilic; it entails only that the use of EBH does not necessarily indicate the text's preexilic origin. This is of course their basis for arguing that the linguistic dating of biblical texts is impossible.

3.6. *The Second Independent Variable: Text Type*

Text type is the second independent variable we will use.[104] In classifying text types, the number of categories will be minimized. Of course, having

---

HS 46 (2005): 347–48; also, idem, *Diversity in Pre-Exilic Hebrew* (FAT 5; Tübingen: J. C. B. Mohr, 1993), 140–57.

[103] Young, Rezetko, and Ehrensvärd, *Linguistic Dating*, 2:72.

[104] In linguistics, 'text type' is different from 'genre'. Genre, which is used more commonly in biblical studies, is determined on the basis of external criteria such as topic and the writer's purpose. Text type, on the other hand, is decided by the text's linguistic form. For example, particular texts from press reportage, biographies, and academic prose

more text types would be more advantageous for some very well attested variables; we might be able to produce a more detailed and precise analysis of them. Since, however, the Hebrew Bible corpus is not large, more text types would usually mean more gaps in the distributions of linguistic variables.[105] I therefore posit two comprehensive text types as the second independent variable: *recorded speech* and *narration*. Below, I will discuss the genre categories that belong to each of the two text types, and then probe the rationale behind this classification.

First, I define the text type of *recorded speech* as any kind of direct quotation of speech. It includes dialogues (even if they are very long, such as the ones in Job), quoted monologues and internal speeches, quoted letters, laws and oracles presented as God's words, Moses' extended speeches in Deuteronomy, songs, and prayers. Although the text type of recorded speech is clearly distinguished by the single criterion of direct quotation, it is widely varied. I will come back to this issue shortly.

Second, the text type of *narration* hardly needs clarification. Logically, it is what remains after one subtracts all the quoted speeches from the Hebrew Bible. There are two kinds of narration in the Hebrew Bible: third-person narration and first-person narration. Examples of third-person narration include narrations in stories and histories in Genesis, DtrH, Chronicles, parts of Ezra and Nehemiah, Ruth, Esther, and the first half of Daniel (note, however, that the Aramaic portion [chs. 2–7] does not belong to our corpus). The narrative frames in Leviticus, Job, and Deuteronomy also include third-person narrations. Biographical materials in prophetic books too belong to this text type. First-person narration includes the narrative portions of Ezekiel, the narrative portions of the latter half of Daniel, sections of prophetic books that are written from the first-person perspective, Ecclesiastes, and parts of Ezra and Nehemiah.

The rationale behind this categorization is an attempt to divide biblical material into oral and literate text types. Dividing a corpus into oral and literate text types is a tried and true convention of historical sociolinguistics. This is based on the belief that some written texts resemble

---

belong to different genres, since the purposes of these texts are different. If, however, all of these texts are written in narrative linguistic form, they may still be categorized into the same text type (Biber, *Speech and Writing*, 206). What I use in the present study is
zation of text types, because texts will be grouped into direct quotation and
e below).
about 300,000 words, it is much smaller than the *CEEC* and the *HC* cited above;
each of those corpora count over a million.

the typical oral mode of expression more than others.[106] As we have seen in Raumolin-Brunberg's study of *you* and *ye*, the spread of *you* was more prominent in the oral genres than in the literate genres. This seems to suggest that the division of data into oral and literate genres (or text types) is not arbitrary.[107]

Douglas Biber describes the characteristics of typical speech and typical writing.[108] He notes three characteristics of typical speech: the production of the message is *interactive*; the references are *situation-dependent*; and the conveyed information is *non-abstract*. In other words, in a typical speech setting (e.g., a conversation), the addressee (and not just the speaker) actively engages in constructing the message (interactive); the speaker frequently uses the first-person and the second-person pronouns and context-dependent demonstratives and adverbs (situation-dependent); and the purpose is more personal, interpersonal, and contextual (non-abstract). On the other hand, typical writing has the contrasting three characteristics: the production of message is *informational*; the references are *explicit*; and the conveyed information is *abstract*. That is, in a typical writing setting, the writer unidirectionally presents propositional information (informational); the writer uses explicit references since he or she does not share time and place with the reader (explicit); and the purpose is to convey abstract ideas (abstract).[109]

Biber's corpus is that of Modern English. His characterization of typical speech and writing, however, may also be applied to biblical literature. I take two examples from the Hebrew Bible, one being an interactive dialogue and the other a third-person narrative. First, look at the following conversation between Esau and Jacob (Gen 25:30–33 NRSV; note that I have omitted narrations and explanatory statements):

---

[106] Raumolin-Brunberg, "Diffusion of *You*," 64, who draws on Biber, *Speech and Writing*.

[107] For example, Nevalainen and Raumolin-Brunberg write as follows: "In the last three decades the notion of *genre* has dominated historical studies of language variation. Their focus has been on the linguistic description and textual embedding of language changes, and they have demonstrated, for instance, that such speechlike genres as drama and personal letters are more likely to foster linguistic innovations than typical written genres, such as legal and other official documents." Nevalainen and Raumolin-Brunberg, *Historical Sociolinguistics*, 2; emphasis original.

[108] It is important to note that Biber has successfully demonstrated that various modes of verbal communication cannot be dichotomously divided into either speech or writing. We should say, instead, that one mode is closer to typical speech and another less so. Nevertheless, Biber himself finds it helpful to talk about typical speech and typical writing. See Biber, *Speech and Writing*, 160–64.

[109] Biber, *Speech and Writing*, 36–46, 160–64.

Esau:	*Let me eat some of that red stuff, for I am famished!*
Jacob:	*First sell me your birthright.*
Esau:	*I am about to die; of what use is a birthright to me?*
Jacob:	*Swear to me first.*

Here, all of the three characteristics of typical speech are prominent. The sentences are *interactive* in constructing the message. Not only Esau, who spoke first, but also Jacob drives the conversation. Also, the statements are *situation-dependent*. Both speakers use the first-person and the second-person pronouns many times. In addition, in Esau's first speech, he says "some of *that* red stuff" instead of saying "some of *the stew*." Had we as the reader not been informed by the narrator, we would not have known what "that red stuff" was. Last, the purpose and content of the communication is *non-abstract*: it is about the "red stuff," hunger, and a birthright (the last of which may be a bit abstract but is still temporal).

Now, contrast the conversation with the following excerpt from the Joseph narrative (Gen 39:1–6 NRSV):

> Now Joseph was taken down to Egypt, and Potiphar, an officer of Pharaoh, the captain of the guard, an Egyptian, bought him from the Ishmaelites who had brought him down there. The LORD was with Joseph, and he became a successful man; he was in the house of his Egyptian master. His master saw that the LORD was with him, and that the LORD caused all that he did to prosper in his hands. So Joseph found favor in his sight and attended him; he made him overseer of his house and put him in charge of all that he had. From the time that he made him overseer in his house and over all that he had, the LORD blessed the Egyptian's house for Joseph's sake; the blessing of the LORD was on all that he had, in house and field.

This is a narrative, which is not the genre that Biber took as an example of typical writing (for which he used academic prose). Nevertheless, Biber's three characteristics of typical writing are conspicuous. First, the statements are not interactive but *informational*, since they unidirectionally tell a story to the reader. Unlike Esau and Jacob in the previous example, the reader passively listens to the message. Second, the references are *explicit* and not dependent on the situation. Thus the first-person and second-person pronouns are not used at all; situation-dependent adverbs such as *here* and *now* are not used either. Last, the purpose is to convey an *abstract* idea, in this case, a story.

The foregoing examples from the Hebrew Bible, I believe, demonstrate that my categorization of text types into speech and narration is valid at least in typical cases, that is, in the cases of interactive dialogue and third-person narration. Now, the problem is that each of the two text types also includes what does not seem to be typical of it. Thus the text type of narration includes not only third-person narration but also first-person narration; the text type of recorded speech includes, apart from interactive dialogue, a variety of quotations such as monologues, internal speeches, letters, laws and oracles presented as God's words, Moses' extended speeches in Deuteronomy, songs, and prayers. The speeches in Job, also, are hardly interactive, though they are formally dialogues. I turn to this issue now.

First, categorizing first-person narration (i.e., autobiography) with third-person narration seems reasonable enough. First-person narration is indeed distinct from third-person narration formally, since it is written from the first-person perspective. Nevertheless, apart from the frequent use of 'I', first-person narration has all of the three characteristics of typical writing. So the production of message is not interactive but *informational*; the references are not situation-dependent but *explicit*; and it conveys an *abstract* idea (usually, story or report) rather than a non-abstract one. Therefore, first-person narration seems to be much closer to third-person narration than to interactive dialogue.

Second, regarding the grouping of all other kinds of direct quotation with interactive reported speech, Cynthia L. Miller provides a solid scholarly support. Miller's extensive study of the speeches in BH narrative distinguishes reported speech into two groups: interactive reported speech and non-interactive reported speech.[110] The dialogue between Esau and Jacob above is an example of the former. Non-interactive reported speeches, on the other hand, refer to speeches "that are not part of a dialogic exchange or that do not report any actual or putative speech event."[111] Even when a speech is directed to another party, if it is unidirectional (i.e., non-interactive), Miller notes, it belongs to this category. So her examples of non-interactive reported speech include the following: God's commands to build and fill Noah's ark (Gen 6:13–21; 7:1–4); the giving of the law (Exod 20–24); the detailed instructions for the construction of the wilderness sanctuary (Exod 25–31; 35:1–36:1); many laws in P; and Moses' exhortation to the Israelites in Deuteronomy. Internal speech too is categorized by Miller with non-interactive reported speech, since it involves no speech event.[112] Important for us is that all of Miller's non-interactive

---

[110] Miller, *Representation* (above, n. 64).
[111] Miller, *Representation*, 234.
[112] Miller, *Representation*, 284–96 (esp. 290).

reported speech amounts to what we have categorized into the text type of recorded speech in addition to interactive dialogues. Also important is her argument that despite a few differences between interactive reported speech and non-interactive reported speech, "non-interactive reported speech takes interactive reported speech as its point of departure."[113] This was a rationale for Miller's treatment in her work of both non-interactive reported speech and interactive reported speech. Consequently, as Miller has done, so we will consider all direct quotations to belong to the same text type of recorded speech, whether they are interactive or non-interactive.

4. *Summary*

The main purpose of this chapter has been to establish the methodological framework. In the first section, we surveyed three Hebraists who have studied BH using sociolinguistic methods. In the second section, we first discussed the characteristics of linguistic variation and the variationist approach. The variation analysis of written data is justified with the established discipline of historical sociolinguistics. We also defended the variation analysis of the BH data. In the last section, we examined the kind of data we will collect, the way we will collect them, and the way we will interpret them. We discussed in detail the basic unit for collecting data, the criteria for choosing linguistic variables, and the rationale for categorizing independent variables.

The question that has motivated this project, whether we can date biblical texts solely on the basis of linguistic evidence, will be translated into the following question in the remaining chapters: when the *dependent linguistic variables* are correlated with the *independent variables* of *time period* and *text type*, does the correlation support Hurvitz's chronological model or the challengers' stylistic model?

---

[113] Miller, *Representation*, 290. Cf. J. MacDonald, "Some Distinctive Characteristics of Israelite Spoken Hebrew," *BO* 32 (1975): 162–75.

CHAPTER FOUR

VARIABILITY, LINGUISTIC CHANGE, AND TWO TYPES
OF CHANGES: A THEORETICAL ASSESSMENT

The question of whether we can date biblical texts solely on the basis of
the linguistic data shall be answered after the next chapter, in which we
will examine eight morphological, syntactical, lexical, and phraseological
variables in BH. Nevertheless, some of the difficult problems in the present
debate may now be tackled with the insights that we have already gleaned
from present-day and historical sociolinguistics. This chapter attempts to
present a theoretical assessment of these problems before we enter into
an empirical analysis of the biblical data in chapter 5.

The major part of this chapter is divided into two sections. The first
section argues that the sociolinguistic conception of linguistic variability
problematizes the challengers' stylistic understanding of EBH and LBH,
while at the same time it potentially weakens the traditionalists' case for
linguistic dating. The second section introduces the sociolinguistic distinction between two types of linguistic changes: changes from below and
changes from above. It is argued that this distinction enables us to accommodate the two opposing views on EBH and LBH, that is, the traditional
chronological model and the challengers' stylistic model.

1. *Variability, EBH and LBH, and Linguistic Dating*

1.1. *Variability, EBH, and LBH*

Most critical for our present discussion is the understanding that a linguistic change occurs only by passing through the state of variation. This
implies that during the period of change an individual *may* or *may not*
adopt the change; in other words, different individuals behave differently
with regard to the change. Raumolin-Brunberg writes the following:

> It is obvious that when there is a linguistic change in progress, everyone
> has to make the choice, usually unconscious, between participating in the
> change or not.
>   If people do participate, they can adopt the innovation in different ways.
> There is always someone who is the innovator, the person who is the first

to use the new form, but tracing innovators in historical texts is impossible. Instead, we can access *early adopters*, people who picked up the new form before most other people. They may have changed their language during their lifetimes or adopted the form during language acquisition. A further division can be made between *people who have had variable grammars*, that is, those who used both the incoming and old forms, and *those who had only one alternative*.[1]

As there are early adopters, so there are late adopters. In some cases, it is possible that the old form is never given up. Nevalainen and Raumolin-Brunberg observe the following:

> It is clear that, if a change has reached ... [a] completed stage, the new form has triumphed and language has changed. But it is not unusual that the old form lingers on in some linguistic environments, some dialects or a genre or two. For instance, the possessive determiner ITS has not ousted its postnominal variants OF IT and THEREOF from the language, and the third-person singular suffix -TH is found in King James Bible, which is still in use today.[2]

The existence of early adopters and conservatives in the process of a linguistic change does not mean that the speakers/writers have freedom in producing the linguistic variable. As Raumolin-Brunberg has noted in the first quotation above, the choice is usually "unconscious."[3] Although "speakers may not be sociolinguistic automata," "neither are they free social agents linguistically,"[4] because

> Apart from their spoken *vernaculars* acquired in early childhood, people have ... *verbal repertoires* which are constrained by their backgrounds. Access to the various regional, social and professional repertoires can only be ensured by sufficient exposure to them.[5]

Therefore, during the period of variability, although there may be individual speakers/writers who deviate from the general tendency of the period, the average use of language by *multiple* speakers/writers is predictable or "orderly,"[6] since the choice that each individual makes is usually *unconsciously constrained* by the linguistic and social context in which she or he is situated.[7]

---

[1] Raumolin-Brunberg, "Diffusion of *You*," 60–61. Emphasis added.
[2] Nevalainen and Raumolin-Brunberg, *Historical Sociolinguistics*, 56.
[3] Raumolin-Brunberg, "Diffusion of *You*," 60.
[4] Nevalainen and Raumolin-Brunberg, *Historical Sociolinguistics*, 20.
[5] Nevalainen and Raumolin-Brunberg, *Historical Sociolinguistics*, 20. Emphasis original.
[6] Weinreich, Labov, and Herzog, "Empirical Foundations," 99–100.
[7] This is especially true when the change itself is an unconscious one (for the distinction between unconscious and conscious changes, see further below).

The foregoing theoretical discussion cautions that the ambiguity of the biblical evidence—that is, the existence of LBH features in preexilic texts and that of EBH features in postexilic texts—does not warrant the challengers' conclusion that EBH and LBH are stylistic choices. In other words, although the challengers have made a correct observation that EBH and LBH were not contrasted by exclusive choice, this observation is irrelevant to, or cannot constitute evidence for, their claim that EBH and LBH were therefore contemporaneous styles which may not be understood in chronological terms.

Since variation is the mechanism that allows a language to remain to be a reliable and efficient mode of communication during the period of change, if there was indeed a change from one linguistic form in EBH to another in LBH, we would expect to see a mixed use of both the EBH and the LBH forms during the change—always across a corpus and many times in an individual text. Even in a case in which one individual text consistently chooses the old form and does not participate in the ongoing change of the period, we cannot say that the change was not occurring at the time. Rather, if we can demonstrate that the particular change was clearly represented in *all or most of the other texts* of the period, we must understand that the change was authentic. It is very likely that this one text was a conservative while the change was in progress, a situation which is not particularly exceptional in the variation model of linguistic change.[8] In order to determine whether or not there was a change, we need to focus on the average uses that are attested in *multiple* texts rather than on the behavior of individual texts. Indeed, for a given change in BH, we will, in theory, always witness the mixed use of the purported EBH and LBH features at least across a corpus, since no change occurs without passing through the state of variation. Conversely, even in the case in which the EBH form is exclusively used in the preexilic corpus and the corresponding LBH form is exclusively used in the postexilic corpus, if we can prove that there was an authentic linguistic shift, we must understand that the record has simply been lost that could have shown the state of variability, rather than assume that the change occurred instantaneously.

Mats Eskhult, a Hebraist, similarly opines regarding the "style" of late BH: "Style is manifested in texts as the consequence of the writer's endeavor to accommodate contents to form; style is, however, *not independent* from language as a system which changes over time." Eskhult, "Traces of Linguistic Development," 369–70; emphasis added.

[8] We will see one case that probably belongs to this situation. See the discussion of הַמֶּלֶךְ אֲאא vs. אאא הַמֶּלֶךְ in chapter 5 (the case of the book of Esther there).

It is important to note that the present discussion does not say that a variation *is* evidence for a change. What we argue is that *when* there was a change, there *was* a variation. Therefore, our case against the challengers is negative. That is, it only *disproves* the challengers' argument that the ambiguity of the biblical data supports their stylistic understanding. On the other hand, in order to demonstrate that a certain BH variation was a facet of change, we need to conduct an empirical analysis, examples of which will appear in the next chapter.

In summary, the variationist understanding of linguistic change suggests that the variability in the BH data may not be interpreted as the evidence for the challengers' stylistic understanding of EBH and LBH. Rather, it raises the possibility that there was indeed a linguistic shift from EBH to LBH.

1.2. *Variability and Linguistic Dating*

Our discussion in the previous subsection certainly supports Hurvitz's and his followers' chronological understanding of EBH and LBH, insofar as it argues that the mixed attestations of the EBH and the LBH features do not support the challengers' non-chronological stylistic model. The concept of variability may not, however, go further and strengthen the traditionalists' argument for the linguistic dating of a particular text. Rather, the fact that a change always involves variation may, in theory, vitiate the case for linguistic dating. The reason is obvious: we do not have an empirical tool with which to decide whether a specific text that we attempt to date was an early adopter, a conservative, or an in-between with regard to individual linguistic changes of the period. We may reasonably assume that the majority of texts were neither early adopters nor conservatives but were average followers of the trend, and we may surely reconstruct the *general* trajectory of a particular linguistic change on the basis of *multiple* texts. But our problem is that linguistic dating always involves an analysis of a *single* text. When it comes to dating a single text, since the text's date is not known, we do not have a methodological tool with which to exclude the possibilities that the text was an early or late adopter of individual linguistic changes. And obviously, without excluding such possibilities, it is hardly justified to date an individual text on the basis of the profile of the language of a certain period.

For example, Hurvitz's linguistic dating of P to the preexilic period[9] can in theory be valid *if* P was neither an early adopter nor a conservative

---

[9] Hurvitz, *Priestly Source and Ezekiel.*

with regard to most of the linguistic shifts from EBH to LBH—a proposition that we cannot defend empirically. If, however, P had been generally conservative in following most of the individual changes of the period—again, we cannot prove this—P could theoretically be placed to the exilic period or later, the position that many biblical scholars subscribe to.

Accordingly, for the reason discussed here and the reasons to be discussed in the following chapter, I will argue that the foundation for linguistic dating is much weaker than its proponents believe.[10]

2. *Two Types of Linguistic Changes and the Opposing Views on EBH and LBH*

There is yet another dimension that is significant to the debate over the linguistic dating of biblical texts. William Labov, the most prominent sociolinguist, distinguishes two types of linguistic changes at their initial stages: *changes from below* (*social awareness*) and *changes from above* (*social awareness*).

2.1. *Changes from Below*

The central concept of changes from below social awareness is that they are socially *unnoticed*, or "completely below the level of social awareness." Labov defines changes from below as follows:

> *Changes from below* are systematic changes that appear first in the vernacular, and represent the operation of internal, linguistic factors. At the outset, and through most of their development, they are completely below the level of social awareness. No one notices them or talks about them, and … [even] trained observers may be quite unconscious of them for many years. It is only when the changes are nearing completion that members of the community become aware of them. Changes from below may be introduced by any social class, although no cases have been recorded in which the highest-status social group acts as the innovating group.[11]

Some points need to be expounded further.

First, as Labov states above, changes from below are caused by "internal, linguistic factors." According to Lyle Campbell and Mauricio J. Mixco, internal, linguistic factors are based on "the limitations and resources of human speech production and perception." They pertain to "physical

---

[10] See further chapters 5 and 6.

[11] Labov, *Principles of Linguistic Change*, vol. 1, *Internal Factors* (Language in Society 20; Oxford: Blackwell, 1994), 78. Emphasis original.

explanations of change stemming from the physiology of human speech organs" and "cognitive explanations involving the perception, processing or learning of language." Internal linguistic factors are largely responsible for the "natural, regular, universal aspects" of language change.[12] To take an example from present English: The form 'data', which is the plural form of the Latin singular 'datum', is now being used as a singular in many contexts except for very formal ones such as academic writings. This ongoing change is readily grasped with cognitive explanations: it reflects our brain's attempt to ease the load of remembering an additional form of a plural noun that does not use -*s*. In other words, by making 'data' a singular form, our brain does not have to remember that the form 'data', which does not end with -*s*, is plural. Thus, the shift in the grammatical number of 'data' is an example of an *internally* induced linguistic change that fits naturally with our cognitive capacity.

Second, changes from below are mostly introduced by the inner classes of the social ladder, such as the lower middle class and the upper working class, but rarely by the highest class. As the above quotation puts it, "*changes from below may be introduced by any social class*," but "*no cases have been recorded in which the highest-status social group acts as the innovating group*" (emphasis added).[13] In her study of the replacement of *ye* by *you* (ch. 3 above), Raumolin-Brunberg found that the social origin of *you* was among the middle classes. Also, R. L. Trask notes that in early Modern English (the sixteenth to seventeenth century), the lower class was the matrix for the merger between the Middle English vowel /ɛ:/, which was represented by the spelling *ea* (as in *meat, seat, read*), and another Middle English vowel /e:/, which was higher than /ɛ:/ and represented by the spelling *ee* (as in *meet, see, heel*).[14] In this sense, the phrase

---

[12] Lyle Campbell and Mauricio J. Mixco, *A Glossary of Historical Linguistics* (Edinburgh: Edinburgh University Press, 2007), s.v. "internal causal factors, internal factors." For a lucid contrast between internal and external causes, see Lyle Campbell, *Historical Linguistics: An Introduction* (2nd ed.; Edinburgh: Edinburgh University Press, 2004), 316–17.

[13] Also, Labov, *Principles*, 1:156; idem, *Principles of Linguistic Change*, vol. 2, *Social Factors* (Language in Society 29; Oxford: Blackwell, 2001), 39, 171–72.

[14] Trask, *Historical Linguistics*, 281–84. Both vowels have now become, of course, the same long high front vowel /i:/ (e.g., the homonyms of *sea, see; meat, meet*; and *read, reed*). Trask provides another example of a change from below. In Old French the spelling *oi*, as in *moi* "me," *loi* "law," and *voix* "voice," was pronounced as [ɔj] (like the diphthong in the English word 'boy'). In medieval French, the spelling came to have two pronunciations: [wɛ] and [wa]. The pronunciation [wɛ] was used by the aristocrats and thus considered prestigious, whereas [wa] was virtually used by everyone else and considered vulgar by the nobility. The situation was reversed after the French Revolution, and it now came to be

from below is a double entendre: not only do the changes occur *below social awareness*, but they also originate from a *lower class*.[15]

Last, since changes from below are unconscious, internally caused, and mostly from the non-highest class of the social ladder, they naturally "develop first in *spontaneous speech* at the most informal level,"[16] then "spread later to the more formal varieties."[17] As for written language, Raumolin-Brunberg notes that "changes from below have been shown to appear first in private writing and *speech-based texts*, such as drama, private letters and autobiographies."[18] We have also seen in chapter 3 that the shift from *ye* to *you* was represented better in the oral genres than in the literate genres when the change was vigorous (68% use of the new form in the oral genres vs. 58% use of the new form in the literate genres; see Table 3 on p. 60).

2.2. *Changes from Above*

The central concept of changes from above social awareness is *social prestige* and *social consciousness*. Labov defines changes from above as follows:

> *Changes from above* are introduced by the dominant social class, often with full public awareness. Normally, they represent borrowings from other speech communities that have higher prestige in the view of the dominant class. Such borrowings do not immediately affect the vernacular patterns of the dominant class or other social classes, but appear primarily in careful speech, reflecting a superposed dialect learned after the vernacular is acquired.[19]

Changes from above show characteristics opposite to those of changes from below.

First, instead of being caused by internal factors, changes from above are caused by external factors, normally taking "the form of the importation of a new prestige feature from outside the speech community."[20]

---

thought that [wa] was prestigious. This is of course the pronunciation now used universally. Trask, *Historical Linguistics*, 285.

[15] Labov, *Principles*, 1:78.

[16] Labov, *Principles*, 2:437. Emphasis added.

[17] Nevalainen and Raumolin-Brunberg, *Historical Sociolinguistics*, 28.

[18] Raumolin-Brunberg, "Historical Sociolinguistics," 16–17. Emphasis added.

[19] Labov, *Principles*, 1:78. Emphasis original.

[20] Labov, *Principles*, 2:272–74. In some cases, changes from above may involve "the re-distribution of forms with known prestige values within the community." Labov, *Principles*, 2:274.

Accordingly, the adopters of the innovative forms have to have access to the prestigious norms.[21] Examples include changes caused by borrowings from a foreign language, because borrowing is often motivated by prestige (e.g., borrowing from French in Europe in the eighteenth century, or borrowing from English in many languages today) and because speakers are aware of their use of foreign language material.[22]

Second, since the adopters of the new norms need to have access to the prestigious norms, this type of change originates with the dominant social class. It starts to diffuse more rapidly when the speakers understand that the innovation is advantageous for their social status.[23] Thus, again, the prepositional phrase *from above* has a double meaning: *from the highest class* of the social ladder as well as *with full public awareness*.[24]

Third, naturally, changes from above "show a higher rate of occurrence in formal styles," and "the more advanced forms are favored in careful speech."[25] Accordingly, in written documents, the literate genre/text type provides a more favorable context for changes from above.[26]

We have seen an example of a change from below in Raumolin-Brunberg's presentation of the replacement of *ye* by *you* (ch. 3 above). Here, I will briefly treat a typical example of a change from above: the decline of multiple negation in the history of English.

External causal factors include "expressive uses of language, positive and negative social evaluations (prestige, stigma), the effects of literacy, prescriptive grammar, educational policies, political decree, language planning, [and] language contact." Campbell, *Historical Linguistics*, 317.

[21] Labov, *Principles*, 2:270–71.

[22] Joan Swann et al., *A Dictionary of Sociolinguistics* (Edinburgh: Edinburgh University Press, 2004), s.v. "change from above." Labov too notes that "shifts from one language to another are conscious shifts and are always changes from above" (Labov, *Principles*, 2:274).

[23] Especially, when "social aspirers" begin to prefer the new form. See Nevalainen and Raumolin-Brunberg, *Historical Sociolinguistics*, 150.

[24] Labov, *Principles*, 1:78.

[25] Labov, *Principles*, 2:274.

[26] Raumolin-Brunberg notes that "changes from above have spread from legal English, expository treatises and official letters to other genres." Raumolin-Brunberg, "Historical Sociolinguistics," 17.

Multiple negation belonged to an English grammar of the upper class; it was not stigmatized until probably the sixteenth century.[27] See the following examples:[28]

(1) And that sawe y *never* yn *no* place but ther (1466[?], John Yeme).

(2) That the dewke of Gelder send me *no* vord vat I sale do, *nor* heelpes me *nat* with *notheng* (1505, Edmund de la Pole).

(3) And I schal *not* put you in *no* more troubul (1516, Margaret Tudor).

(4) I'l *never* be so lasie *no* more but rise by five a cloke (1677[?], Mary Stuart).[29]

As Nevalainen notes, this usage started to lose ground supralocally in the early sixteenth century, being replaced by single negation followed by nonassertive indefinites (*any, ever,* etc.). The shift was completed by the end of the seventeenth century.[30] Importantly, this avoidance of multiple negation originated with administrative language and was led by professional men and social aspirers; so it disappeared first in formal writings.[31]

One final note regarding changes from above is significant for our discussion: in changes from above, the distribution of the old and the new linguistic forms are typically *less predictable*. Unlike changes from below,

---

[27] Terttu Nevalainen, "Social Mobility and the Decline of Multiple Negation in Early Modern English," in *Advances in English Historical Linguistics* (1996) (ed. Jacek Fisiak and Marcin Krygier; Trends in Linguistics: Studies and Monographs 112; Berlin: M. de Gruyter, 1998), 285; Manfred Görlach, *Introduction to Early Modern English* (Cambridge: Cambridge University Press, 1991), 102.

[28] The examples have been taken from Terttu Nevalainen, "Gender Differences in the Evolution of Standard English: Evidence from the *Corpus of Early English Correspondence*," *Journal of English Linguistics* 28 (2000): 50. Emphasis was added by Nevalainen.

[29] The sentences in modern spelling are as follows: (1) And that saw I never in no place but there; (2) That the duke of Gelder send me no word what I shall do, nor helps me not with nothing; (3) And I shall not put you in no more trouble; (4) I'll never be so lazy no more but rise by five o'clock. I thank my old friend Hyoungbae Lee for helping me with these sentences.

[30] Nevalainen, "Gender Differences," 39, 49; idem, "Multiple Negation," 273.

[31] Nevalainen and Raumolin-Brunberg, *Historical Sociolinguistics*, 128, 150; Nevalainen, "Multiple Negation," 281, 284; and Matti Rissanen, "Syntax," in *The Cambridge History of the English Language*, vol. 3, *1476–1776* (ed. Roger Lass; Cambridge: Cambridge University Press, 1999), 263, 272. Accordingly, it is not surprising that we see multiple negation in the year 1677 in a writing by Mary Stuart (above, (4)), since this document belongs to the genre of private letter, which is considered to be closest to the spoken mode of expression. For a fuller discussion of the decline of multiple negation, see Nevalainen, "Multiple Negation," 263–91; idem, "Gender Differences," 49–52.

these changes may look sporadic or unsystematic.[32] This is due to the fact that in a change from above, the direction is usually *unnatural* and the process is normally *uneven*, while the old form tends to occur *persistently*. So it is not surprising that the speakers easily and frequently slip into the existing, natural forms.

Again, multiple negation is exemplary. One might argue, with good reason, that the shift from multiple negation to single negation has never been completed. Indeed, multiple negation has not died out in some (social) dialects of English, where it is instead a norm; and in some other dialects, even though it may be completely avoided in a formal context, it is still used in the vernacular in a less formal context.[33] J. K. Chambers observes that multiple negation belongs to the cases in which a specific variant occurs in the vernacular repeatedly and ubiquitously.[34]

From another perspective, the unevenness of a change from above is explained in regard to the time when the individual speaker acquires the forms promoted by this change. As Labov says in the above quotation, the new forms in changes from above are "learned after the vernacular is acquired."[35] In other words, the speakers acquire them during their adulthood, not during their childhood. In such a situation, it is only a matter of course that the old form is persistent and the change looks sporadic.

2.3. *The Opposing Views on EBH and LBH*

I argue that the idea of the two types of linguistic changes allows us to accommodate the two opposing views on EBH and LBH. Hurvitz and his followers maintain that the shift from EBH and LBH was irreversible, which means that the postexilic biblical writers had no choice but to use LBH; the challengers argue that the postexilic biblical writers were able

---

[32] Labov, *Principles*, 1:453.

[33] Nevalainen, "Gender Differences," 49. This situation, of course, suggests that the variation between multiple negation and single negation could constitute a case of *stable sociolinguistic variables*, like the variation between *-in'* and *-ing*. Indeed, on the basis of vast sociolinguistic studies, Labov notes that changes from above much resemble stable sociolinguistic variables. See further Labov, *Principles*, 2:266–71, 274.

[34] Chambers, *Sociolinguistic Theory*, 265–66. Chambers lists five variables that appear to be recurrent in vernacular English: (1) the variation between *-ing* and *-in'*; (2) the deletion or retention of the final consonant in the consonant cluster, as in *firs'* for *first* and *wes' side* for *west side*; (3) default singulars, as in *David and I was the last ones* instead of *David and I were . . .*; (4) conjugation regularization, for example, using *mowed, proved,* or *sawed* for historically correct *mown, proven,* or *sawn*; and (5) multiple negation. See further Chambers, *Sociolinguistic Theory*, 265–66.

[35] Labov, *Principles*, 1:78.

to write flawless EBH. The situation may not be as simple as either group argues, and it seems to make much more sense—and I shall demonstrate this in the remaining chapters—that some individual changes were largely irreversible and others were rather stylistic. And I suggest that the former kind of changes belongs to changes from below and the latter kind to changes from above. From a different perspective, if a particular change from EBH to LBH proves to be a change from below social awareness, it is understood that the change was unconscious and its direction was natural. The writers during this ongoing change must have participated in the trend of the period unconsciously and naturally. In this case, we can reasonably assume that the use of the variant forms during this change is, *in general*, a reliable indicator of the chronology of BH.[36] On the other hand, if a specific change from EBH to LBH was a change from above social awareness, it follows that its process was uneven, its direction was unnatural, and the old form recurred persistently. The writers must have consciously chosen the new form, which was promoted by this *unnatural* change. They had freedom—of which they were aware—to participate in the change or not, although they were probably pressed by their peers within their scribal culture. In this case, the use of the variant forms during the change may not be understood to be a reliable indicator of the development of BH; it is more or less what the challengers would call stylistic.[37]

How can we decide whether a change—if it proves to be a change—is from below or from above? We may do it by correlating the linguistic variable with the independent variable of text type. When we see an individual book/text *vigorously participating* in a certain change, we will compare the uses of both the old and the new variants in our two text types (recorded speech and narration), which represent oral- and written-based text types (see ch. 3). When the change is more prominent in the oral-based text type (i.e., recorded speech), we shall understand that this change is a change from below. When the change is more prominent

---

[36] Only *in general*, because the situation should be different for a text that does not follow the general trend of the period (i.e., a text that is a late adopter or an early one).

[37] It is important and helpful to distinguish between the chronological understanding of EBH and LBH and the argument for linguistic dating. The chronological understanding of EBH and LBH may entail a *description* of the profiles of EBH and LBH (particularly on the basis of the texts whose dates are agreed upon), whereas linguistic dating presupposes a *prescriptive* use of the outcome of the description. The validity of a chronological understanding does not automatically lead to a case for linguistic dating. See further chapters 5 and 6.

in the written-based text type (i.e., narration), it shall be considered a change from above. That a change is "vigorous" shall mean that the use of the newer form has reached at least 15 percent. This number has been taken from Nevalainen and Raumolin-Brunberg's adoption of Labov's system of the stages of a linguistic change. Labov posits five stages of an ongoing linguistic change (incipient, new and vigorous, mid-range, nearing completion, and completed). Nevalainen and Raumolin-Brunberg set 15 percent as the boundary between the first, "incipient" stage and the second, "new and vigorous" stage.[38]

3. *The Questions for the Empirical Analysis*

The theoretical assessment that we have conducted in this chapter has argued the following points with regard to the chronological understanding of EBH and LBH and the linguistic dating of biblical texts. First, the notion of variability as the mechanism of linguistic change reveals a logical gap between the challengers' correct observation of the biblical evidence and their non-chronological stylistic understanding of EBH and LBH. Second, Labov's idea of two types of changes raises the possibility that some changes in BH were unconsciously adopted by the users of BH and proceeded in a more natural direction while others were consciously imposed and proceeded in a less natural direction.

These tentative answers, which are based on a theoretical assessment, cannot be fully substantiated without actual data being examined. Therefore, in the following chapter, we will analyze eight morphological, syntactical, lexical, and phraseological variables in BH. In the analysis of each variable, we will ask two questions. The first question is whether the shift of tendency from EBH to LBH represents an authentic change in the history of BH. If the answer to this question is in the affirmative, we will then ask whether this change was a change from below or from above. For the first question we will depend on a correlation of the BH variable in question with the independent variable of time period. For the second question we will attempt a correlation with the independent variable of text type.

---

[38] The breakdown of the percentage is as follows: incipient, below 15 percent; new and vigorous, between 15 and 35 percent; mid-range, between 36 and 65 percent; nearing completion, between 66 and 85 percent; and completed, above 85 percent. Nevalainen and Raumolin-Brunberg, *Historical Sociolinguistics*, 54–55; see also Labov, *Principles*, 1:79–83.

CHAPTER FIVE

VARIABLES OF BIBLICAL HEBREW: A SOCIOLINGUISTIC ANALYSIS OF THE PURPORTED EBH AND LBH FEATURES

In this chapter, we will examine the following eight morphological, syntactical, phraseological, and lexical variables in BH:

(1)	־וֹתָם	vs.	־וֹתֵיהֶם
(2)	וְהָיָה/וַיְהִי + כְּ/בְּ + inf. const.	vs.	וְ + כְּ/בְּ + inf. const.
(3)	הַמֶּלֶךְ + king's name	vs.	king's name + הַמֶּלֶךְ
(4)	בֵּין...וּבֵין...	vs.	בֵּין...לְ...
(5)	בֵּית יְהוָה	vs.	בֵּית הָאֱלֹהִים
(6)	מַמְלָכָה	vs.	מַלְכוּת
(7)	עֵדָה	vs.	קָהָל
(8)	צָעַק	vs.	זעק

These eight items have been chosen because their variations are explained completely differently by the two groups of scholars who participate in the debate over the linguistic dating of biblical texts: whereas the advocates of linguistic dating understand them to indicate a decisive shift from preexilic EBH to postexilic LBH, the challengers argue that the variant forms of each linguistic item are merely stylistic and may not be explained in chronological terms.

It is important to note that, for Hurvitz and those who agree with him, these eight items constitute a very strong case for the argument for the linguistic dating of biblical texts. All of them meet the first two of Hurvitz's three criteria for identifying an LBH feature (linguistic distribution and linguistic contrast; see ch. 2), and, except for one case (בֵּית יְהוָה vs. בֵּית הָאֱלֹהִים; see below), all meet the third criterion of extrabiblical attestations. Accordingly, to speak in terms of the debate, if a few of these items prove to be inadequate for linguistic dating, we would have to reconsider seriously the validity of the project.

There are hundreds of linguistic items that scholars have identified as markers of the change within BH.[1] I have chosen only the above eight

---

[1] Young, Rezetko, and Ehrensvärd have collected 460 grammatical and lexical items. See Young, Rezetko, and Ehrensvärd, *Linguistic Dating*, 2:160–214.

for two reasons. First, each pair of the purported EBH forms and the corresponding purported LBH forms constitutes a linguistic variable, that is, the two forms are equivalent in their linguistic meaning. This condition, of course, is a prerequisite to our application of the variationist approach to these linguistic items. Second, of hundreds of the purported EBH and LBH contrasts, these eight items are among the most frequently used. This situation will enable us to obtain statistically more reliable results.

There is one notable omission: אָנֹכִי and אֲנִי. Clearly, אָנֹכִי and אֲנִי constitute a true linguistic variable, and this variable is one of the most frequently attested in the Bible (occurring 1,233 times). Also, many understand that the two forms have chronological implications (אָנֹכִי being the marker of EBH, אֲנִי that of LBH). Nevertheless, this variable has been excluded from our discussion because, as the first-person pronoun, the two forms hardly occur in the text type of narration. It is virtually impossible to compare their uses across the two text types (recorded speech and narration). I have identified only 58 cases (1 אָנֹכִי and 57 אֲנִי's) in which either form is used in the text type of narration (which is first-person narration). This is less than five percent of the total use of אָנֹכִי and אֲנִי.[2]

The discussion of each variable will proceed as follows. First, it begins by summarizing the traditional understanding of the contrast between the purported EBH form and the purported LBH form and the challengers' objection to it. To our great advantage, the challengers have discussed all of the eight items in several of their studies. Second, the discussion will then establish that the relationship of the pair is one of a true variable. Third, we will briefly discuss the linguistic contexts in which the variant forms are used. Last, a sociolinguistic analysis of the variable will follow, in which we will try to correlate the linguistic variable with the independent variable of time period and then with the independent variable of text type. In this part of the analysis, we will ask two questions. First, does the linguistic variable, as realized in two variant forms, represent an authentic linguistic shift from EBH to LBH? In our sociolinguistic model, this question is translated into the following: is the choice between the

---

[2] Another interesting variable, לֵב and לֵבָב, will not be treated because the two forms are not understood in chronological terms and thus not relevant to the present discussion. The sociolinguistic understanding of linguistic variation suggests that the variants were not chosen freely or meaninglessly by the writers of BH. It is also possible, however, that we will not be able to discern the factors and the contexts that contributed to the choice between the two forms. As we have noted in chapter 3, many important social variables are not available in the study of BH. Cf. Young, Rezetko, and Ehrensvärd's brief treatment of לֵב and לֵבָב in their *Linguistic Dating*, 2:108–11.

variant forms meaningfully correlated with time period? If the answer to this question is affirmative, we can argue that the use of the variable was constrained by a chronological factor. If a meaningful correlation is not found, the linguistic variable should be explained without recourse to the diachronic model. Second, once we establish that a particular BH variable reflects an authentic change from EBH to LBH, we will then ask whether this change was from below or from above. In our sociolinguistic analysis, we will answer this question by attempting to correlate the choice with the independent variable of text type. We will see whether the change appeared first in the written-based text type (narration) or in the oral-based text type (recorded speech) when the change was vigorous (i.e., when the use of the new form is more than 15%; see ch. 4).

1. וֹתֵיהֶם- *vs.* וֹתָם-[3]

1.1. *The Debate*

The traditional understanding. When it follows the (typically) feminine plural ending וֹת-, the BH third-person masculine plural pronominal suffix is realized in two forms: ◌ָם- and ◌ֵיהֶם-. Thus we encounter the combination וֹתָם- sometimes (as in מוֹשְׁבוֹתָם and אֲבוֹתָם) and the combination וֹתֵיהֶם- at other times (as in מוֹשְׁבוֹתֵיהֶם and אֲבוֹתֵיהֶם). The proponents of the diachronic understanding believe that EBH favors the shorter combination וֹתָם-, whereas LBH favors the longer form וֹתֵיהֶם-. Hurvitz understands that there was a gradual replacement of the shorter form (וֹתָם-) by the longer one (וֹתֵיהֶם-) in the biblical period.[4] He presents the following parallel passages:[5]

| 1 Kgs 8:34 | הָאֲדָמָה אֲשֶׁר נָתַתָּ לַאֲבוֹתָם | the land that you gave to their ancestors[6] |
| 2 Chr 6:25 | הָאֲדָמָה אֲשֶׁר־נָתַתָּה לָהֶם וְלַאֲבֹתֵיהֶם | the land that you gave to them and to their ancestors |

---

[3] In this and the following headings, the first variant always represents the purported EBH feature as understood by the advocates of linguistic dating, and the second variant represents the purported LBH feature as understood by the same scholars.

[4] Hurvitz, *Priestly Source and Ezekiel*, 25–26.

[5] Hurvitz, *Priestly Source and Ezekiel*, 26.

[6] Unless otherwise noted, all English translations of biblical passages in this chapter follow the New Revised Standard Version (New York: Division of Christian Education of the National Council of Churches of Christ in the United States of America, 1989).

Isa 59:8   וְאֵין מִשְׁפָּט בְּמַעְגְּלוֹתָם   and there is no justice in their paths
1QIsa[a]   במעגלותיהמה

Exod 36:34   וְאֶת־טַבְּעֹתָם עָשָׂה זָהָב   and [he] made rings of gold for them
Samaritan Pentateuch   טבעתיהם

Accordingly, Hurvitz argues as follows:

> The ending -ōthām is dominant in classical BH. Though its rival -ōthēyhem
> may turn up here and there in early compositions, its employment in these
> texts is extremely rare and hardly noticeable. Only in the later period does
> the wide use of the extended suffix -ēyhem replace the shorter -ām. In cer-
> tain words, the earlier ending -ōthām has managed to survive throughout
> the entire biblical period, without being forced off stage by the equivalent
> -ōthēyhem even in late biblical books. In other cases, in contrast, the older
> suffix shows signs of weakness already in books definitely belonging to clas-
> sical Hebrew; but all these cases are linguistically exceptional and do not
> distort the overall picture: biblical literature as a whole exhibits faithfully
> the gradual substitution of -ōthām by -ōthēyhem. The process reflected in
> the Bible illustrates very clearly the transitional period which LBH repre-
> sents between the fading away of -ōthām in the Bible on the one hand, and
> the taking over of -ōthēyhem in the Mishnah on the other.[7]

In short, Hurvitz maintains that though the change from -ōtām to -ōtêhem
was not completed in LBH, each form clearly represents one of the two
main stages of BH.

Following Hurvitz, Wright uses the contrast between -ōtām and -ōtêhem as
a criterion for dividing BH chronologically. Thus, for Wright, J's preexilic
provenance is supported by the fact that J does not use the longer form.[8]

The challengers' argument. Young, Rezetko, and Ehrensvärd do not, however, understand this contrast in chronological terms. They have counted
the occurrences of both forms in the core EBH books and the core LBH
books:[9]

---

[7] Hurvitz, *Priestly Source and Ezekiel*, 26.

[8] Wright, *Yahwistic Source*, 29–30. For a similar understanding of -ōtām/-ōtêhem, see Paul
Joüon and T. Muraoka, *A Grammar of Biblical Hebrew* (rev. ed.; SubBi 27; Rome: Editrice
Pontificio Istituto Biblico, 2006), 264–65 (§94g).

[9] "The core EBH books" and "the core LBH books" are the terms Young, Rezetko, and
Ehrensvärd use throughout their *Linguistic Dating*. The former designation refers to Genesis through Kings, whose language is exemplary of EBH, and the latter designation refers
to Esther, Daniel, Ezra, Nehemiah, and Chronicles, which are undisputed postexilic books
written in clear LBH.

If we compare the core EBH and LBH books, we find ratios of 6 EBH וֹתִם-
vs. 1 LBH occurrence [i.e., 6 וֹתִם-'s in Gen–Kgs per 1 וֹתִם- in Esth–Chr], and
1 EBH וֹתֵיהֶם- vs. 2 LBH occurrences [i.e., 1 וֹתֵיהֶם- in Gen–Kgs per 2 וֹתֵיהֶם-'s
in Esth–Chr]. Or, from a different perspective, in core EBH וֹתִם- prevails
over וֹתֵיהֶם- by about 12 to 1, whereas in core LBH וֹתֵיהֶם- occurs only slightly
more often than וֹתִם-. The difference between EBH and LBH is the *frequency*
of the endings. Consequently, this is not an issue of early vs. late but rather
stylistic preference. EBH mostly shuns 'younger' וֹתֵיהֶם- whereas less conservative LBH uses both suffixes evenly.[10]

Thus while admitting that the ratios are distinct, Young, Rezetko, and
Ehrensvärd argue that since both forms were used throughout the biblical period, they represent a stylistic difference rather than a chronological
one.

Elisha Qimron's evidence from QH may further support Young, Rezetko,
and Ehrensvärd's position. Although Hurvitz cited the use of the longer
form in 1QIsaᵃ (see above) and tried to show LBH's connection to QH,
Qimron notes the following on QH's use of וֹתִם- and וֹתֵיהֶם-:

> After the ending וֹת-, the form ם- (or מה-) is preferred to the form םיהם- (or
> יהמה-): forms like אבותם occur some 70 times, as opposed to 15 times for
> forms like אבותיהם. This is somewhat surprising, since the short form is
> older.[11]

Qimron's surprise is due to his adherence to the traditional understanding. But in a footnote, referring to Hurvitz's discussion of the contrast,
Qimron writes,

> The fact, unnoticed by Hurvitz, that the short form predominates in DSS
> Hebrew and is not absent from MH (contra Hurvitz), shows that both forms
> were in use in pre-exilic Hebrew, in post-exilic Hebrew and perhaps in MH
> as well.[12]

One might ask Hurvitz: when we know that the form וֹתִם- was preferred
in QH and was not defunct in MH, and that the form וֹתֵיהֶם- was in use
throughout the biblical period, can we still understand that the two forms
represent a linguistic change from EBH to LBH and thus may be used as
an indicator of EBH or of LBH?

---

[10] Young, Rezetko, and Ehrensvärd, *Linguistic Dating*, 1:76. Emphasis added.

[11] Elisha Qimron, *The Hebrew of the Dead Sea Scrolls* (HSS 29; Atlanta: Scholars,
1986), 63.

[12] Qimron, *Hebrew of the DSS*, 63 n. 81. Note, however, that Qimron does not say that the
shorter form is predominant in MH. Tannaitic literature clearly prefers the longer form.
See Wright's discussion of postbiblical literature in his *Yahwistic Source*, 28–29.

1.2. *A True Variable?*

The two forms וָתְמ- and וָתֵיהֶם- are a clear case of a true variable. They are grammatically equivalent, as Hurvitz's examples at the beginning of this section illustrate. Although the longer form is not used with some words in the Bible (such as שֵׁם, אֶרֶץ, דּוֹר, נֶפֶשׁ, and תּוֹלְדוֹת), it is productive, and there seems to be no grammatical restrictions on its usage.[13]

1.3. *Variation Analysis*

In order to see whether the variation has chronological implications, I present the following table, which arranges the variable וָתְמ-/וָתֵיהֶם- according to books/texts and time periods. Note that in this and the following tables and charts, the percentages always represent the use of the purportedly late form out of the use of both forms. Also, I have presented only the raw numbers for the cases in which the variable occurs less than five times in either form in one unit. In order to be cautious in our analysis, we will not consider the ratios of these data statistically relevant. When the variable occurs between five and nine times in one unit, I have italicized the percentage, again for cautioning. We might use them supplementarily with other data, but will not interpret them independently.

Table 4. The use of וָתְמ- and וָתֵיהֶם- according to books/texts (the synoptic passages in Chr and books/texts with disputed dates excluded)[14]

		וֹתם-	וֹתיהם-	Use of וֹתיהם-
	Non-P	13	4	24%
	Deut	7	2	22%
Preexilic	Isa¹	2	1	
	Hos	10	1	9%
	Amos	2	1	
	Mic	4	4	*50%*

---

[13] Wright, *Yahwistic Source*, 27. Wright cites Friedrich Böttcher, who has found 22 nouns that appear with both suffixes. Probably more importantly, the longer form's productivity is demonstrated by its use with nouns that occur frequently, such as אָחוֹת, אָב, מִזְבֵּחַ, בַּת, עֶצֶם, and מִשְׁפָּחָה. See Böttcher, *Ausführliches Lehrbuch der hebräischen Sprache* (ed. Ferdinand Mühlau; 2 vols.; Leipzig: J. A. Barth, 1866–1868), 2:42.

[14] The numbers that are not included in the table (the occurrences of וָתְמ- vs. those of וָתֵיהֶם-): synoptic Chronicles—7 vs. 1; P—187 vs. 4; the passages in the Pentateuch that have not been identified as either Non-P (J/E) or P (see ch. 3)—4 vs. 1; Joel—1 vs. 1; Psalms—23 vs. 14; Proverbs—5 vs. 3; the prose section of Job—0 vs. 1; and the poetry section of Job—5 vs. 0.

Table 4. (*cont.*)

		-וֹתָם	-וֹתֵיהֶם	Use of -וֹתֵיהֶם
	Nah	1	0	
	Zeph	3	0	
Preexilic to	DtrH	67	16	19%
early exilic	Jer	18	18	50%
	Isa²	5	1	*17%*
Exilic	Ezek	26	12	32%
	Lam	3	1	
	Isa³	5	6	55%
	Mal	1	0	
Postexilic	Ezra–Neh	6	20	77%
	Chr (non-syn.)	36	38	51%

Note: Isa¹ designates Isaiah 1–39, excluding chs. 13–14, 24–27, 34–35; Isa² designates Isaiah 40–55 plus chs. 13–14 and 34–35; and Isa³ designates Isaiah 24–27; 56–66 (see ch. 3 for more discussion).

With numerous data and rather uneven numbers, it may be difficult for us to identify a pattern. However, when we transfer the statistically relevant data to a chart, a pattern is discernible.

Figure 3 shows that the variable וֹתֵיהֶם-/וֹתָם- is *meaningfully correlated* with the independent variable of *time period* in the way that the use of וֹתֵיהֶם- *increases*. Of course, we see unevenness among individual books/texts. However, with the sociolinguistic understanding that there can be early adopters and conservatives in a linguistic change, the simplest and most reasonable interpretation of the data is that *a change was in progress during the biblical period.*[15] This understanding may be

---

[15] In connection with the relatively diverging tendencies of individual texts' uses of the variable, Hurvitz comments on Chronicles, which uses the shorter form rather frequently as a postexilic text (51%; cf. Ezra–Nehemiah's 77%): "In regard to the *Book of Chronicles* we know that both old and new elements appear there simultaneously, the explanation of this specific peculiarity in Chronicles is simple: the occurrence of the earlier form *mōšᵉbhōthām* must be regarded as one of the Chronicler's successful attempts to reproduce faithfully the classic style of the Pentateuch" (Hurvitz, *Priestly Source and Ezekiel*, 27; emphasis original). This comment by Hurvitz is double-edged. If the Chronicler *was* successful in attempting to reproduce the classic style in his own time, why not other biblical writers? Hurvitz quickly qualifies the foregoing comment in a footnote: "As is well known, in many cases the Chronicler's attempts to adhere to classical BH were unsuccessful. For example, Ch. contains 26 occurrences of the late form *ᵃbhōthêyhem* but only 12 of the early *ᵃbhōthām*" (Hurvitz, *Priestly Source and Ezekiel*, 27 n. 13). A simpler explanation is that the Chronicler's use of the two forms was in accord with the linguistic milieu of his

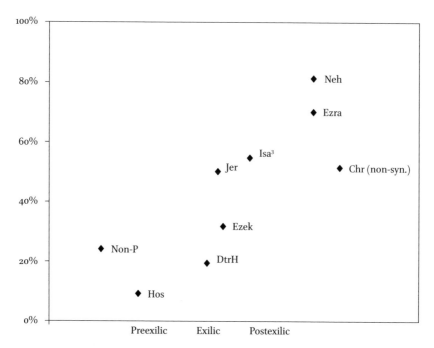

Figure 3. The use of וֹתֵיהֶם- in the books/texts in which וֹתָם- and וֹתֵיהֶם- occur ten or more times

strengthened by scholarly observation that the longer form became predominant in MH.[16]

As we have seen above, the challengers argue that "the difference between EBH and LBH is the *frequency* of the endings" and thus this is a matter of "*stylistic preference*."[17] However, the *observation* that the difference is in frequency does not lead to the *interpretation* that it was a matter of "style." On the other hand, the sociolinguistic model of linguistic change provides an empirical link between the same observation and the interpretation that there *was* a change.[18]

---

own period, while simultaneously showing a fluctuation that is expected in the variation model of linguistic change. To be sure, the Chronicler uses the longer form more than most of the preexilic and exilic books.

[16] Wright, *Yahwistic Source*, 28–29. See his extensive discussion of Qumran and Tannaitic literature there.

[17] Young, Rezetko, and Ehrensvärd, *Linguistic Dating*, 1:76. Emphasis added.

[18] If Young, Rezetko, and Ehrensvärd want to argue that the choice between וֹתָם- and וֹתֵיהֶם- was a matter of style—a scenario which is certainly possible—it is *their* obligation

There is one significant problem in the foregoing understanding of the variable וֹתָם-/וֹתֵיהֶם-, however. As Qimron has observed above, the increase of וֹתֵיהֶם- which the biblical data represent is reversed in QH (70 occurrences of the shorter form and 15 of the longer form, according to Qimron). Thus, the process is apparently not straightforward: the use of the longer form increased in the biblical period, then reduced in QH, and then resumed its original increase in MH. To consider this problem, we will now use our second independent variable.

This time, we are allowed to include the books/texts whose dates are disputed, because we correlate the linguistic variable with text types (and not with time periods). But only P has been added, because the other books/texts do not present data in both text types of narration and recorded speech.

Table 5. The use of וֹתָם- and וֹתֵיהֶם- according to books/texts and text types (only the texts in which either form occurs in both text types included)

		Narration			Recorded speech		
		וֹתם-	וֹתיהם-	Use of וֹתיהם-	וֹתם-	וֹתיהם-	Use of וֹתיהם-
Preexilic	Non-P	7	1	*13%*	6	3	*33%*
Preexilic to early exilic	DtrH	54	12	18%	13	4	24%
Exilic	Ezek	1	1		25	11	31%
Postexilic	Ezra–Neh	6	12	67%	0	8	*100%*
	Chr (non-syn.)	35	34	49%	1	4	80%
Disputed	P	126	1	1%	61	3	5%

The table is illuminating. When we set aside the statistically irrelevant narration text type of Ezekiel (1 occurrence of each form), in all of the texts and books that are vigorously participating in the change (more than 15% total use of the newer form; all books/texts except for P), the recorded speech text type provides a more favorable context for the form וֹתֵיהֶם- than the narration text type. The implication may be solidly stated: the shift from וֹתָם- to וֹתֵיהֶם- in the biblical period was used first in the

_____

to provide an explanation that is based on non-chronological factors such as dialect, diglossia, and editorial and scribal activity (cf. Rezetko, "Dating Biblical Hebrew," 222).

vernacular or in the text type that is closer to it and only later permeated the text type that approaches typical writing.

Accordingly, the shift from ‑וֹתָם to ‑וֹתֵיהֶם as represented by the biblical data is an example of *changes from below social awareness*, or "systematic changes that appear first in the *vernacular*, and represent the operation of *internal, linguistic* factors."[19] On the one hand, we have seen that the vernacular, or the text type that is closer to it (i.e., recorded speech) is the context in which this change was represented better. On the other hand, Hurvitz has correctly observed that this change was probably caused by an internal, linguistic factor. He has argued that the change from ‑וֹתָם to ‑וֹתֵיהֶם is a case in which the language adopted "a more 'transparent' form, in which the possessive pronoun also acquires its own morpheme of plurality" (i.e., ‑ֵ◌-). The resulting combination ‑וֹתֵי- is redundant, as Hurvitz notes, because the plural meaning is expressed by two morphemes (i.e., תֹו- and ‑ֵ◌-).[20]

The biblical data—which are our immediate concern—then strongly suggest that the change from ‑וֹתָם to ‑וֹתֵיהֶם was a change from below. Yet, a difficult question remains: how do we explain the reversal of development in QH? Without analyzing the data from Qumran, a tentative answer might be provided with recourse to Schniedewind's theory about QH. As we have seen in chapter 3, Schniedewind argues that QH was an example of "antilanguage," in which the speakers of QH manipulated the linguistic forms in order to differentiate themselves from others.[21] If Schniedewind is correct, the reversal of the trend in QH does not have to compromise our understanding that the change from ‑וֹתָם to ‑וֹתֵיהֶם was an unconscious natural change. We could argue that the speakers of QH

---

[19] Labov, *Principles*, 1:78. Emphasis added.

[20] Hurvitz, *Priestly Source and Ezekiel*, 25. English provides a similar example: In Old English, the negation of a verb was expressed by *ne* alone. Later in Middle English, without adding any further meaning, an additional word, *naht*, had to be used alongside *ne* to express a negation. See Olga Fischer, "Syntax," in *The Cambridge History of the English Language*, vol. 2, *1066–1478* (ed. Norman Blake; Cambridge: Cambridge University Press, 1992), 280.

Hurvitz proposes an additional external causal factor for the change from ‑וֹתָם to ‑וֹתֵיהֶם. He claims that there was also Aramaic influence. According to Hurvitz, the corresponding Aramaic form (אֲבָהָתְהֹם) influenced the change, because this form has "two plural morphemes, both in the word itself *(-āhāth)* and the suffixed pronoun *(-hōm)*" (Hurvitz, *Priestly Source and Ezekiel*, 25 and n. 8). This remark by Hurvitz, however, is incorrect, because in the combined ending *-āhāthōm*, the meaning for plurality is not expressed by two morphemes: the plural meaning in the suffix *(-hōm)* is not for the preceding noun but for the pronoun's antecedent.

[21] Schniedewind, "Antilanguage," 235–36. See my brief survey of Schniedewind in chapter 3.

deliberately used the older form, which did not die out but was still in their linguistic competence.[22]

In summary, the biblical evidence, as we have analyzed, suggests the following understanding of the variation between וֹתָם- and וֹתֵיהֶם-. First, since our analysis shows a meaningful correlation between the variable וֹתֵיהֶם-/וֹתָם- and the independent variable of time period, we have to reject the challengers' non-chronological, stylistic understanding of the variation, notwithstanding their correct observation of the two forms' availability through the biblical period. Rather, our sociolinguistic analysis shores up Hurvitz's argument that the shorter form וֹתָם- was gradually replaced by the longer form וֹתֵיהֶם-, and we should understand the variation between וֹתָם- and וֹתֵיהֶם- as a facet of change during the biblical period. Second, the change that this variation represents should be understood to be a change from below social awareness, that is, a change that is natural and unconscious. This suggests that the choice between וֹתָם- and וֹתֵיהֶם- should in general be considered to be a reliable indicator of the chronology of BH.

2. וְהָיָה/וַיְהִי + כְּ/בְ + Inf. Const. vs. וְ + כְּ/בְ + Inf. Const.

2.1. *The Debate*

The traditional understanding. Scholars have long believed that the use of the introductory וְהָיָה/וַיְהִי before a temporal clause has chronological implications. In narrative, for example, time may be marked by וַיְהִי + the preposition כְּ/בְ + inf. const. or by the preposition כְּ/בְ + inf. const. (i.e., without the introductory וַיְהִי). It has been argued that the structure with the introductory וַיְהִי decreased during the biblical period.[23]

See the following parallel passages:

1 Kgs 8:54	וַיְהִי כְּכַלּוֹת שְׁלֹמֹה לְהִתְפַּלֵּל	When Solomon finished offering... prayer
2 Chr 7:1	וּכְכַלּוֹת שְׁלֹמֹה לְהִתְפַּלֵּל	When Solomon had ended his prayer

---

[22] If this understanding is correct, the situation in Qumran would probably qualify as a case of a change from above social awareness, in which the speakers/writers were consciously encouraged, or demanded, to use one form—which was probably considered prestigious—over the other.

[23] See, for example, Driver, *Introduction*, 538; Kropat, *Syntax der Chronik*, 22–23.

2 Kgs 12:11	וַיְהִי כִּרְאוֹתָם כִּי־רַב הַכֶּסֶף	Whenever they saw that there was a great deal of money
2 Chr 24:11	וְכִרְאוֹתָם כִּי־רַב הַכֶּסֶף	When they saw that there was a large amount of money
2 Kgs 22:3	וַיְהִי בִּשְׁמֹנֶה עֶשְׂרֵה שָׁנָה לַמֶּלֶךְ יֹאשִׁיָּהוּ	In the eighteenth year of King Josiah[24]
2 Chr 34:8	וּבִשְׁנַת שְׁמוֹנֶה עֶשְׂרֵה לְמָלְכוֹ	In the eighteenth year of his reign

In all three cases, the Chronicler deleted the introductory וַיְהִי that is found in his source (if, of course, we accept that MT Samuel–Kings was the Chronicler's source).

Using a concordance, Polzin has counted the forms כְּכַלּוֹת and כִּשְׁמֹעַ in the whole Bible. He states as follows:

> Confer the concordance where *kᵉ* plus *kallôt* occurs twenty-five times. It occurs sixteen times with *hāyāh* and nine times without *hāyāh*; *hāyāh* never occurs in a book later than Jeremiah and the lack of *hāyāh* is found seven times in Chr, Ezr and Dan, and once in Ex and II Sam. Again, the introductory phrase, *wayhî kišmoaᶜ* occurs 14 times in Kgs and not at all in the Chronicler's language, whereas the introductory phrase *wᵉkišmoaᶜ* occurs twice in the Chronicler's language: II Chr 15.8, Ezr 9.3, and not at all in Kgs.[25]

Bergey observes Esther's "marked preference" for the construction without וַיְהִי or וְהָיָה.[26] Rooker too argues that Ezekiel's decided preference for the same construction "certainly indicates that this feature was firmly established in the exilic period."[27] The decrease of the introductory וְהָיָה/וַיְהִי in LBH also meets the criterion of extrabiblical attestations. Bergey and Rooker note that the introductory וְהָיָה/וַיְהִי is rarely used in the DSS and that, when it is, it occurs only in biblical citations and allusions.[28]

---

[24] Note here that the preposition is followed by a numeral, not by an infinitive. The implication remains to be the same, nevertheless.

[25] Polzin, *Late Biblical Hebrew*, 46. Cf., however, Hurvitz's critique of Polzin's use of this feature in dating P. Hurvitz agrees with Polzin that the structure with הָיָה fell into disuse in LBH, but this particular feature, which is used frequently in narrative, is not a good criterion for dating P, since P includes many lists and genealogies but relatively few narratives. Hurvitz, *Priestly Source and Ezekiel*, 166–67.

[26] Bergey, "Book of Esther," 52.

[27] Rooker, *Biblical Hebrew in Transition*, 104.

[28] Bergey, "Book of Esther," 54–55; Rooker, *Biblical Hebrew in Transition*, 104. The data from MH are not helpful, because MH does not use בְּ or כְּ with the infinitives (Bergey, "Book of Esther," 54). For a similar understanding of the use and non-use of the introductory וְהָיָה/וַיְהִי before כְּ/בְּ + inf. const., see Wright, *Yahwistic Source*, 42–45; Qimron, *Hebrew of the DSS*, 72–73; Joüon and Muraoka, *Grammar*, 590 (§166q); Sáenz-Badillos, *History*, 119, 144–45; and W. Th. van Peursen, *The Verbal System in the Hebrew Text of Ben Sira* (Studies in Semitic Languages and Linguistics 41; Leiden: Brill, 2004), 340–43. Eskhult discusses

The challengers' argument. Rezetko thinks differently. Regarding the use of וַיְהִי, he argues, "A close look at the three synoptic passages *routinely* cited in the literature and at a fourth synoptic passage that is neglected shows that a trend of 'replacement' does not occur in Chronicles."[29] The three synoptic passages Rezetko addresses are those we have seen above (1 Kgs 8:54//2 Chr 7:1; 2 Kgs 12:11//2 Chr 24:11; 2 Kgs 22:3//2 Chr 34:8). Of these, his comment on 2 Kgs 12:11//2 Chr 24:11 is worth noting. Below I cite the passages with his fourth additional example (2 Kgs 10:13 and 2 Chr 22:8).

2 Kgs 12:11	וַיְהִי כִּרְאוֹתָם כִּי־רַב הַכֶּסֶף	Whenever they saw that there was a great deal of money
2 Chr 24:11	וַיְהִי בְּעֵת יָבִיא אֶת־הָאָרוֹן... וְכִרְאוֹתָם כִּי־רַב הַכֶּסֶף	Whenever the chest was brought... when they saw that there was a large amount of money
2 Kgs 10:13	וְיֵהוּא מָצָא	Jehu met...
2 Chr 22:8	וַיְהִי כְּהִשָּׁפֵט יֵהוּא עִם־בֵּית אַחְאָב וַיִּמְצָא	When Jehu was executing judgment on the house of Ahab, he met...

For the first parallel, Rezetko correctly notes that "Chronicles' reading lies within an expansion that in fact *does begin* with ויהי."[30] Also, as for 2 Chr 22:8, into which the Chronicler inserted וַיְהִי, he calls it the "counter example to the supposed 'trend'" and says that it "seems virtually unknown" to scholarship.[31]

Rezetko closes his discussion of the use and non-use of וַיְהִי by quoting Rendsburg's critique of Polzin: "The figures presented by Polzin do not show a tremendous decrease in the use of *wayhî*... That Chronicles uses *wayhî* less than Kings is still correct, but the difference is not as great as

---

this feature in several essays and concludes that the variation has diachronic implications. See Eskhult, "Verbal Syntax in Late Biblical Hebrew," in *Diggers at the Well: Proceedings of a Third International Symposium on the Hebrew of the Dead Sea Scrolls and Ben Sira* (ed. T. Muraoka and J. F. Elwolde; STDJ 36; Leiden: Brill, 2000), 91–92; idem, "Markers of Text Type in Biblical Hebrew from a Diachronic Perspective," in *Hamlet on a Hill: Semitic and Greek Studies Presented to Professor T. Muraoka on the Occasion of His Sixty-Fifth Birthday* (ed. M. F. J. Baasten and W. Th. van Peursen; OLA 118; Leuven: Peeters, 2003), 154–56; and idem, "Traces of Linguistic Development," 367–68.

29 Rezetko, "Dating Biblical Hebrew," 236. Emphasis original.
30 Rezetko, "Dating Biblical Hebrew," 236. Emphasis original.
31 Rezetko, "Dating Biblical Hebrew," 236.

Polzin's statistics suggest."[32] We may safely observe that Rezetko again believes that this difference is no more than stylistic.

Supplementarily, Young, Rezetko, and Ehrensvärd comment on the use and non-use of וְהָיָה in discourse, which Rezetko did not treat in his earlier essay. They muster various observations and argue that "this issue [i.e., the use and non-use of the introductory וְהָיָה], once again, is stylistic preference."[33]

2.2. *Linguistic Context*

Two of the parallel passages cited at the beginning of the present discussion (1 Kgs 8:54//2 Chr 7:1; 2 Kgs 22:3//2 Chr 34:8) suggest that the two constructions וַיְהִי + כְ/בְ + inf. const. (e.g., וַיְהִי כְּכַלּוֹת) and Ø + כְ/בְ + inf. const. (e.g., כְּכַלּוֹת) are grammatically equivalent, constituting a true variable. Nevertheless, there seems to be a confusion with regard to exactly *which construction and usage* of כְּכַלּוֹת is contrasted with וְהָיָה/וַיְהִי + כְּכַלּוֹת. For example, Eskhult argues that our discussion should examine constructions such as וּכְכַלּוֹת but not ones without וֹ.[34] On the other hand, as Young, Rezetko, and Ehrensvärd note, other scholars do not make this distinction and argue that the constructions both with and without וֹ are characteristic of LBH.[35] In order to address this problem, we should look more closely at the usage of the constructions with וְהָיָה/וַיְהִי and the context in which they are used.

First, the functional markers וַיְהִי and וְהָיָה always begin a clause, since וֹ is their first element (hence "the *introductory* וְהָיָה/וַיְהִי"). Second, וַיְהִי and וְהָיָה may be followed by various temporal expressions. According to GKC, וַיְהִי may accompany a prepositional noun phrase (e.g., וַיְהִי מִמָּחֳרָת "on the next day" [Gen 19:34]); כְ/בְ with an infinitive (e.g., וַיְהִי כְּכַלּוֹת שְׁלֹמֹה "when Solomon finished" [1 Kgs 8:54]); an independent sentence with the perfect (e.g., וַיְהִי־הוּא טֶרֶם כִּלָּה לְדַבֵּר "before he had finished speaking" [Gen 24:15]); a temporal clause with כִּי, כַּאֲשֶׁר, or מֵאָז (e.g., respectively, Gen 26:8; 12:11; and 39:5); and a noun clause (e.g., וַיְהִי הֵם מְרִיקִים שַׂקֵּיהֶם "as they were emptying their sacks" [Gen 42:35]).[36] Similarly, וְהָיָה may be followed by various structures such as a prepositional noun phrase, a noun

---

[32] Rendsburg, "Late Biblical Hebrew" (review of Polzin), 70.
[33] Young, Rezetko, and Ehrensvärd, *Linguistic Dating*, 1:76–78 (quotation from p. 78).
[34] Eskhult, "Verbal Syntax in LBH," 92 n. 46. Eskhult observes, "The difference is thus not in the use of b^e or k^e plus infinitive, but rather the proclitic *waw*."
[35] Young, Rezetko, and Ehrensvärd, *Linguistic Dating*, 1:77 n. 64.
[36] GKC §111g (p. 327).

clause, and a temporal clause (in this case, וְהָיָה is used with כַּאֲשֶׁר, or
אִם, since it expresses the future). Third, the functions of וַיְהִי and those of
וְהָיָה are different. וַיְהִי marks past time and is thus mostly used in narratives. Even when וַיְהִי is used in speech, the speech acquires the characteristic of a narrative (e.g., Gen 39:15, 18; Deut 5:23). On the other hand, וְהָיָה
marks a situation that has not occurred yet, and is thus usually used in
speech. Or, when it is used in narratives, it usually expresses an iterative
aspect (translated "whenever" as in Judg 2:19; 1 Sam 16:23; 2 Sam 15:5).[37]

The third point, that the functions of וַיְהִי and וְהָיָה are different, provides
a warrant for treating the two constructions together (i.e., the one with
וַיְהִי and the one with וְהָיָה; as all previous scholars have done). The uses of
וַיְהִי and וְהָיָה do not overlap, and therefore the two should be understood
as two manifestations of one semantic function, that is, the marking of
time (or aspect; וַיְהִי for the past and וְהָיָה for the future or the iterative
aspect). The speaker/writer cannot choose between the two freely; rather,
meaning dictates the choice of one form over the other. The second point,
that various temporal expressions can follow וְהָיָה/וַיְהִי, tells us that when
we treat only the contrast between וְהָיָה/וַיְהִי + כְ/בְ + inf. const. (e.g., וַיְהִי
כְּכַלּוֹת) and כְ/בְ + inf. const. (e.g., וּכְכַלּוֹת) we will not cover every possible
contrast between the expression with the introductory וְהָיָה/וַיְהִי and the
one without, since the phrase כְ/בְ + inf. const. is only one of several possibilities to which וְהָיָה/וַיְהִי may be attached. Nevertheless, in the following
discussion, we will focus only on כְ/בְ + infinitive, since this is the most
common and has been treated in previous studies more than any other
structure. The first point, that וְהָיָה/וַיְהִי are functional markers that begin a
clause, is important for our discussion. From it, we understand that not all
constructions of כְ/בְ + inf. const. without the introductory וְהָיָה/וַיְהִי can be

---

[37] Note, however, that וְהָיָה sometimes occurs in the narrative passages in which the
iterative meaning hardly makes sense. For example, GKC notes that וְהָיָה in 1 Sam 1:12; 10:9;
17:48; 25:20; 2 Sam 6:16; 2 Kgs 3:15; Jer 37:11; and Amos 7:2 is a mistake and should be read
as וַיְהִי. GKC §112uu (p. 339).

For a thorough review of the scholarship on the introductory וְהָיָה/וַיְהִי, see the recent
work by Viktor Ber, *The Hebrew Verb HYH as a Macrosyntactic Signal: The Case of wayhy and
the Infinitive with Prepositions Bet and Kaf in Narrative Texts* (Studies in Biblical Hebrew;
Frankfurt am Main: Peter Lang, 2008), 13–35. This study comprehensively examines the
constructions וְהָיָה/וַיְהִי + בְ/כְ + inf. const., clause-initial וְ + בְ/כְ + inf. const., clause-initial
בְ/כְ + inf. const., and clause-final בְ/כְ + inf. const. Ber discusses all of these constructions
in the Bible and attempts to synthesize his analyses. Although it is very exhaustive and
detailed, Ber's study does not seek to discuss possible chronological implications in the use
of these different constructions, which we will do here. Another important study on וַיְהִי is
C. H. J. van der Merwe, "The Elusive Biblical Hebrew Term וַיְהִי: A Perspective in terms of
Its Syntax, Semantics, and Pragmatics in 1 Samuel," *HS* 40 (1999): 83–114.

an alternative expression for וְהָיָה/וַיְהִי + כְ/בְ + inf. const. Examples of כְ/בְ + inf. const. must be clause-initial, as is וְהָיָה/וַיְהִי + כְ/בְ + inf. const. Accordingly, we should exclude from our analysis non–clause-initial כְ/בְ + inf. const. and the coordinating וּ + כְ/בְ + inf. const. We should also exclude clause-initial כְ/בְ + inf. const. (i.e., without וּ), since, as Eskhult observes, the expression without וּ (e.g., כְּכַלּוֹת) occurs frequently in Samuel–Kings.[38] The contrast does not lie between וְהָיָה/וַיְהִי + כְ/בְ + inf. const. and Ø + כְ/בְ + inf. const.: we cannot argue that the structure כְּכַלּוֹת is grammatically equivalent to the structure וְהָיָה/וַיְהִי + כְּכַלּוֹת, for example. Rather, וְהָיָה/וַיְהִי + כְ/בְ + inf. const. is contrasted with *the proclitic* וּ + כְ/בְ + *inf. const.*, and only these two structures seem to constitute a true variable. Consequently, our analysis will examine the following cases only: וְהָיָה/וַיְהִי + כְ/בְ + inf. const. and the proclitic וּ + כְ/בְ + inf. const.[39]

2.3. *Variation Analysis*

I combine the occurrences of the constructions with the preposition בְ and the ones with the preposition כְ, instead of treating them separately. Thus, what we examine is the variation between וְהָיָה/וַיְהִי + בְ or כְ + inf. const. and the proclitic וּ + בְ or כְ + inf. const. See the following table:

---

[38] Eskhult, "Verbal Syntax in LBH," 92 n. 46. Also, since וַיְהִי and וְהָיָה are *functional* markers, we should exclude the cases in which וַיְהִי or וְהָיָה is used as a full verb, meaning "to be."

[39] I have counted 88 occurrences of וּ + בְ + inf. const., of which I have identified 48 as the cases with the proclitic וּ (the remaining 40 are the cases with coordinating וּ): Exod 34:34; 40:36; Lev 12:6; 19:9; 23:22; Num 1:51 (first occurrence); 7:89; 9:19; 10:7; 11:9; Deut 9:23; 2 Sam 14:26; Isa 1:15; Ezek 1:19 (first occurrence); 3:20, 27; 10:16 (first occurrence); 16:34; 18:24, 27; 20:31; 23:39; 29:7; 33:33; 45:1; 46:8, 9; Ps 22:25; Esth 1:5; 2:12, 15, 19; 9:25; Dan 8:17, 18; 10:11, 15; 11:34; Ezra 9:5; 1 Chr 5:1; 2 Chr 12:7, 12; 16:8; 20:20; 22:7; 24:25; 26:19; 34:14. The following are the remaining cases with the conjunctive וּ: Gen 19:33, 35; 30:42; Exod 28:35; 30:8; 40:32; Num 1:51 (second occurrence); 9:22; 10:36; Deut 6:7 (3x; all occurrences); 11:19 (3x; all occurrences); 2 Kgs 11:8; Isa 32:7; Ezek 1:19 (second occurrence), 21 (2x; both occurrences); 10:16 (second occurrence), 17; 17:17; 33:14, 19; 37:13; 44:19; 46:10; Ps 46:3; Prov 11:10; 21:11; 24:17; 28:12, 28; 29:2; Job 17:2; Esth 2:8; Ezra 3:11; 2 Chr 5:13; 23:7.
    I have counted 33 occurrences of וּ + כְ + inf. const., of which I have identified 29 as the cases with the proclitic וּ: Deut 23:12; Josh 3:15; 8:29; 1 Sam 17:55, 57; Isa 10:14; Hos 6:9; Esth 5:9; Dan 8:8; 10:9, 19; 11:4; 12:7; Ezra 9:1, 3; 10:1 (first occurrence); Neh 8:5; 9:28; 1 Chr 21:15; 2 Chr 5:13; 7:1; 15:8; 20:23; 24:14, 22; 29:29; 31:1, 5; 33:12. The following are the remaining cases with the conjunctive וּ: Gen 24:30; Isa 18:3; Ezra 10:1 (second occurrence); 2 Chr 24:11.

Table 6. The use of וְהָיָה/וַיְהִי + כְ/בְ + inf. const. and the proclitic וְ + כְ/בְ + inf. const. according to books/texts (the synoptic passages in Chr and books/texts with disputed dates excluded)[40]

		כ' + והיה/ויהי	ובכלות	Use of ובכלות
	Non-P	22	1	4%
	Deut	9	2	18%
Preexilic	Isa¹	3	2	40%
	Hos	0	1	
Preexilic to	DtrH	95	5	5%
early exilic	Jer	9	0	0%
	Isa²	1	0	
Exilic	Ezek	4	14	78%
	Isa³	1	0	
	Esth	3	6	67%
Postexilic	Dan	2	10	83%
	Ezra–Neh	2	6	75%
	Chr (non-syn.)	4	20	83%

If we take into account only the data with ten or more occurrences, we obviously see an increase in the non-use of וְהָיָה/וַיְהִי. We should therefore understand that there was an authentic linguistic change during the biblical period from the use of the introductory וְהָיָה/וַיְהִי to the non-use of it. There is a big break between DtrH and Ezekiel: until DtrH the highest percentage is 18 (Deuteronomy; Isa¹ being excluded because of its low attestations of the variable), whereas from Ezekiel onward the lowest percentage is 78 (Ezekiel). It may seem a bit surprising to see a big leap between exilic Ezekiel and late preexilic/early exilic DtrH (and also Jeremiah, though it uses the structures less than ten times), since the authorship and redaction of DtrH (and Jeremiah) probably overlap in time with the same of Ezekiel. Nevertheless, this is not unexpected in the variationist understanding of a linguistic change. As we have noted, some speakers/writers may be early adopters of some innovations; some others may be conservatives. Both traditionalists and challengers have observed that Ezekiel tends to be an early adopter of many LBH features.[41]

---

[40] The numbers that are not included in the table (וְהָיָה/וַיְהִי + כְ vs. וּבְ): synoptic Chronicles—7 vs. 0; P—6 vs. 8; the passages in the Pentateuch that have not been identified as either Non-P (J/E) or P—1 vs. 1; Jonah—1 vs. 0; and Psalms—0 vs. 1.

[41] For example, Hurvitz, *Priestly Source and Ezekiel*; Rooker, *Biblical Hebrew in Transition*; and also Young, "Concluding Reflections," in Young (ed.), *Biblical Hebrew*, 314–17.

As an attempt to exploit all the data, I group them into time periods:[42]

Table 7. The use of וְהָיָה/וַיְהִי + בְּ/כְ + inf. const. and the proclitic וְ + בְּ/כְ + inf. const. according to time periods (the synoptic passages in Chr and books/texts with disputed dates excluded)

	כ'+והיה/ויהי	וכבלות	Use of וכבלות
Preexilic	34	6	15%
Preexilic to early exilic	104	5	5%
Exilic	5	14	74%
Postexilic	12	42	78%

Again, the increase is noticeable, and our initial observation is confirmed.

We now use our second independent variable in order to see if this change was a change from below or from above.

Table 8. The use of וְהָיָה/וַיְהִי + בְּ/כְ + inf. const. and the proclitic וְ + בְּ/כְ + inf. const. according to books/texts and text types (only the texts in which either form occurs in both text types included)

		Narration			Recorded speech		
		ו' כ'	וכ'	Use of וכ'	ו' כ'	וכ'	Use of וכ'
	Non-P	18	1	5%	4	0	
Preexilic	Deut	1	0		8	2	20%
	Isa¹	1	0		2	2	
Preexilic to	DtrH	87	5	5%	8	0	0%
early exilic	Jer	8	0	0%	1	0	
Exilic	Ezek	3	2	40%	1	12	92%
	Dan	2	7	78%	0	3	
Postexilic	Ezra–Neh	2	5	71%	0	1	
	Chr (non-syn.)	4	19	83%	0	1	
Disputed	P	4	3	43%	2	5	71%

If this table might be of any help, it is so only in that it provides all the raw numbers originally obtained from individual books/texts. Most of these

---

[42] One might raise a question about my decision to combine data from different books/texts. However, when we group data according to time periods, we do not mingle dissimilar elements. The data from each group share, and are defined by, the property of coming from the same time period.

statistics, however, are not helpful, since they are based on too few occurrences of the variants. So I combine the numbers for each period.

Table 9. The use of וְהָיָה/וַיְהִי + כְ/בְ + inf. const. and the proclitic וְ + כְ/בְ + inf. const. according to time periods and text types (the synoptic passages in Chr excluded; books/texts with disputed dates that do not show either form in both text types excluded)

	Narration			Recorded speech		
	ו' כ'	וכ'	Use of וכ'	ו' כ'	וכ'	Use of וכ'
Preexilic	20	1	5%	14	5	26%
Preexilic to early exilic	95	5	5%	9	0	0%
Exilic	3	2	40%	1	12	92%
Postexilic	8	31	79%	0	5	100%
Disputed (P)	4	3	43%	2	5	71%

The percentages should be used with caution, as several are based on less than ten occurrences of the two forms. Nevertheless, we identify a consistent correlation between the linguistic variable and the independent variable of text type: when books/texts are vigorously participating in the change (i.e., 15% or more overall use of the new form; all groups except for the late preexilic/early exilic groups and the narration group of the preexilic period), the text type of recorded speech always provides a more favorable context for the structure without the introductory וְהָיָה/וַיְהִי (i.e., וְ + כְ/בְ + inf. const.).[43] In other words, the shift from וְהָיָה/וַיְהִי + כְ/בְ + inf. const. to the proclitic וְ + כְ/בְ + inf. const. was represented first in the vernacular or in the text type that is closer to it; it permeated the written-based text type only in the later period. We may accordingly conclude that this shift as represented by the biblical data is another example of changes from below social awareness, which must have been part of a natural, language internal development in BH.

In summary, the biblical evidence, as we have analyzed, suggests the following understanding of the variation between וְהָיָה/וַיְהִי + כְ/בְ + inf. const. and the proclitic וְ + כְ/בְ + inf. const. First, despite Rezetko's discussion of וַיְהִי and Young, Rezetko, and Ehrensvärd's of וְהָיָה, since the variation shows a meaningful correlation with the independent variable

---

[43] The same is also true for the preexilic period, in which the change is vigorous in the recorded speech text type but not so in the narration text type.

of time period, we should accept the traditional chronological under-standing that the variation represents a facet of change during the bibli-cal period. Rezetko's "counter example"—in which the Chronicler uses וַיְהִי in the place where the Deuteronomist does not (2 Chr 22:8//2 Kgs 10:13; see above)—does not weaken this understanding, because, as we have emphasized repeatedly, it is not unexpected to see in an ongoing lin-guistic change a few isolated examples that go against the general trend. More significant is the fact that the non-synoptic portions of Chronicles conform to the general trend by choosing the newer structure much more frequently than the older structure (83%; see Table 6). Second, according to our sociolinguistic analysis, the change that this variation represents was a change from below social awareness, that is, a change that was nat-ural and unconscious. Therefore, the choice between the two structures may in general be considered to be a reliable indicator of the develop-ment of BH.[44]

3. אאא הַמֶּלֶךְ *vs.* הַמֶּלֶךְ אאא

3.1. *The Debate*

The traditional understanding. Biblical Hebrew uses two different word orders when it juxtaposes the title 'king' and the king's name: for example, 'King Solomon' may be expressed by הַמֶּלֶךְ שְׁלֹמֹה or שְׁלֹמֹה הַמֶּלֶךְ. Tradition-ally, scholars have argued that EBH predominantly favors the structure the title + king's name (e.g., הַמֶּלֶךְ שְׁלֹמֹה), whereas in LBH the usage is mixed (e.g., הַמֶּלֶךְ שְׁלֹמֹה *and* שְׁלֹמֹה הַמֶּלֶךְ).

Representative of the traditional opinion is Bergey's discussion of the language of Esther. He argues that the pattern of אֶסְתֵּר and וַשְׁתִּי הַמַּלְכָּה הַמַּלְכָּה in Esther "reflects an overall development in LBH."[45] Since outside Esther there is no further example of a queen's name apposed with the title, Bergey uses the more common example of male rulers.

---

[44] The understanding that the present change (from וְהָיָה/וַיְהִי + כְ/בְ + inf. const. to the proclitic וּ + כְ/בְ + inf. const.) was a change from below, I believe, is potentially significant. Virtually all scholars—including Hurvitz's challengers—believe or assume that verbal syn-tax would be one of the most reliable indicators of the change from EBH to LBH (see, for example, Eskhult, "Traces of Linguistic Development," 369–70, and our discussion in ch. 2). Our sociolinguistic analysis provides an *empirical* explanation of why it is so in the case of the introductory וְהָיָה/וַיְהִי. As an unconscious change, this particular syntax was not something one could choose or avoid consciously.

[45] Bergey, "Book of Esther," 60.

The dominant EBH pattern is title (הַמֶּלֶךְ) + name which is found ca. eighty times in comparison to the relative absence of the name + title order. . . .

In LBH, the appositional name + title (הַמֶּלֶךְ) syntax appears nearly forty times and the title + name pattern occurs in ca. fifty instances, excluding parallel passages. Clearly then, there is a marked trend, in comparison with EBH, toward the use of the name + title syntax.[46]

To meet Hurvitz's third criterion of extrabiblical attestations, Bergey supports his argument with the corpora in QH and MH. He notes that the syntax in these corpora is "identical to the emerging LBH syntax."[47]

The challengers' argument. Young, Rezetko, and Ehrensvärd disagree, however. Bergey's subject matter, the book of Esther, poses a problem, because when the book refers to King Ahasuerus, it uses exclusively the purported EBH pattern: הַמֶּלֶךְ אֲחַשְׁוֵרוֹשׁ. Young, Rezetko, and Ehrensvärd argue as follows:

> Non-synoptic Chronicles has an even mixture of ZYX הַמֶּלֶךְ ('[the] king X') and הַמֶּלֶךְ ZYX ('X the king'), whereas other books, including Samuel and Kings, prefer ZYX הַמֶּלֶךְ, and yet others, including Esther, absolutely prefer ZYX הַמֶּלֶךְ. Interpreting this variation as LBH vs. EBH misses the different treatments of this feature in core LBH Chronicles and Esther, the latter being more consistently 'EBH' than core EBH Samuel and Kings in this case.[48]

In his earlier study, Rezetko has made a similar point: "Noteworthy among many relevant observations are Song of Songs' use of the 'early' phrase twice and Esther's use of it 25 times, but neither book has the 'late' phrase."[49] The date of Song of Songs is disputed, and thus it cannot support Rezetko's position in this regard. On the other hand, Esther's exclusive use of הַמֶּלֶךְ אֲחַשְׁוֵרוֹשׁ, regardless of its predominant use of the structures אֶסְתֵּר הַמַּלְכָּה and וַשְׁתִּי הַמַּלְכָּה, remains to be a problem for those who would argue that the structure אאא הַמֶּלֶךְ is an LBH feature.

---

[46] Bergey, "Book of Esther," 58–59. Note that, in addition to the undisputed postexilic books, Bergey includes in his LBH corpus Jeremiah and the Aramaic portion of the Bible.

[47] Bergey, "Book of Esther," 60. See his citations on pp. 59–60. For a similar understanding of the choice between אאא הַמֶּלֶךְ and הַמֶּלֶךְ אאא, see Kropat, *Syntax der Chronik*, 48; Hurvitz, *Transition Period*, 45; and Sáenz-Badillos, *History*, 120.

[48] Young, Rezetko, and Ehrensvärd, *Linguistic Dating*, 2:103.

[49] Rezetko, "Dating Biblical Hebrew," 229.

3.2. *A True Variable?*

It is clear that the two structures הַמֶּלֶךְ אאא and הַמֶּלֶךְ אאא are a true variable. They are grammatically equivalent, which may be easily demonstrated by parallel passages:

1 Kgs 12:2	וְהוּא עוֹדֶנּוּ בְמִצְרַיִם אֲשֶׁר בָּרַח מִפְּנֵי הַמֶּלֶךְ שְׁלֹמֹה	For he was still in Egypt, where he had fled from King Solomon
2 Chr 10:2	וְהוּא בְמִצְרַיִם אֲשֶׁר בָּרַח מִפְּנֵי שְׁלֹמֹה הַמֶּלֶךְ	For he was in Egypt, where he had fled from King Solomon
1 Kgs 15:22	וְהַמֶּלֶךְ אָסָא הִשְׁמִיעַ אֶת־כָּל־יְהוּדָה	Then King Asa made a proclamation to all Judah
2 Chr 16:6	וְאָסָא הַמֶּלֶךְ לָקַח אֶת־כָּל־יְהוּדָה	Then King Asa brought all Judah

Also, since the two structures occur in parallel passages, the linguistic
contexts in which they are used are identical. Thus the choice between
the two variants does not seem to be conditioned by different linguistic
contexts.

3.3. *Variation Analysis*

Accordingly, we should consider non-linguistic factors that may have
influenced some postexilic writers to use הַמֶּלֶךְ אאא as well as הַמֶּלֶךְ אאא.
The following table (Table 10) presents all of the occurrences in the Bible
of the two patterns of apposition, הַמֶּלֶךְ אאא and הַמֶּלֶךְ אאא, except for the
cases of synoptic Chronicles and Song of Songs, for which I provide the
data in a footnote.

Four books/texts are statistically relevant: DtrH (5%), Jeremiah (11%),
Esther (0%), and non-synoptic Chronicles (51%). Of these four books/
texts, only the non-synoptic portions of Chronicles stand out; the other
three use the purported new structure sparingly. The data as presented in
Table 10 may be interpreted in two different ways.

First, one may argue that the use of the syntax הַמֶּלֶךְ אאא is idiolectal and thus may not be understood in chronological terms, since, of the
four books/texts that are statistically relevant, only Chronicles uses this
syntax vigorously. Second, following the variation model of change, one
may argue that there was an authentic change toward the syntax אאא
הַמֶּלֶךְ in the postexilic period and that Esther was actually a late adopter
of this change. The present data support either model, and there is a good
reason for the debate between the advocates of linguistic dating and the

Table 10. The use of אאא הַמֶּלֶךְ and הַמֶּלֶךְ אאא according to books/texts
(the synoptic passages in Chr and books/texts with disputed dates excluded)[50]

		המלך א׳	א׳ המלך	Use of א׳ המלך
Preexilic	Isa[1]	6	0	*0%*
Preexilic to	DtrH	98	5	5%
early exilic	Jer	17	2	11%
Exilic	Isa[2]	1	0	
	Ezek	1	0	
Postexilic	Zech 1–8	0	1	
	Hag	0	2	
	Esth	25	0	*0%*
	Dan	0	2	
	Ezra–Neh	3	4	57%
	Chr (non-syn.)	18	19	51%

challengers. We could observe that the remaining pieces of evidence—
the other postexilic texts (see the data from Haggai, Zechariah 1–8, Ezra–
Nehemiah, and Daniel in Table 10) and the data from QH and MH (see
Bergey's discussion above)—give a little more weight to the understanding that there was a change in the postexilic period and that Esther was
conservative. This understanding may be strengthened by the fact that
Esther predominantly uses the purported newer syntax when referring to
Queens Esther and Vashti (18 out of 20 times). Nevertheless, it is true that
the evidence is not decisive, and it is more prudent not to draw a conclusion at this stage.

Our foregoing discussion sounds like little more than a careful observation of the available data or a paraphrase of the current debate. No doubt,
with the same data that have always been there, one can add little to the
present discussion. A sociolinguistic categorization, however, may enable
us to do more than just observe. See the following table, in which I have
arranged the same data according to text types:

---

[50] The numbers that are not included in the table (the occurrences of הַמֶּלֶךְ אאא vs.
אאא הַמֶּלֶךְ): synoptic Chronicles—22 vs. 2; Song of Songs—2 vs. 0.

Table 11. The use of הַמֶּלֶךְ אאא and אאא הַמֶּלֶךְ according to books/texts and text types (only the texts in which either form occurs in both text types included)

		Narration			Recorded speech		
		א' המ'	המ' א'	Use of המ' א'	א' המ'	המ' א'	Use of המ' א'
Preexilic to early exilic	DtrH	86	4	4%	12	1	8%
Postexilic	Esth	21	0	0%	4	0	
	Ezra–Neh	2	4	67%	1	0	
	Chr (non-syn.)	16	18	53%	2	1	?

Statistically, this table is not very helpful. When the data are categorized into text types, we naturally see more gaps. Thus, for those two periods in which we see either variant in both text types (the late preexilic/early exilic period and the postexilic period), I count all the occurrences.[51]

Table 12. The use of הַמֶּלֶךְ אאא and אאא הַמֶּלֶךְ according to time periods and text types (only the texts from the late preexilic/early exilic and the postexilic periods included)

	Narration			Recorded speech		
	א' ה'	ה' א'	Use of ה' א'	א' ה'	ה' א'	Use of ה' א'
Preexilic to early exilic	103	6	6%	12	1	8%
Postexilic	39	26	40%	7	2	22%

We have proposed above two different interpretations of the use of the syntax הַמֶּלֶךְ אאא in Chronicles. It may represent an idiolect or a general linguistic change in the postexilic period. If we assume, for the moment, that postexilic Hebrew experienced an increase in the use of הַמֶּלֶךְ אאא, it does not seem to have been a change from below, or an unconscious change. The change—if there was a change—is represented vigorously in the texts from the postexilic period, and with due caution about the statistics for the text type of recorded speech, the purported innovation is represented better in the written-based text type (narration) than in the

---

[51] That is, I have included the data from Jeremiah, Zechariah 1–8, Haggai, and Daniel, which have not been included in Table 11.

oral-based one (recorded speech). Accordingly, the data, as they are correlated with text types, suggest that if there was a change, it was a change from above, which is "introduced by the dominant social class, often with full public awareness" and which normally represents "borrowings from other speech communities that have higher prestige."[52] This empirical decision—that the use of אאא הַמֶּלֶךְ in the postexilic period would represent a change from above if there had been a change—may concur with scholars' observation that the syntax אאא הַמֶּלֶךְ was dominant in Aramaic.[53] The possible change could have been a result of a borrowing from a foreign language through the highest members of the Jews who had access to it—a typical situation for a change from above (see ch. 4).

In summary, our sociolinguistic analysis of the choice between הַמֶּלֶךְ אאא and אאא הַמֶּלֶךְ suggests two possible scenarios. The less likely scenario is that the use of אאא הַמֶּלֶךְ was idiolectal, and the more likely one is that it reflected a change from above. If we accept the first scenario, we agree to the challengers' position that the choice between the two variant forms should not be understood in chronological terms. If we accept the second scenario, our understanding of the variation between הַמֶּלֶךְ אאא and אאא הַמֶּלֶךְ becomes subtler. On the one hand, we would agree with the traditionalists and consider that there was an authentic change from הַמֶּלֶךְ אאא to אאא הַמֶּלֶךְ. On the other hand, since this change was a conscious one, the choice between הַמֶּלֶךְ אאא and אאא הַמֶּלֶךְ may not be understood to be a reliable indicator of the chronology of BH. The new syntax was not something unavoidable during the period of change. The choice must have been made consciously, and the postexilic writers were probably able to go against the general trend, especially since, in a change from above, the older form recurs persistently. The book of Esther is a telling example: as we have seen, the book shows a neat split in referring to the male ruler and the female ones. The simplest explanation for this "artificial" split would be that the author was consciously choosing between the two structures, both being legitimate in his period.

---

[52] Labov, *Principles*, 1:78. See chapter 4 of the present study.
[53] Joüon and Muraoka, *Grammar*, 450–51 (§131k) n. 5; Hurvitz, *Transition Period*, 45.

4. ‏...בֵּין...וּבֵין‎ vs. ‏בֵּין...לְ...‎

4.1. *The Debate*

The traditional understanding. Hurvitz draws on Gideon Hannemann's comprehensive discussion of the preposition ‏בֵּין‎ in the Bible and the Mishnah, in which he argues that there was a gradual diachronic transition from ‏...בֵּין...וּבֵין‎ to ‏...בֵּין...לְ‎ through the biblical period, which originated from classical BH and which was being completed in late biblical literature.[54] Hannemann is cautious to note that the choice may have been constrained by dialect as well as chronology. Nevertheless, he affirms that "the distribution of this model [i.e., ‏...בֵּין...לְ‎] indicates that it is indeed this structure which expanded and penetrated into the realm of model A [i.e., ‏...בֵּין...וּבֵין‎]."[55] Following Hannemann, Hurvitz argues the following:

> It should be emphasized...that *bēyn...le...* is not a *total innovation* of the later period. This expression occurs already in classical biblical literature...What characterizes the later period is, rather, an *intensified application* of *bēyn...le...*—at the expense of the classical *bēyn...bēyn.*[56]

This understanding of ‏...בֵּין...וּבֵין‎ and ‏...בֵּין...לְ‎ further meets Hurvitz's third criterion. Scholars note that the older form ‏...בֵּין...וּבֵין‎ is absent from the DSS and Ben Sira and is rarely used in rabbinic literature.[57]

The challengers' argument. On the other hand, Young, Rezetko, and Ehrensvärd argue that "the data do not support the view that ‏...בֵּין...לְ‎ gradually increased in frequency in BH compared to ‏...בֵּין...וּבֵין‎."[58] Their argument rests on three observations. First, they observe that "it is largely

[54] Gideon Hannemann, "On the Preposition ‏בין‎ in the Mishnah and in the Bible," *Leshonenu* 40 (1975–1976): 44 [in Hebrew].

[55] Hannemann, "Preposition ‏בין‎," 45. Hurvitz's translation (Hurvitz, *Priestly Source and Ezekiel,* 114).

[56] Hurvitz, *Priestly Source and Ezekiel,* 114 n. 179. Emphasis original.

[57] For postbiblical attestations of the two structures, see the discussions and the citations in Hannemann, "Preposition ‏בין‎," 37; Hurvitz, *Priestly Source and Ezekiel,* 114; Qimron, *Hebrew of the DSS,* 83; Rooker, *Biblical Hebrew in Transition,* 117–18; and Wright, *Yahwistic Source,* 47.

In addition to ‏...בֵּין...וּבֵין‎ and ‏...בֵּין...לְ‎, there are two related expressions, each of which occurs only once in the Hebrew Bible: ‏...בֵּין...לְבֵין‎ in Isa 59:2 and ‏...בֵּין...וְל‎ in Joel 2:17. These expressions will not be included in the present discussion, since they may not be categorized with either of our two forms (i.e., ‏...בֵּין...וּבֵין‎ and ‏...בֵּין...לְ‎), and they occur only once and are not statistically relevant. See further p. 123 n. 62 below for Young, Rezetko, and Ehrensvärd's discussion of the latter expression.

[58] Young, Rezetko, and Ehrensvärd, *Linguistic Dating,* 1:123.

unnoticed that there are altogether more instances of ...לְ...בֵּין *in EBH*
than in (mostly) undisputed postexilic BH, 12 to 8, respectively."[59] Second, when they focus on Numbers, which is generally considered EBH,
they find four occurrences of ...בֵּין...וּבֵין (17:13; 21:13; 31:27; 35:24) and
three occurrences of ...בֵּין...לְ (26:56; 30:17 [2×]).[60] The use of ...בֵּין...לְ
in Numbers (3 out of 7) is quite heavy for an EBH text. Third, in Chronicles, they count five cases of ...בֵּין...וּבֵין in the passages parallel with
Kings (and no cases of ...בֵּין...לְ). More importantly for their argument, in
non-synoptic passages they find one case of the purportedly early form
(1 Chr 21:16) and only two cases of ...בֵּין...לְ (2 Chr 14:10; 19:10).[61] They
conclude, "both ...בֵּין...וּבֵין and ...בֵּין...לְ were stylistic choices available
to all BH writers, whether EBH or LBH."[62]

4.2. *A True Variable?*

The two expressions ...בֵּין...וּבֵין and ...בֵּין...לְ seem to be two realizations of one meaning and thus constitute a true variable. The passages
that Hurvitz presents are illustrative:[63]

---

[59] Young, Rezetko, and Ehrensvärd, *Linguistic Dating*, 1:123. Emphasis original. Note
here that Young, Rezetko, and Ehrensvärd include Jonah in the "(mostly) undisputed
postexilic BH" books.

[60] As is well known, much of Numbers is identified as the P source. We have grouped P
with texts with a disputed date, but Hurvitz and many of his followers consider P to belong
to the EBH corpus following Hurvitz's pressing demonstration of P's typological anteriority to exilic Ezekiel. Engaging in the debate, Young, Rezetko, and Ehrensvärd accept this
convention.

[61] Young, Rezetko, and Ehrensvärd, *Linguistic Dating*, 1:123. Note, however, that their
counting is different from mine. In synoptic passages I have found *six* cases of ...בֵּין...וּבֵין
(2 Chr 4:17; 13:2; 16:3 [2×]; 18:33; 23:16) and no cases of ...בֵּין...לְ, and in non-synoptic
passages, one case of ...בֵּין...וּבֵין (1 Chr 21:16) and *three* cases of ...בֵּין...לְ (2 Chr 14:10;
19:10 [2×]).

[62] Young, Rezetko, and Ehrensvärd, *Linguistic Dating*, 1:123. Young, Rezetko, and
Ehrensvärd discuss whether the expression ...בֵּין...וְלִ in Joel 2:17 may be used as evidence for a late dating of the book (we remember that Joel was classified as a book with
an unknown date). For them, it is difficult for two reasons. First, the expression is not the
same as the supposed late expression ...בֵּין...לְ. Second, even if it is granted that Joel's
unique expression is associated with ...בֵּין...לְ, we have seen that Young, Rezetko, and
Ehrensvärd argue that ...בֵּין...לְ may not be understood to have "gradually increased in
frequency in BH compared to ...בֵּין...וּבֵין" (Young, Rezetko, and Ehrensvärd, *Linguistic
Dating*, 1:123). We attempt to evaluate their second point below.

[63] As is expected, Hurvitz presents these parallel passages to show that P's expression is
the one that early biblical literature preferred, whereas the exilic prophet Ezekiel's expression is the one that later biblical writers preferred. Hence, for Hurvitz and his followers,
they furnish further support for the argument for P's preexilic provenance.

Lev 10:10	וּֽלֲהַבְדִּיל בֵּין הַקֹּדֶשׁ וּבֵין הַחֹל וּבֵין הַטָּמֵא וּבֵין הַטָּהוֹר	To distinguish between the holy and the common, and between the unclean and the clean
Ezek 22:26	בֵּין־קֹדֶשׁ לְחֹל לֹא הִבְדִּילוּ וּבֵין־הַטָּמֵא לְטָהוֹר לֹא הוֹדִיעוּ	They have made no distinction between the holy and the common, neither have they taught the difference between the unclean and the clean

4.3. *Linguistic Context*

There are similarities and differences in the linguistic contexts in which the two forms are used.

As for similarities, first, there seem to be no restrictions as to the semantics of the objects of the prepositions (i.e., בֵּין or -לְ). The objects may be either opposite (as in the above passages) or identical (e.g., בֵּין עֵדֶר וּבֵין עֵדֶר [Gen 32:17] and בֵּין מַיִם לָמָיִם [Gen 1:6]). Also, unlike the English preposition 'between', both expressions may govern more than two items (e.g., בֵּין־תּוֹרָה לְמִצְוָה לְחֻקִּים וּלְמִשְׁפָּטִים [Gen 9:15] and בֵּינִי וּבֵינֵיכֶם וּבֵין כָּל־נֶפֶשׁ חַיָּה [2 Chr 19:10]).

On the other hand, there are differences in their usage. As Wright observes, when one or both of the objects are pronouns, the expression בֵּין...לְ... is never used, but only בֵּין...וּבֵין... (e.g., בֵּינִי וּבֵין בְּנֵי יִשְׂרָאֵל [Exod 31:17] and בֵּינֵנוּ וּבֵינֵיכֶם [Josh 22:25]). Wright also notes that in the cases in which the objects are the same word, בֵּין...לְ... is preferred.[64] He excludes these two cases from his statistics, without providing a rationale. I will, however, include these cases in order to be as comprehensive as possible. It is important to remember that if this was indeed a linguistic change (as the traditionalists argue), one linguistic/non-linguistic context may have been more favorable to the innovation than another linguistic/non-linguistic context. The diffusion of a linguistic change occurs when an innovated form is used in more diverse contexts.[65]

---

[64] Wright, *Yahwistic Source*, 45 n. 25. I have found one example of בֵּין...וּבֵין... with the identical words (Gen 32:17) and nine examples of בֵּין...לְ... with the identical words (Gen 1:6; Deut 17:8 [3x]; 2 Chr 19:10; Ezek 18:8; 34:17, 22; 41:18).

[65] See also chapter 3, p. 53, Table 2, "Variation Model of Change," which illustrates the process of linguistic change through variation.

4.4. *Variation Analysis*

See the following table for the variable ...וּבֵין...בֵּין and ...לְ...בֵּין:

Table 13. The use of ...וּבֵין...בֵּין and ...לְ...בֵּין according to books/texts (the synoptic passages in Chr and books/texts with disputed dates excluded)[66]

		בֵּין...וּבֵין...	בֵּין...לְ...	Use of בֵּין...לְ...
Preexilic	Non-P	24	0	0%
	Deut	3	3	50%
	Isa[1]	1	0	
Preexilic to early exilic	DtrH	42	2	5%
	Jer	1	0	
Exilic	Ezek	9	9	50%
Postexilic	Zech 1–8	1	0	
	Zech 9–14	1	0	
	Mal	1	2	
	Dan	0	1	
	Ezra–Neh	0	1	
	Chr (non-syn.)	1	3	

With the fewest attestations of the eight variables that the present study analyzes (152 occurrences of both ...וּבֵין...בֵּין and ...לְ...בֵּין), the variable presents many gaps in its distribution across biblical books and texts. It seems best to avoid deriving any conclusions from the correlation with individual books/texts. In order to exploit the data as much as possible, I group them by time period.

Table 14. The use of ...וּבֵין...בֵּין and ...לְ...בֵּין according to time periods (the synoptic passages in Chr and books/texts with disputed dates excluded)

	בֵּין...וּבֵין...	בֵּין...לְ...	Use of בֵּין...לְ...
Preexilic	28	3	10%
Preexilic to early exilic	43	2	4%
Exilic	9	9	50%
Postexilic	4 ·	7	64%

---

[66] The numbers that are not included in the table (...וּבֵין...בֵּין vs. ...לְ...בֵּין): synoptic Chronicles—6 vs. 0; P—32 vs. 7; Jonah 0 vs. 1; and Ruth 1 vs. 0.

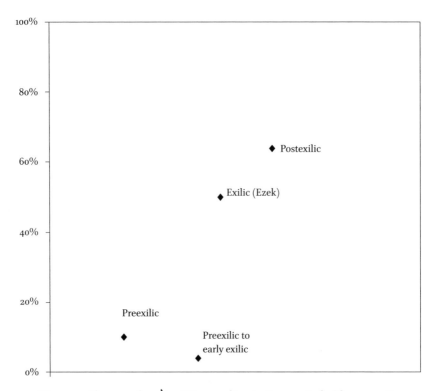

Figure 4. The use of ...בְּ...לְ...בֵּין according to time periods (the synoptic passages in Chronicles and books/texts with disputed dates excluded)

The implication is clear: as Hannemann and Hurvitz have argued, the use of the pattern ...בֵּין...לְ... increased during the biblical period. At the same time, however, Young, Rezetko, and Ehrensvärd's observation also remains true: the two expressions were "available to all BH writers, whether EBH or LBH."[67] That both groups of scholars are correct is not surprising, since Hurvitz and the challengers—and we too—look at the same data. With the variationist model of linguistic change and the method we have established in chapter 3, however, we can reevaluate Young, Rezetko, and Ehrensvärd's three observations above, which have been the basis for their claim that "both ...בֵּין...וּבֵין and ...בֵּין...לְ... were stylistic choices."[68]

First, Young, Rezetko, and Ehrensvärd have pointed that more instances of ...בֵּין...לְ... are found in the EBH texts than in the undisputed postexilic BH (12 to 8). Counting occurrences this way, however, is methodologi-

67 Young, Rezetko, and Ehrensvärd, *Linguistic Dating*, 1:123.
68 Young, Rezetko, and Ehrensvärd, *Linguistic Dating*, 1:123.

cally unsound. We should compare not the *raw numbers* of the writers' choices, but their *ratios* (i.e., the ratios that the writer chooses one form over the other). When we compare the ratios of the use of the newer form, a contrast is clear between the preexilic/early exilic period (4–10%) and the exilic/postexilic period (50–64%). Second, Young, Rezetko, and Ehrensvärd's argument on the basis of Numbers is problematic. They have argued that Numbers's use of the purportedly late form is quite heavy for an EBH text (4 occurrences of בֵּין...וּבֵין... and 3 of בֵּין...לְ...). However, as I have argued in chapter 3, each "book" of the Pentateuch is not a methodologically legitimate unit for collecting data. The data should be arranged with sources such as P and Non-P, each of which is relatively distinct and consistent. The ratio of the "book" of Numbers is irrelevant to our discussion. Third, the challengers pay attention to one case of the purportedly early form (בֵּין...וּבֵין...) in non-synoptic Chronicles (1 Chr 21:16). However, within the variationist framework of understanding language change, the Chronicler's use of the purportedly early form in a non-synoptic passage does not pose a problem. It is correct that the postexilic writers had both forms in their linguistic repertoire. The point, however, is that the Chronicler shows variability in his grammar (1 case of בֵּין...וּבֵין... and 3 cases of בֵּין...לְ...), which is expected and essential for a change in progress.[69] According to the variationist understanding of linguistic change, we should pay attention to the overall use (i.e., the ratios), but not to isolated examples.[70]

In summary, our analysis of the biblical data supports Hannemann's and Hurvitz's understanding but rejects the challengers' position. It is difficult to defend the challengers' claim that "the data do not support the view that בֵּין...לְ... gradually increased in frequency in BH compared to בֵּין...וּבֵין..."[71] The use of בֵּין...וּבֵין... and בֵּין...לְ... is meaningfully correlated with chronology, and the variation between the two during the exilic/postexilic period must be understood as a facet of a change in progress, whose completion we may witness in postbiblical literature (above, p. 122). It should not now surprise us that there was a big leap between DtrH's use of the variable and Ezekiel's (5% to 50%), since in a language change, we will always see early adopters and conservatives.

---

[69] Admittedly, the statistics are not very useful with four total uses of either variant. This, of course, is a problem for Young, Rezetko, and Ehrensvärd as well.

[70] This argument of course presupposes that the pluses in Chronicles in comparison with Samuel–Kings did not depend on any other sources. Both Young, Rezetko, and Ehrensvärd and I presuppose this for the sake of argument.

[71] Young, Rezetko, and Ehrensvärd, *Linguistic Dating*, 1:123.

Last, I correlate the present linguistic variable with the variable of text type.

Table 15. The use of בֵּין...וּבֵין... and בֵּין...לְ... according to time periods and text types (the synoptic passages in Chr excluded; Jonah and Ruth excluded)[72]

	Narration			Recorded speech		
	ב׳ וב׳	בין ל ב׳	Use of ל ב׳	ב׳ וב׳	בין ל ב׳	Use of ל ב׳
Preexilic	9	0	0%	19	3	14%
Preexilic to early exilic	27	0	0%	16	2	11%
Exilic	2	2		7	7	50%
Postexilic	3	1		1	6	86%
Disputed (P)	7	2	22%	25	5	17%

It is difficult to identify a correlation between the variable בֵּין...וּבֵין.../בֵּין...לְ... and text types. The change is vigorously attested in P, the exilic texts, and the postexilic texts. We cannot, however, compare the ratios across text types for the exilic and the postexilic texts, on account of the scantiness of the data in the text type of narration. Also, for the same text type, the evidence from P is tentative. Therefore, it seems best not to decide whether this change was one from below or from above.

5. בֵּית הָאֱלֹהִים *vs.* בֵּית יְהוָה

5.1. *The Debate*

The traditional understanding. It is generally understood that the personal name of the God of Israel (the Tetragrammaton) became less and less used in the Hebrew Bible. In relation to this, some scholars think that the two designations of the temple בֵּית יְהוָה and בֵּית הָאֱלֹהִים have chronological significance. So Polzin writes the following:

> This phrase [בֵּית הָאֱלֹהִים] appears 51 times in Chr, Ezr, Neh and Dan, and of this number 33 are in Chr, as S. R. Driver has pointed out. The only other occurrence of this phrase is Jd 18.31, the temple at Shiloh. The phrase is most probably LBH. It replaces the older *bêt YHWH* (e.g., Ex 23.19, 34.26) or simply *habbayit* (Ez 41.7ff, Mic 3.12, Hagg 1.8). Chronicles'

---

[72] Synoptic Chronicles has 4 occurrences of בֵּין...וּבֵין... in narration and 2 of בֵּין...וּבֵין... in recorded speech; Jonah has 1 occurrence of בֵּין...לְ... in speech; and Ruth has 1 occurrence of בֵּין...וּבֵין... in narration.

preference for this phrase concurs with the fact that Chronicles uses *'ĕlōhîm* twice as often as Kings does.[73]

In short, Polzin argues that בֵּית הָאֱלֹהִים is an LBH feature because it is used almost exclusively by postexilic books.

Unfortunately, with regard to Hurvitz's third criterion of extrabiblical sources, scholars have nothing to say because neither of the two expressions seems to be used in non-biblical Qumran texts, Ben Sira, or the Mishnah.[74]

The challengers' argument. Rezetko objects to this idea. Concerning בֵּית הָאֱלֹהִים, the purported innovation, he argues that the phrase was not totally unknown to preexilic biblical writers, since "similar *phraseology* occurs outside the Writings."[75] The following are his examples: בֵּית אֱלֹהִים (Gen 28:17, 22; Judg 17:5; cf. 2 Chr 34:9); בֵּית אֱלֹהֵי (Josh 9:23; cf. 1 Chr 29:2, 3 [2×]); בֵּית אֱלֹהֵינוּ (Joel 1:16); בֵּית אֱלֹהֵיכֶם (Joel 1:13; cf. 2 Chr 24:5); בֵּית אֱלֹהָיו (Hos 9:8; cf. 2 Chr 32:21); בֵּית אֱלֹהֵיהֶם (Judg 9:27; Amos 2:8; cf. 1 Chr 10:10); and בֵּית אֱלֹהֵי יַעֲקֹב (Isa 2:3; Mic 4:2).[76] On the other hand, as for the purportedly early בֵּית יְהוָה, Rezetko argues that it was a viable choice in the postexilic period; he supports his argument by the fact that בֵּית יְהוָה occurs most frequently in Chronicles (95 times)—more than in Kings (74 times).[77] Hence Rezetko concludes, "Evidence suggests that these were alternative expressions in the Second Temple period."[78]

---

[73] Polzin, *Late Biblical Hebrew*, 130. For a similar understanding of the uses of בֵּית יְהוָה and בֵּית הָאֱלֹהִים, see also Driver, *Introduction*, 535–36.

With regard to the otherwise unique appearance of בֵּית הָאֱלֹהִים in Judg 18:31, F. W. Dobbs-Allsopp suggests that it may have derived from the northern dialect (Dobbs-Allsopp, "Linguistic Evidence for the Date of Lamentations," *JANES* 26 [1998]: 22 n. 111).

[74] In the Mishnah, there is one occurrence of בית יהוה [*m. Bik.* 3:2], but it is a biblical citation. I have consulted the following concordances: Martin G. Abegg Jr. et al., *The Dead Sea Scrolls Concordance*, vol. 1, *The Non-Biblical Texts from Qumran* (Leiden: Brill, 2003); *The Book of Ben Sira: Text, Concordance and an Analysis of the Vocabulary* (Jerusalem: The Academy of the Hebrew Language and the Shrine of the Book, 1973); and Chayim Y. Kasovsky, *Thesaurus Mishnae: concordantiae verborum quae in sex Mishnae ordinibus repreiuntur* (4 vols.; Jerusalem: Massadah, 1956–1960).

[75] Rezetko, "'Late' Common Nouns," 386. Emphasis original.

[76] Rezetko, "'Late' Common Nouns," 386. Note that Rezetko here discusses *phraseology*, not the designations for the temple of the Israelite God. I have found that three of these examples refer to the temple of foreign gods (Judg 9:27; 1 Chr 10:10; 2 Chr 32:21).

[77] The numbers are from my counting, which is different from Rezetko's: he counts 77 occurrences of בֵּית יְהוָה in Kings. Rezetko, "'Late' Common Nouns," 387.

[78] Rezetko, "'Late' Common Nouns," 387. Likewise, Young argues that "'house of the Lord' [i.e., בֵּית יְהוָה] is well attested also in LBH sources, and thus should be seen as a 'common Hebrew' feature, not a specific marker of SBH." Young, "Hebrew Inscriptions," 287.

One must note a flaw in the first point of Rezetko's argument, that pre-exilic texts knew phrases similar to בֵּית הָאֱלֹהִים. Many of Rezetko's examples include the noun אֱלֹהִים + a pronominal suffix or a personal name (e.g., אֱלֹהֵי יַעֲקֹב, and אֱלֹהָי, אֱלֹהֵיכֶם, אֱלֹהֵינוּ, אֱלֹהָיו, אֱלֹהֵיהֶם). And BH does not allow a pronominal suffix (or a personal name) to be attached to a personal name (here, the Tetragrammaton). So, if a preexilic biblical writer wanted to add a pronominal suffix to the nomen rectum of בֵּית יְהוָה, there was no way but to replace יְהוָה with אֱלֹהִים.[79]

On the other hand, Rezetko's second observation, that בֵּית יְהוָה was a viable option in the postexilic period, remains true, and this situation deserves our further attention.

5.2. *A True Variable?*

It seems that the two designations בֵּית יְהוָה and בֵּית הָאֱלֹהִים constitute a true variable, although the genitives of both phrases (יְהוָה and הָאֱלֹהִים) are not grammatically equivalent (one being a personal name and the other a common noun). It is obvious that the two expressions most often refer to the same physical entity (i.e., Solomon's temple). In addition, there are occasions in which the Chronicler uses the expression בֵּית הָאֱלֹהִים when the parallel passages in Kings use the expression בֵּית יְהוָה. See the following parallel passages:

1 Kgs 8:11	כִּי־מָלֵא כְבוֹד־יְהוָה אֶת־ בֵּית יְהוָה	For the glory of YHWH filled the house of YHWH
2 Chr 5:14	כִּי־מָלֵא כְבוֹד־יְהוָה אֶת־ בֵּית הָאֱלֹהִים	For the glory of YHWH filled the house of God
2 Kgs 11:3	וַיְהִי אִתָּהּ בֵּית יְהוָה מִתְחַבֵּא שֵׁשׁ שָׁנִים	He remained with her six years, hidden in the house of YHWH
2 Chr 22:12	וַיְהִי אִתָּם בְּבֵית הָאֱלֹהִים מִתְחַבֵּא שֵׁשׁ שָׁנִים	He remained with them six years, hidden in the house of God[80]

Accordingly, we are justified to analyze the uses of these two designations with the variationist approach.

---

[79] I thank Joel S. Baden for bringing this issue to my attention.

[80] Additional examples include, for example, 1 Kgs 8:63//2 Chr 7:5 and 1 Kgs 15:15// 2 Chr 15:18. There are no cases in which the Chronicler replaced בֵּית הָאֱלֹהִים with בֵּית יְהוָה, since the former never occurs in Samuel–Kings.

5.3. *Variation Analysis*

See the following table in which I have arranged the uses of the two variant forms according to books/texts:

Table 16. The use of בֵּית יְהוָה and בֵּית הָאֱלֹהִים according to books/texts (the synoptic passages in Chr and books/texts with disputed dates excluded)[81]

		בית יהוה	בית האלהים	Use of ב׳ האלהים
Preexilic	Non-P	1	0	
	Deut	1	0	
	Isa[1]	5	0	0%
	Hos	2	0	
	Mic	1	0	
Preexilic to	DtrH	80	1	1%
early exilic	Jer	33	0	0%
Exilic	Ezek	6	0	0%
	Lam	1	0	
Postexilic	Isa[3]	1	0	
	Hag	2	0	
	Zech 1–8	2	0	
	Zech 9–14	3	0	
	Dan	0	1	
	Ezra–Neh	9	18	67%
	Chr (non-syn.)	66	34	34%

Only four books/texts are statistically relevant: DtrH, Jeremiah, Ezra–Nehemiah, and non-synoptic Chronicles. Nevertheless, a contrast is observed between the almost exclusive use of בֵּית יְהוָה till the early exilic period (1% and 0% in DtrH and Jeremiah) and the active variability in the postexilic period (34% and 67% in non-synoptic Chronicles and Ezra–Nehemiah). That variability is attested in two postexilic texts (Chronicles and Ezra–Nehemiah) raises the possibility that the mixed use of בֵּית יְהוָה and בֵּית הָאֱלֹהִים during this period is more than idiolectal. The fact that only two works present evidence should duly caution us, but with little to no data from other postexilic books such as Daniel and Esther (1 occurrence of the variable in Daniel and none in Esther), the simplest understanding

---

[81] The numbers that are not included in the table (בֵּית יְהוָה vs. בֵּית הָאֱלֹהִים): synoptic Chronicles—29 vs. 0; the passages in the Pentateuch that have not been identified as either Non-P (J/E) or P—1 vs. 0; Joel—3 vs. 0; Psalms—9 vs. 0; and Ecclesiastes 0 vs. 1.

is that there was an authentic change toward variability in the postexilic period. Admittedly, as we have mentioned, we do not have any data to tell us whether this change developed further or reached a completion later in the postbiblical period. The biblical data, nevertheless, are solid.

As an attempt to incorporate all the relevant data, I present below the combined numbers according to time periods:

Table 17. The use of בֵּית יְהוָה and בֵּית הָאֱלֹהִים according to time periods (the synoptic passages in Chr and books/texts with disputed dates excluded)

	בית יהוה	בית האלהים	Use of האלהים 'ב
Preexilic	10	0	*0%*
Preexilic to early exilic	113	1	*1%*
Exilic	7	0	*0%*
Postexilic	83	53	*39%*

Again, we see the same contrast. The choice of the variable changed suddenly after the exilic period.

In order to see if this change was from below or from above, I arrange the data according to text types. In this case, I have included only the data from Ezra–Nehemiah and non-synoptic Chronicles, since the other books/texts hardly show variability in their uses of the variants: outside Ezra–Nehemiah and Chronicles, there are only three occurrences of the newer form (one in each of DtrH, Daniel, and Ecclesiastes).

Table 18. The use of בֵּית יְהוָה and בֵּית הָאֱלֹהִים according to books/texts and text types (only the texts that actively participate in the change are included)

		Narration			*Recorded speech*		
		בית ה′	בית ′י	Use of בית ה′	בית ה′	בית ′י	Use of בית ה′
Postexilic	Ezra–Neh	4	14	*78%*	5	4	*44%*
	Chr (non-syn.)	54	32	*37%*	12	2	*14%*

With due caution regarding the recorded speeches of Ezra–Nehemiah (9 total occurrences), the statistics show meaningful differences in the uses of the linguistic variable between the narration text type and the recorded speech text type. The correlation of the linguistic variable with the independent variable of text type suggests that the change from the (almost) exclusive use of בֵּית יְהוָה to the variation between בֵּית יְהוָה and בֵּית הָאֱלֹהִים was one from above social awareness. Accordingly, although we cannot know how the change began at the very outset—as is often the case in historical linguistics—we have good reason to assume regarding its spread that the change was imposed and carried out consciously by those who were at the top of the society.[82]

To summarize our discussion: Polzin has argued that בֵּית הָאֱלֹהִים is an LBH feature because it is used almost exclusively by the postexilic books. Rezetko, on the other hand, has argued that בֵּית יְהוָה and בֵּית הָאֱלֹהִים "were alternative expressions in the Second Temple period."[83] First, our correlation of the linguistic variable with the independent variable of time period has suggested that Rezetko's position may be accepted as long as it remains an observation (i.e., of the availability of the two expressions in the Second Temple period). However, concerning the implications of the uses of the two expressions, we should agree with Polzin, since the biblical data, as interpreted by the sociolinguistic understanding of language change, clearly suggest a linguistic shift from the absence of variation toward the presence of variation. Second, our correlation with text types has suggested that this change was one from above social awareness. Thus it is unlikely that the new trend was unavoidable, since in a change from above, the old form typically persists. According to our theoretical model, therefore, the use of בֵּית יְהוָה and בֵּית הָאֱלֹהִים may not be considered to be a reliable indicator of the chronology of BH.

6. מַלְכוּת vs. מַמְלָכָה

6.1. The Debate

The traditional understanding. For the advocates of the chronological approach to BH, מַמְלָכָה and מַלְכוּת, both meaning "kingdom," are exemplary of Hurvitz's method of identifying a contrast between EBH and LBH. See the following parallel passages:[84]

---

[82] As a change from above, we may speculate that the new form בֵּית הָאֱלֹהִים was invented by the religious leaders or elitist scribes and that the change toward its use were fostered by the same personnel at least in the initial stages. This understanding might be supported by the abrupt shift in usage—from the near absence of בֵּית הָאֱלֹהִים in the early literature to its sudden appearance and vigorous use in the late literature.

[83] Rezetko, "'Late' Common Nouns," 387.

[84] The following passages are discussed in Hurvitz, *Transition Period*, 81; Bergey, "Book of Esther," 32; and Rooker, *Biblical Hebrew in Transition*, 56.

2 Sam 5:12	וְכִי נִשָּׂא מַמְלַכְתּוֹ בַּעֲבוּר עַמּוֹ יִשְׂרָאֵל	And that he had exalted his kingdom for the sake of his people Israel
1 Chr 14:2	כִּי־נִשֵּׂאת לְמַעְלָה מַלְכוּתוֹ בַּעֲבוּר עַמּוֹ יִשְׂרָאֵל	And that his kingdom was highly exalted for the sake of his people Israel
2 Sam 7:12	וַהֲכִינֹתִי אֶת־מַמְלַכְתּוֹ	And I will establish his kingdom
1 Chr 17:11	וַהֲכִינוֹתִי אֶת־מַלְכוּתוֹ	And I will establish his kingdom
2 Sam 7:16	וְנֶאְמַן בֵּיתְךָ וּמַמְלַכְתְּךָ עַד־עוֹלָם לְפָנֶיךָ	Your house and your kingdom shall be made sure forever before you
1 Chr 17:14	וְהַעֲמַדְתִּיהוּ בְּבֵיתִי וּבְמַלְכוּתִי עַד־הָעוֹלָם	But I will confirm him in my house and in my kingdom forever

Rooker comments on the above passages:

> The occurrence of these terms in Samuel and Chronicles illustrates not only that the two terms are synonymous but that מלכות appears to be the later linguistic equivalent for ממלכה. This is the principle of linguistic contrast or linguistic opposition [i.e., Hurvitz's second criterion; see ch. 2 above]. Next, we observed that מלכות which does not occur in EBH, occurs very frequently in LBH literature. This observation takes into account the diffusion of the lexeme—the principle of linguistic distribution [i.e., Hurvitz's first criterion]. That מלכות is the later LBH equivalent for ממלכה is reinforced by the [sic] what is found in post-biblical literature. There we saw an unequivocal preference for מלכות over the earlier ממכלה.[85]

Accordingly, for Rooker, the contrast between מַמְלָכָה and מַלְכוּת is "a classic illustration" for the use of Hurvitz's three criteria in identifying an LBH feature.[86]

---

[85] Rooker, *Biblical Hebrew in Transition*, 57. With regard to postbiblical usage, Polzin notes, "*malkût* appears at least 11 times at Qumrân, whereas *mamlākāh* appears only once there. *malkût* occurs at least 15 times in the Mishna, whereas *mamlākāh* seems to be lacking in mhe1 [= early MH before ca. 200 C.E., i.e., Tannaitic Hebrew]" (Polzin, *Late Biblical Hebrew*, 142). For the citations from the DSS and the Mishnah, see Bergey, "Book of Esther," 33.

[86] Rooker, *Biblical Hebrew in Transition*, 56. For a similar understanding of the use of מַמְלָכָה and מַלְכוּת, see also Kutscher, *History*, 43, 81, 84; Bergey, "Book of Esther," 31–34 (cf. pp. 157–59); Wright, *Yahwistic Source*, 135–37; and Sáenz-Badillos, *History*, 117.

The challengers' argument. Young, Rezetko, and Ehrensvärd, however, object to this traditional understanding. They observe the following:

- Some EBH books have מַמְלָכָה only, namely, Genesis, Exodus, Deuteronomy, Joshua and Isaiah 1–39, *but* so do Isaiah 40–55, 56–66, Ezekiel and Haggai.
- Other EBH books have both מַמְלָכָה and מַלְכוּת, namely Numbers, Samuel and Kings, *but* so do Jeremiah, Ezra, Nehemiah and Chronicles.
- Finally, only three books have מַלְכוּת to the exclusion of מַמְלָכָה: LBH Qoheleth, Esther and Daniel.[87]

The key point is that מַמְלָכָה was actively used in the postexilic period: some texts used it alongside מַלְכוּת, and some other texts used it to the exclusion of מַלְכוּת. On another occasion, Rezetko emphasizes "the nearly equal number of occurrences of מלכות and ממלכה in non-synoptic portions of Chronicles."[88]

Young, Rezetko, and Ehrensvärd also criticize scholars' use of the criterion of *extrabiblical sources*. They note that מלכות occurs in Old Aramaic (from the tenth to the seventh centuries B.C.E.) and thus cannot be used to corroborate the postexilic provenance of מַלְכוּת in BH. They maintain, "The appearances of מַלְכוּת in later Aramaic by themselves tell us nothing about the chronology of the word in BH."[89]

6.2. *A True Variable?*

מַלְכוּת/מַמְלָכָה is the first of the three lexical variables that we examine in the present study. It is often difficult to establish that two or more synonymous lexemes constitute a true variable. It is rarely the case that the glosses in dictionaries completely overlap. Nevertheless, on the basis of the dictionary definitions and the usages in context, we can reasonably argue that the three lexical variables that we treat in this chapter constitute true or almost true variables.

With regard to the case of מַלְכוּת/מַמְלָכָה, we first see that the linguistic contexts in which the two forms are used can be identical. This is demonstrated by the parallel passages cited at the beginning of this section. Second, the glosses in BDB generally overlap: מַמְלָכָה is glossed as "kingdom,

---

[87] Young, Rezetko, and Ehrensvärd, *Linguistic Dating*, 1:88. Emphasis original.
[88] Rezetko, "Dating Biblical Hebrew," 224. Cf., however, my counting below.
[89] Young, Rezetko, and Ehrensvärd, *Linguistic Dating*, 1:91.

sovereignty, dominion, reign," and מַלְכוּת as "royalty, royal power, reign, kingdom."

It should be noted, however, that מַלְכוּת has an additional nuance which מַמְלָכָה does not have. When it is said of God, מַלְכוּת means his royal dominion, and, as Wright notes, with this meaning it can refer to God as a circumlocution that replaces the Tetragrammaton.[90] See the following examples:[91]

Ps 103:19	יְהוָה בַּשָּׁמַיִם הֵכִין כִּסְאוֹ וּמַלְכוּתוֹ בַּכֹּל מָשָׁלָה	YHWH has established his throne in the heavens, and his kingdom rules over all
Ps 145:11	כְּבוֹד מַלְכוּתְךָ יֹאמֵרוּ וּגְבוּרָתְךָ יְדַבֵּרוּ	They shall speak of the glory of your kingdom, and tell of your power
Ps 145:12	לְהוֹדִיעַ לִבְנֵי הָאָדָם גְּבוּרֹתָיו וּכְבוֹד הֲדַר מַלְכוּתוֹ	To make known to all people his mighty deeds, and the glorious splendor of his kingdom

Wright observes that the word מַלְכוּת in each of the above passages replaces God's name. This usage is similar to P's and Ezekiel's well-known uses of כְּבוֹד יְהוָה (e.g., Lev 9:23; Ezek 1:28), which avoids referring directly to YHWH, but it is even more indirect by completely avoiding the name.[92]

מַמְלָכָה does not have such usage, although it can be used for God's dominion (as in 1 Chr 29:11). This difference in usage, however, does not necessarily lead us to the understanding that מַמְלָכָה and מַלְכוּת are not linguistically equivalent. The circumlocutory use of מַלְכוּת is a metaphorical extension of the primary meaning "kingdom" or "reign," which befits the theological milieu of the Second Temple period.[93] There is no a priori reason to argue that מַמְלָכָה, which has the same primary meaning as מַלְכוּת, was unable to extend its meaning so as to have a similar function. The difference in usage between מַמְלָכָה and מַלְכוּת is not so much linguistic or grammatical as theological. Therefore, we should consider the two forms to constitute a true or almost true variable, since a linguistic variation is defined by linguistic meaning but not by pragmatics.

---

[90] Wright, *Yahwistic Source*, 135–37; also, *HALOT*, s.v. "מַלְכוּת."

[91] The examples are from Wright, *Yahwistic Source*, 136.

[92] Wright, *Yahwistic Source*, 135–37. According to Wright, this is a later development to emphasize God's remoteness and transcendence.

[93] Indeed, BDB and *HALOT* do not offer a separate gloss for this usage of מַלְכוּת.

6.3. *Variation Analysis*

See the following table in which I have arranged the uses of מַמְלָכָה and מַלְכוּת according to books/texts:

Table 19. The use of מַמְלָכָה and מַלְכוּת according to books/texts (the synoptic passages in Chr and books/texts with disputed dates excluded)[94]

		ממלכה	מלכות	Use of מלכות
Preexilic	Non-P	3	1	
	Deut	7	0	0%
	Isa¹	9	0	0%
	Amos	3	0	
	Mic	1	0	
	Nah	1	0	
	Zeph	1	0	
Preexilic to early exilic	DtrH	31	2	6%
	Jer	17	3	15%
Exilic	Isa²	4	0	
	Ezek	4	0	
	Lam	1	0	
Postexilic	Isa³	1	0	
	Hag	2	0	
	Esth	0	26	100%
	Dan	0	16	100%
	Ezra–Neh	2	8	80%
	Chr (non-syn.)	18	28	61%

In the statistically relevant data, a contrast is noticeable: until the late preexilic/early exilic period, the use of מַלְכוּת does not exceed 15 percent; only after the exilic period is מַלְכוּת used significantly. Thus the evidence leads us to consider that there was an authentic change during the biblical period. The change seems to have gained momentum sometime between the exilic and the postexilic periods and to have been reaching a

---

[94] The numbers that are not included in the table (מַמְלָכָה vs. מַלְכוּת): synoptic Chronicles—4 vs. 0; the passages in the Pentateuch that have not been identified as either Non-P (J/E) or P—2 vs. 0; Psalms—6 vs. 6; and Ecclesiastes—0 vs. 1.

completion when Esther and Daniel were written.[95] The data also suggest that the replacement was quite rapid.

When we group the data into different periods, the result is similar.

Table 20. The use of מַמְלָכָה and מַלְכוּת according to time periods (the synoptic passages in Chr and books/texts with disputed dates excluded)

	ממלכה	מלכות	Use of מלכות
Preexilic	25	1	4%
Preexilic to early exilic	48	5	9%
Exilic	9	0	0%
Postexilic	23	78	77%

Now, in order to see whether this change was one from below or from above, I arrange the data according to text types.

Table 21. The use of מַמְלָכָה and מַלְכוּת according to books/texts and text types (only the texts that participate in the change are included)

		Narration			*Recorded speech*		
		ממלכה	מלכות	Use of מל׳	ממלכה	מלכות	Use of מל׳
Preexilic to	DtrH	9	1	10%	22	1	4%
early exilic	Jer	4	2	*33%*	13	1	7%
	Esth	0	15	100%	0	11	100%
Postexilic	Dan	0	6	*100%*	0	10	100%
	Ezra–Neh	0	7	*100%*	2	1	
	Chr (non-syn.)	12	19	61%	6	9	60%

The evidence is not conclusive, since several ratios are statistically irrelevant. To exploit the data as much as possible, I group them by time period.

---

[95] The postbiblical evidence too is definitive. Scholars note that מַמְלָכָה appears very few times in the DSS and is absent from MH. See p. 134 n. 85 above.

Table 22. The use of מַמְלָכָה and מַלְכוּת according to time periods and text types (only the periods that participate in the change are included)

	Narration			Recorded speech		
	ממלכה	מלכות	Use of מלכות	ממלכה	מלכות	Use of מלכות
Preexilic to early exilic	13	3	19%	35	2	5%
Postexilic	12	47	80%	11	31	74%

In the periods that participate in the change, the written-based text type (narration) always provides a more favorable context for the new form than the oral-based text type (recorded speech). We have to be cautious since the difference in percentage is not significant in the postexilic period (80% vs. 74%). Nevertheless, on the basis of all the available data, we should reasonably understand that the change from מַמְלָכָה to מַלְכוּת was one from above, a change that is consciously imposed and whose trajectory is generally uneven. This empirical decision—that this change was one from above—is coherent with, though not prove, the possibility that the newer form came from Aramaic, in which the nominal suffix -וּת was common.[96] Of course, we cannot exclude the possibility that the cause for this change was internal to BH, since the suffix -וּת was not absent from it. The borrowing from Aramaic, however, is a plausible scenario, since, as a change from above, it must have been initiated and diffused by the highest classes of the Jews during the exilic and postexilic periods, who had access to Aramaic.

To summarize: The debate over the variable מַלְכוּת/מַמְלָכָה is typical of many of those between Hurvitz and his followers and the challengers. Whereas the challengers emphasize the fact that מַמְלָכָה was not defunct but actively used in some postexilic texts, the traditionalists underscore the near-absence of מַלְכוּת from preexilic material and the sudden appearance of the same in postexilic literature. Within the sociolinguistic framework of understanding linguistic change, our analysis suggests the following: First, the shift from the almost exclusive use of מַמְלָכָה to a preference for מַלְכוּת must be understood as an authentic linguistic change. Second, at the same time, since this change was one from above social awareness, or

---

[96] See Joüon and Muraoka, *Grammar*, 243 (§88Mj) n. 2.

a conscious change, we should not consider the change to have been irreversible or the newer form to have been unavoidable during the postexilic period. Accordingly, the contrast between מַמְלָכָה and מַלְכוּת may not be understood to be a reliable indicator of the chronology of BH.

7. קָהָל vs. עֵדָה

7.1. *The Debate*

According to BDB, the primary meaning of עֵדָה is "congregation" or "company." It may designate a congregation of angels, peoples, the righteous, the evil, or animals, but most frequently, it refers to the Israelites or their descendants. Likewise, קָהָל is defined by BDB as "assembly" or "congregation." It may be used for evil counsel, civil affairs, war or invasion, angels, or a group of people. Again, it most frequently refers to the Israelites or their descendants.[97]

The traditional understanding. Traditionally, it has been understood that עֵדָה and קָהָל were used side by side during the preexilic period, while in the postexilic period קָהָל became predominant, ousting עֵדָה completely. Hurvitz writes the following:

> The total absence of *'ēdhāh* in the distinctively late biblical works—Ezra, Nehemiah and Chronicles—is, therefore, a clear indication of the term's gradual falling into disuse. The "assembly" of Israel still plays an important rôle in these three compositions; but they all use the alternate Pentateuchal term *qāhāl*, synonymous—or, at any rate, interchangeable—with *'ēdhāh.*[98]

Rooker also notes that in the non-synoptic passages of Chronicles, קָהָל occurs on 27 occasions (out of 33 occurrences of קָהָל in the whole book). This, Rooker argues, supports the conclusion that קָהָל belonged to the lexicon of the postexilic community, since it occurs much more frequently when the Chronicler was not following his source.[99] Likewise,

---

[97] BDB, s.v. "עֵדָה" and "קָהָל."

[98] Hurvitz, *Priestly Source and Ezekiel,* 66. Note, however, as Milgrom and Rooker observe, that Chronicles has one occurrence of עֵדָה in 2 Chr 5:6. Nevertheless, to Hurvitz's advantage, this passage is parallel to 1 Kgs 8:5, and it is likely that the Chronicler copied this term from his source. Milgrom, "Priestly Terminology and the Political and Social Structure of Pre-Monarchic Israel," *JQR* 69 (1978): 68 n. 20; Rooker, *Biblical Hebrew in Transition,* 143 n. 61.

[99] Rooker, *Biblical Hebrew in Transition,* 144 and n. 63. Note, however, that I have found 29 occurrences of קָהָל in the places where the Chronicler's reading differs from his biblical parallel (see Table 23 below).

in his detailed study of the priestly terms pertaining to premonarchic Israel's social and political structure, Milgrom argues that עֵדָה referred to one of Israel's premonarchic political bodies. He asserts on the basis of עֵדָה's absence from Deuteronomy that this term was no longer used after the ninth century.[100] Scholars also note the use of קָהָל in postbiblical sources.[101]

The challengers' argument. The challengers see the situation differently. Young, Rezetko, and Ehrensvärd note: "The standard diachronic view is difficult if not impossible to sustain. For instance, both words are often used synonymously in EBH (e.g. עֵדָה and קָהָל are used for Israel's assembly in Num. 16.3), and קָהָל, which is far from absent in EBH, is actually used to the exclusion of עֵדָה in Deuteronomy (11 to 0)."[102] Rezetko further challenges the traditional view by pointing out the abundance of the root קָהָל in the EBH corpus: about 40 percent of the root's manifestations are from Genesis–Kings.[103] He asserts that "Milgrom's explanation of Deuteronomy's קהל, Rooker's of Chronicles' עדה, and Hurvitz's of the preference in QH for עדה fall short."[104] In short, the challengers observe that both the noun קָהָל and its root were actively used in EBH and thus argue that the contrast between עֵדָה and קָהָל may not be used as an indicator of the chronology of BH.

7.2. *A True Variable?*

As we have seen above, the glosses in BDB of the two terms overlap considerably. We can say that the two nouns are semantically very similar. See each of the following passages in which the two words refer to the same entity:

---

[100] See further Milgrom, "Priestly Terminology," 66–76.

[101] For documentations, see Rooker, *Biblical Hebrew in Transition*, 144–45.

[102] Young, Rezetko, and Ehrensvärd, *Linguistic Dating*, 1:74. Note here that the same fact that Deuteronomy does not use עֵדָה is interpreted differently by Milgrom and the challengers (see above for Milgrom).

[103] Rezetko, "'Late' Common Nouns," 412.

[104] Rezetko, "'Late' Common Nouns," 413. Cf. Hurvitz's statement that עֵדָה "was later artificially revived by DSS and Ben-Sira, both of which are marked by their strong tendency to adopt antiquarian biblical expressions." Hurvitz, *Priestly Source and Ezekiel*, 66 n. 33.

וְאִם כָּל־עֲדַת יִשְׂרָאֵל יִשְׁגּוּ וְנֶעְלַם Lev 4:13
דָּבָר מֵעֵינֵי הַקָּהָל

If the whole congregation of Israel errs unintentionally and the matter escapes the notice of the assembly

וַיֹּאמְרוּ אֲלֵהֶם רַב־לָכֶם כִּי כָל־ Num 16:3
הָעֵדָה כֻּלָּם קְדֹשִׁים וּבְתוֹכָם יְהוָה
וּמַדּוּעַ תִּתְנַשְּׂאוּ עַל־קְהַל יְהוָה

And [they] said to them, "You have gone too far! All the congregation are holy, every one of them, and YHWH is among them. So why then do you exalt yourselves above the assembly of YHWH?"

Clearly, עֵדָה and קָהָל in each passage refer to the same body of people, that is, all Israel.

Some idiomatic phrases show that עֵדָה and קָהָל are completely interchangeable. So we meet expressions such as כָּל־עֲדַת יִשְׂרָאֵל (e.g., Exod 12:3; Lev 4:13; Josh 22:18) and כָּל־קְהַל יִשְׂרָאֵל (e.g., Lev 16:17; Deut 31:30; Josh 8:35). To this pair, one may add a very similar but more periphrastic expression כָּל־עֲדַת בְּנֵי־יִשְׂרָאֵל (e.g., Exod 16:1; Lev 19:2; Num 1:2; Josh 18:1). Likewise, there are כֹּל עֲדַת יְהוָה and קְהַל יְהוָה, which too may testify to their semantic similarity (for the former, Josh 22:16; for the latter, e.g., Num 16:3; 1 Chr 13:2; Ezek 23:46).

It seems that the two words can constitute a hendiadys:

כִּמְעַט הָיִיתִי בְכָל־רָע בְּתוֹךְ קָהָל Prov 5:14
וְעֵדָה

Now I am at the point of utter ruin in *the public assembly*

In summary, עֵדָה and קָהָל seem to be interchangeable in most cases, constituting an almost true variable.[105]

Admittedly, it may be impossible to prove that עֵדָה and קָהָל are a true linguistic variable. For example, Milgrom has attempted to argue that in the premonarchic period קָהָל functioned as a verbal noun (i.e., gerund) meaning "gathering" rather than being a synonym of עֵדָה.[106] Nevertheless, it seems justified to employ the variationist approach to עֵדָה and קָהָל, since קָהָל is equivalent to עֵדָה in both meaning and usage in the many cases that we have seen above.

---

[105] See also Abraham Malamat, "Organs of Statecraft in the Israelite Monarchy," *BA* 28 (1965): 37–38, who argues that קָהָל is virtually synonymous with עֵדָה. At the same time, Malamat does not exclude the possibility that קָהָל in 1 Kings 12, who conducted negotiations with Rehoboam, may refer to the group who acted as the representative of, and was therefore smaller than, עֵדָה.

[106] See further Milgrom, "Priestly Terminology," 68–69.

7.3. *Variation Analysis*

See the following table in which I have arranged the uses of עֵדָה and קָהָל according to books/texts:

Table 23. The use of עֵדָה and קָהָל according to books/texts
(the synoptic passages in Chr and books/texts with disputed dates excluded)[107]

		עדה	קהל	Use of קהל
Preexilic	Non-P	0	2	100%
	Deut	0	11	
	Hos	1	0	
	Mic	0	1	
Preexilic to early exilic	DtrH	22	11	33%
	Jer	2	4	67%
Exilic	Ezek	0	15	100%
	Lam	0	1	
Postexilic	Ezra–Neh	0	10	100%
	Chr (non-syn.)	0	29	100%

If compared with other studies that treat עֵדָה and קָהָל, our table would be markedly different because it does not include the data from the P source, which, as is well-known, supplies the absolute majority of the occurrences of עֵדָה in the Hebrew Bible (107 occurrences in P out of 149 in the whole Bible, according to our source division). Of course, it has been our methodological decision to exclude P from the correlation of the linguistic variable with the independent variable of time period (ch. 3 above).

Scholars who work in a chronological model have argued that עֵדָה belonged to EBH and קָהָל belonged to LBH. The data in the above table, however, present a somewhat different view. When statistics are relevant with ten or more occurrences of עֵדָה and קָהָל, עֵדָה is used only in late preexilic/early exilic DtrH. Preexilic Deuteronomy uses קָהָל exclusively as well as exilic Ezekiel and postexilic Ezra–Nehemiah and Chronicles. What we see is less a shift over time than a deviation of one individual book (i.e., DtrH).

When we group all the data into the four time periods (Table 24), the result is similar: קָהָל was predominant before the late preexilic period and

---

[107] The numbers that are not included in the table (עֵדָה vs. קָהָל): synoptic Chronicles—1 vs. 4; P—107 vs. 20; the passages in the Pentateuch that have not been identified as either Non-P (J/E) or P—3 vs. 1; Joel—0 vs. 1; Psalms—10 vs. 9; Proverbs 1 vs. 3; and the poetry section of Job—2 vs. 1.

Table 24. The use of עֵדָה and קָהָל according to time periods
(the synoptic passages in Chr and books/texts with disputed dates excluded)

	עדה	קהל	Use of קהל
Preexilic	1	14	93%
Preexilic to early exilic	24	15	38%
Exilic	0	16	100%
Postexilic	0	39	100%

was the only attested form from the exilic period onward; עֵדָה, with one exception in the preexilic period, occurs only in the texts from the late preexilic/early exilic period, of which DtrH comprises a major portion.

Consequently, the data examined with our method—which excludes P when correlating with the independent variable of time period—reject the chronological understanding of the choice between עֵדָה and קָהָל. The traditionalists are correct inasmuch as they *observe* that עֵדָה was not used in the late literature. However, we cannot accept their *claim* that עֵדָה was characteristic of EBH and later fell into disuse by giving way to קָהָל, because the evidence suggests that קָהָל had always been available and that the use of עֵדָה belonged to the Deuteronomist's idiolect.[108] Therefore, with regard to the choice between עֵדָה and קָהָל, we must concur with the challengers: the use of עֵדָה and קָהָל cannot serve as a marker for the linguistic shift from EBH to LBH.[109]

8. זעק *vs.* צעק

8.1. *The Debate*

The traditional understanding. Scholars have traditionally understood that the use of the roots צעק and זעק has chronological implications. This understanding rests on two observations.

---

[108] This understanding is based on our methodological decision to ignore the data from Jeremiah, which provide only 2 occurrences of עֵדָה and 4 occurrences of קָהָל. One might wonder if the use of עֵדָה was not a vogue of one particular period, since Jeremiah and DtrH belong to the same period according to our periodization. This idea, though interesting, cannot be corroborated because of the scantiness of the evidence.

[109] If this understanding of the use of עֵדָה and קָהָל is correct, we may also understand P's predominant use of עֵדָה (107 occurrences against 20 occurrences of קָהָל) to be an individual preference rather than a preservation of the older usage.

First, while the two roots occur in approximately the same numbers in the whole Bible, their distribution is uneven. Thus Kutscher writes as follows:

> Upon closer scrutiny one discovers that the two words are very unequally distributed between the early and late parts of the Bible. Whereas in the Pentateuch צעק is used almost exclusively, (the ratio there of צעק : זעק = 26:2), in Chron., Neh. and Esther... the ratio of צעק : זעק = 3:11! We thus see that זעק (apparently thanks to Aramaic influence) was commoner by far during the Second Temple period.[110]

Second, Kutscher and Rooker extensively discuss the attestations of the root זעק in postbiblical literature. For example, Kutscher pays attention to the fact that the scribe of 1QIsaᵃ replaced צעק of the MT with זעק twice (in Isa 33:7; 42:2) but that he preserved appearances of זעק in the MT nine times. According to Kutscher, this is an example of replacing an EBH word, which had become rare by the time, with an LBH word, which became more familiar in the period.[111]

Following his predecessors' argument, Hill, for example, considers the verb זעק in Zech 6:8 to be a possible LBH feature.[112]

The challengers' argument. However, Ehrensvärd's opinion is different. Opposing the view that זעק in Zech 6:8 is a possible LBH feature, he writes the following:

> The root זעק is used once in Zech. 6.8, and צעק is not found in the book. Both roots are found throughout EBH and LBH even though there is a preference for זעק in LBH writings. However, of the 91 BH occurrences of the root, only ten are found in Esther, Daniel, Ezra, Nehemiah, and Chronicles, and there are, for example, 15 occurrences in Samuel, 11 in Judges, and seven

---

[110] Kutscher, *Isaiah Scroll*, 34. Note, however, that I have counted 27 occurrences of the forms derived from צעק in the Pentateuch.

[111] Kutscher, *Isaiah Scroll*, 34, 233. For more extrabiblical uses of the root זעק, see Rooker, *Biblical Hebrew in Transition*, 134–38. Polzin also understands that the use of צעק and זעק has chronological significance. Citing Kutscher, he considers זעק to be "the more popular spelling in the later language." At the same time, he cautiously emphasizes that "both spellings appear early and late." Polzin, *Late Biblical Hebrew*, 137.

[112] Hill, "Malachi: Its Place," 93. In his dissertation, Hill lists 100 lexical items that possibly indicate LBH (pp. 84–108). זעק is among them. To be fair to Hill, however, it is important to note his precautionary comment on the list: "I admit, however, that factors other than chronological ones may account for the differences in lexical selection (*e.g.* individual writing style, literary genre, geographic location, subject matter and purpose of the writer)." Hill, "Malachi: Its Place," 84–85.

in Isaiah 1–39. Usage of the root can therefore not be said to point in the direction of LBH.[113]

In other words, since it occurs frequently in some preexilic texts (such as Samuel, Judges, and Isaiah 1–39) and since about 80 occurrences of it are found outside the undisputed LBH books, זעק in Zech 6:8 may not be interpreted as evidence for the claim that the book's language is LBH.[114]

At the center of the debate are scholars' different decisions as to what evidence is more relevant. On the one hand, Kutscher and other traditionalists emphasize the contrast between the rare use of זעק in the Pentateuch and the predominance of the same root in the undisputed late books. On the other hand, Ehrensvärd focuses on the active use of זעק in preexilic texts such as Judges, Samuel, and Isaiah 1–39.

8.2. *A True Variable?*

The two roots צעק and זעק "to cry, cry out, call" seem to be semantically equivalent. In BDB and *HALOT*, the glosses are the same, and the usages are almost parallel. The two lexicons say that one is a by-form of the other.[115] Both roots have the same noun formations (צְעָקָה and זְעָקָה), whose meanings are again the same.[116] See the following passage that demonstrates the interchangeability of the two roots in a single context:[117]

| Gen 18:20–21 | וַיֹּאמֶר יְהוָה זַעֲקַת סְדֹם
וַעֲמֹרָה כִּי־רָבָּה וְחַטָּאתָם כִּי כָבְדָה
מְאֹד: אֵרֲדָה־נָּא וְאֶרְאֶה
הַכְּצַעֲקָתָהּ הַבָּאָה אֵלַי עָשׂוּ כָּלָה
וְאִם־לֹא אֵדָעָה | Then YHWH said, "How great is the outcry against Sodom and Gomorrah and how very grave their sin! I must go down and see whether they have done altogether according to the outcry that has come to me; and if not, I will know." |

---

[113] Ehrensvärd, "Linguistic Dating," 179. Note, however, that I have counted 11 occurrences of זעק in Esther, Ezra, Nehemiah, and Chronicles (but none in Daniel), and 13 occurrences in Judges. This does not affect, of course, Ehrensvärd's overall argument.

[114] Likewise, Young, Rezetko, and Ehrensvärd observe that "זעק ('cry out') is preferred in Judges, Samuel, Jeremiah, Ezekiel, the Twelve and Chronicles, whereas צעק is preferred in the Pentateuch and Kings." They argue, "This is another good example of a linguistic variation that is real, but is hard to explain by conventional EBH vs. LBH models" (Young, Rezetko, and Ehrensvärd, *Linguistic Dating*, 2:104).

[115] BDB, s.v. "זָעַק" and "צָעַק"; *HALOT*, s.v. "זעק" and "צעק." When used as a verb, both forms can be *qal*, *nip'al*, and *hip'il*. The only difference is that צעק is attested as the *pi'el* participle, which occurs only once in 2 Kgs 2:12.

[116] BDB, s.v. "זְעָקָה" and "צְעָקָה"; *HALOT*, s.v. "זְעָקָה" and "צְעָקָה."

[117] I thank Joel S. Baden for bringing this example to my attention.

Accordingly, we can conclude that the roots צעק and זעק constitute a true variable.[118]

8.3. *Variation Analysis*

To see whether the use of זעק/צעק should be explained chronologically, I present below the uses of the variable in the texts with agreed-upon dates:[119]

Table 25. The use of צעק and זעק according to books/texts
(the synoptic passages in Chr and books/texts with disputed dates excluded)[120]

		צעק	זעק	Use of זעק
	Non-P	22	1	4%
	Deut	3	0	
	Isa¹	3	5	63%
Preexilic	Hos	0	2	
	Mic	0	1	
	Hab	0	2	
	Zeph	1	0	
Preexilic to	DtrH	20	30	60%
early exilic	Jer	7	14	67%
	Isa²	2	1	
Exilic	Ezek	0	5	*100%*
	Lam	1	1	

---

[118] It is interesting that we are able to say that this is an example of a *true* (not an *almost true*) variable, despite the fact that this variation is a lexical one. As I have mentioned above, it is generally difficult to prove that lexemes constitute a true variable.

One might think that the two forms are an example of a phonological variation (i.e., between the emphatic sibilant צ and the voiced sibilant ז). I agree with Rooker, however, who notes that if such a case is to be argued, it should be demonstrated that the same vacillation between the phonemes צ and ז is seen across many other words. Such is not the case in BH. Rooker, *Biblical Hebrew in Transition*, 134 n. 28.

[119] I choose to treat the noun forms and the verb forms together. Of course, it would be more desirable to treat the two parts of speech separately instead of mixing them, since theoretically, we might be able to describe the usage of the different forms more accurately. However, with only 21 occurrences of צְעָקָה and 18 of זְעָקָה, an analysis only of the noun forms would not be statistically trustworthy. The noun forms will surely be helpful, on the other hand, by supplementing the data mustered from the verb forms.

[120] The numbers that are not included in the table (צעק vs. זעק): non-synoptic Chronicles—0 vs. 1; P—0 vs. 1; the passages in the Pentateuch that have not been identified as either Non-P (J/E) or P—2 vs. 0; Joel—0 vs. 1; Jonah—0 vs. 2; Psalms—6 vs. 5; Proverbs—0 vs. 1; the poetry section of Job—5 vs. 3; and Ecclesiastes—0 vs. 1.

Table 25 (*cont.*)

		צעק	זעק	Use of זעק
	Isa[3]	1	3	
	Zech 1–8	0	1	
Postexilic	Esth	0	3	
	Ezra-Neh	2	4	67%
	Chr (non-syn.)	1	3	

Useful statistics are provided only by Non-P, DtrH, and Jeremiah. We might observe an increase from preexilic Non-P to late preexilic/early exilic DtrH and Jeremiah, but we should not be conclusive at the moment. In order to see if this initial impression is correct for all the available data, I combine the occurrences according to time periods.

Table 26. The use of צעק and זעק according to time periods
(the synoptic passages in Chr and books/texts with disputed dates excluded)

	צעק	זעק	Use of זעק
Preexilic	29	11	28%
Preexilic to early exilic	27	44	62%
Exilic	3	7	70%
Postexilic	4	14	78%

Looking at a more general picture according to time periods, we identify a clear pattern: there was a shift in the dominant form from צעק to זעק (from 28% use of זעק to 62% to 70% to 78%). There is a leap between the preexilic period and the late preexilic/early exilic period. The leap may represent a decisive period in the diffusion of the newer form זעק. This understanding, of course, differs from Hurvitz's opinion that the divide between EBH and LBH falls in the exilic period (ch. 2 above). It is also different from some other scholars who would place the divide between the dedication of the second temple and the ministry of Ezra and Nehemiah (e.g., Driver; see ch. 2 above). In the case of זעק/צעק, the divide apparently falls earlier: before the beginning of the exile.[121]

Now in order to see if this change was from below or from above, I arrange the uses of the variable according to text types. When we divide

---

[121] This point will be elaborated further in the concluding chapter.

the data into text types, we will naturally have more gaps than we had in Table 25. Hence I combine the numbers by time period.

Table 27. The use of צעק and זעק according to time periods and text types (the synoptic passages in Chr and books/texts with disputed dates excluded)

	Narration			Recorded speech		
	צעק	זעק	Use of ז'	צעק	זעק	Use of ז'
Preexilic	9	0	*0%*	20	11	35%
Preexilic to early exilic	17	22	56%	10	22	69%
Exilic	0	2		3	5	63%
Postexilic	2	8	80%	2	6	75%

A meaningful comparison may be made only for the late preexilic/early exilic period. Here, the recorded speech text type proves to be a more favorable context for the new form by statistically significant difference (13%). The other time periods do not offer us statistically reliable evidence, a situation that cautions us not to be conclusive. Nevertheless, I think the data from the late preexilic/early exilic period should be taken seriously, since this period is, as we have understood above, immediately after the decisive period in the diffusion of the new form (זעק). As we have seen in chapter 4, the most critical period for distinguishing the two types of changes is the initial stages of the particular change.[122] Accordingly, I would argue, with due caution, that the change from the root צעק to the root זעק was a change from below social awareness.[123]

---

[122] Cf. Raumolin-Brunberg's study of *ye* and *you* ("Diffusion of *You*"; ch. 3 above). Raumolin-Brunberg's argument that the change from *ye* to *you* was one from below is based on the statistics that are close to ours (58% of the new form *you* in the literate genre vs. 68% of the same in the oral-based genre). We may also comment on the statistics provided by the preexilic texts and the postexilic texts, although the uses of the variable are less than ten times in the narration of the preexilic texts and in the recorded speech of the postexilic texts. Labov's distinction between the two types of changes focuses more on the initial stages of a particular change. Thus, our understanding that this change was one from below might secondarily be supported by the statistics of the earliest period (i.e., the preexilic period; *0%* in narration and 35% in speech). The statistics of the postexilic period (80% in narration and 75% in speech) pose little challenge because the change was approaching completion in this period and also the difference in percentage is relatively small in comparison with those of the preexilic and the late preexilic/early exilic texts.

[123] Kutscher's conjecture that there was Aramaic influence (i.e., a borrowing from Aramaic) is not incompatible with our decision that this change was one from below (Kutscher, *Isaiah Scroll*, 34, or our quotation on p. 145 above). It is possible that a change that originally started with an internal factor may have been expedited further by an external factor.

To summarize: Our first correlation of the variable זעק/צעק with time periods suggests that the use of צעק and זעק in the Bible reflects a change in progress, in which the newer form זעק became decisively predominant sometime between the preexilic period and the late preexilic/early exilic period. Importantly, this understanding of ours embraces the challengers' *observation* while it does not accept their *claim*. That is, it is true, as the challengers state, that the root זעק was used frequently in some preexilic books: the evidence suggests that זעק became predominant *before* the exile. At the same time, our analysis cannot accept the challengers' stylistic understanding of EBH and LBH, because the variation is meaningfully correlated with the independent variable of time period.

Our second correlation of the linguistic variable with text types leads to the understanding that the change was one from below, that is, a natural linguistic shift in the development of BH. Accordingly, we should understand that the choice between צעק and זעק was made unconsciously by the biblical writers, and the use of the two forms was not stylistic but reflected the general tendency of the time. Therefore, the choice between the roots צעק and זעק may in general be considered to be a reliable indicator of the development of BH.

9. *Summary*

Our sociolinguistic analyses of the eight linguistic variables are summarized as follows:

(1) ‑וֹתֵיהֶם vs. ‑וֹתָם	An authentic change, from below
(2) וְהָיָה/וַיְהִי + כְּ/בְּ + inf. const. vs. the proclitic וֹ + כְּ/בְּ + inf. const.	An authentic change, from below
(3) אאא הַמֶּלֶךְ vs. הַמֶּלֶךְ אאא	An authentic change, from above; or the latter possibly belonging to the Chronicler's idiolect
(4) בֵּין...וּבֵין... vs. בֵּין...לְ...	An authentic change, but the direction undecided
(5) בֵּית הָאֱלֹהִים vs. בֵּית יְהוָה	An authentic change, from above
(6) מַלְכוּת vs. מַמְלָכָה	An authentic change, from above
(7) קָהָל vs. עֵדָה	Not a change, the former probably related to an individual preference
(8) זעק vs. צעק	An authentic change, from below

In the following concluding chapter, we will attempt to seek the implications of these analyses for the current debate over the linguistic dating of biblical texts.

CHAPTER SIX

A SOCIOLINGUISTIC EVALUATION OF THE LINGUISTIC DATING OF BIBLICAL TEXTS: SUMMARY AND CONCLUSIONS

This concluding chapter comprises three sections. The first section summarizes the central problems in the debate over the linguistic dating of biblical texts. The second section summarizes and synthesizes the arguments propounded in the previous chapters. This section provides what I believe is an answer to the problem of the linguistic dating of biblical texts. It also provides answers to other questions that are closely related to the issue of linguistic dating. The third and final section reflects on the significance of the present study.

1. *Summary of the Problem*

Regarding the issue of the linguistic dating of BH texts, Hurvitz and his followers would say the following:

> The question "Late Biblical Hebrew—Fact or Fiction?," used as the title of a recently published article, may, therefore, be answered quite decidedly and safely. By any and every standard accepted and implemented in our field, Late Biblical Hebrew is a viable linguistic variety, with a recognizable, distinctive profile, which replaced the older Standard Biblical Hebrew [i.e., EBH]. It is the emergence of the Late Biblical Hebrew components on the biblical scene which marks a new phase in the development of Biblical Hebrew—that of the post-classical era. The distinctive linguistic nature of these late elements makes them, further, valid chronological markers which may be utilized . . . for dating purposes in approaching biblical texts whose historical age is debated.[1]

In other words, Hurvitz and his followers argue the following: First, LBH is clearly distinct from EBH in form, thus constituting a well-established entity within BH. Second, LBH is distinct from EBH also in chronology: that is, LBH completely and successfully replaced EBH, and the two

---

[1] Hurvitz, "Recent Debate," 210. The article Hurvitz mentions is Sverrir Ólafsson, "Late Biblical Hebrew: Fact or Fiction?" in *Intertestamental Essays: In Honour of Józef Tadeusz Milik* (ed. Zdzislaw J. Kapera; Qumranica mogilanensia 6; Kraców: Enigma, 1992), 135–47.

did not coexist even for a short period of time. Third, accordingly, with
the distinctive profile of LBH, one can date a biblical text whose date
is problematic, depending on whether it shows an accumulation of
LBH features.

On the other hand, Young, Rezetko, and Ehrensvärd argue precisely the
opposite. First, although EBH and LBH are admittedly not identical, the
two are not so distinct in form from each other as has been traditionally
understood. The challengers highlight the fact that the distinction between
EBH and LBH most often depends on frequencies. That is, an LBH text is
not a text that uses LBH features to the exclusion of EBH features, but one
that uses more LBH features than EBH features. Likewise, an EBH text is
a text that shows more EBH features than LBH features. Second, Young,
Rezetko, and Ehrensvärd maintain that LBH and EBH are not distinct in
chronology. They argue, for example, that there are postexilic texts whose
language should properly be identified as EBH rather than LBH (e.g., Haggai, Zechariah, Malachi, and Isaiah 40–66). They also discern LBH features
in preexilic biblical texts and inscriptions. So, for the challengers, EBH and
LBH coexisted probably throughout the biblical period. Third, as LBH is
not distinct from EBH in form or in chronology, it is impossible to identify a biblical text as an LBH text (and, for that matter, to date the same
text to the postexilic period), no matter how much accumulation of LBH
features the text shows.

See, for example, what the challengers have to say regarding מַלְכוּת,
which may be considered a strong case of an LBH feature since it meets
all of Hurvitz's three criteria for identifying an LBH feature (linguistic distribution, linguistic contrast, and extrabiblical sources):

> For example, the form מַלְכוּת ('kingdom') is clearly a characteristic of LBH.
> It occurs 91 times in the Hebrew Bible, 78 of them in the core LBH books,
> and a further six times in LBH-related psalms and Qoheleth. Thus it has
> a very strong LBH distribution, and an impeccable linguistic contrast with
> other BH words for 'kingdom' such as מַמְלָכָה. Yet, still, the remaining seven
> of those 91 occurrences in the Hebrew Bible are found in EBH texts like
> Samuel and Kings.
>
> This phenomenon raises questions about the chronological approach
> that are not adequately explored by its proponents. Is מַלְכוּת actually a 'late'
> linguistic item after all? If so, its appearance in a text should indicate that
> therefore the text is to be dated late. And if EBH texts that use מַלְכוּת were
> dated late, this means late texts need not exhibit an 'accumulation' of LBH
> features. If against this is it argued that the LBH linguistic feature found in
> the EBH text is not actually 'late' but was also available in an early period,
> then its value for dating texts 'late' is negated. Despite the claims of the cri-
> terion of accumulation, ... *there is no reason to assume that an early author*

could not produce a text with a clustering of LBH elements if they were available to him.[2]

Accordingly, Young, Rezetko, and Ehrensvärd argue, "If EBH texts are early, and most LBH features are attested in EBH texts, then LBH features already existed in an early period, and were available to early authors." Their thesis and conclusion, which is repeated throughout their *Linguistic Dating*, is therefore that the use of EBH and LBH was "a matter of style, not chronology."[3]

At the very center of the debate is the characteristic of the data that are typically not categorical (i.e., ambiguous). This is also the reason that Hurvitz and his followers have to employ the fourth criterion of accumulation in order to define a text to be one of LBH, a situation that the challengers argue to be logically unjustifiable. Therefore, our central question has been this: when EBH and LBH—or the EBH features and the LBH features—are contrasted by frequency rather than by exclusive distribution, *should we understand that the two forms of BH are still discretely identifiable, or that they are in the realm of biblical writers' free styles?*

2. *Summary of the Arguments*

2.1. *The Method and the Presuppositions*

The present study has attempted to solve the above problem with a sociolinguistic understanding of variability in language. The rationale was that many of the contrasts between one EBH feature and the corresponding LBH feature are good examples of linguistic variables in sociolinguistic terms.

Our working principles in applying the variationist approach to the BH data were the following: First, as a prerequisite for evaluating the chronological significances of the purported EBH and LBH features, we have accepted the classical datings of biblical materials, although we have minimized the number of books/texts to which we have assigned a date. So, for example, we have accepted the internal datings of prophetic books such as Ezekiel, Haggai, and Zechariah 1–8. Also, despite a few challenging voices, we have not questioned the anteriority of Samuel–Kings to Chronicles. Second, drawing on the sociolinguistic understanding of the

---

[2] Young, Rezetko, and Ehrensvärd, *Linguistic Dating*, 2:84–85. Emphasis added.
[3] Young, Rezetko, and Ehrensvärd, *Linguistic Dating*, 1:86.

written mode of communication, we have accepted that different text types represent the typical form of vernacular to different degrees. So, of the two text types into which we have categorized all the biblical data, we have understood that the text type of narration is closer to the typical writing and that the text type of recorded speech is closer to the typical vernacular.

These two working principles, which served as the basis for establishing the independent variables in the subsequent correlations, could arguably be called a consensus, the former being one among the majority of biblical scholars and the latter among sociolinguists.

2.2. *Argument 1: EBH and LBH Are Not Stylistic*

We have argued in chapter 4 that the variationist understanding of linguistic change renders the challengers' observations irrelevant to their conclusions. That is, although the challengers are indeed correct in observing that the evidence regarding the proposed linguistic shift within BH is ambiguous, this ambiguity of the evidence, or the variability of the biblical data, cannot warrant the challengers' conclusion that EBH and LBH should not be understood in terms of linguistic diachrony and that EBH and LBH were free stylistic choices that coexisted throughout the biblical period. On the contrary, the variability in the biblical evidence—i.e., the mixed attestations of EBH and LBH features—attests to the possibility that there was an authentic linguistic change from EBH to LBH, since every linguistic change passes through the state of linguistic variation.

Indeed, our empirical analysis of the BH variables in chapter 5 has suggested that there was an authentic language change from earlier Hebrew in the preexilic period to later Hebrew in the postexilic period. Of the eight linguistic variables that the traditional view has understood to indicate the linguistic shift from EBH to LBH, seven have shown a meaningful correlation between the choices of the variants and the independent variable of time period—that is, the choices were constrained by chronology.[4] Only in one case ((7) עֵדָה vs. קָהָל) should the choice be explained by individual preferences rather than chronology.

When the challengers highlighted the fact that most of the contrasts between EBH and LBH are represented by frequency, it seemed that they transferred the burden of proof to Hurvitz and his followers.

---

[4] Note, however, that we have not excluded the possibility that the use of הַמֶּלֶךְ אאא vs. אאא הַמֶּלֶךְ involves the Chronicler's idiolect.

However, with the variationist understanding of linguistic change, it is now the challengers' obligation to prove that EBH and LBH were a matter of style, since style, like other linguistic choices, is contingent upon different situations. If one is to argue that EBH and LBH were a matter of style which had nothing to do with chronology, one must provide an explanation for what kind of non-chronological factors and situations were more favorable to one style than to the other and thus made the speaker/writer choose a particular style. Of course, it is always possible that we should come across non-chronological factors that can explain the choices of the biblical writers. For now, however, our empirical study has demonstrated that chronology *can* explain most of our samples (seven of eight).

2.3. *Argument 2: Linguistic Dating Is Not Viable*

Even though the sociolinguistic understanding of linguistic variation and change serves to support the chronological explanation for EBH and LBH, it does not automatically lead to the understanding that linguistic dating is therefore possible. Rather, our sociolinguistic study argues the opposite.

To begin with, it is always possible that a particular biblical text is an early adopter or a late adopter with regard to the general linguistic trend of the period. If that is the case, it makes no sense to compare the linguistic profile of a particular text with the linguistic profile of LBH or of EBH.

Moreover, even in the case that a text follows the general linguistic trend of a particular period,[5] the linguistic characteristics of LBH or of EBH as the traditionalists have presented are not as reliable as they believe. Rather, Labov's concept of two types of linguistic change (changes from below social awareness and changes from above social awareness) cautions that not all linguistic changes bear the same implications.

Thus, if a particular change in BH was a change from below, the biblical writer who had to make a choice in this ongoing change must have been unaware of the change or the innovation. His choice was unconsciously constrained by independent variables, among which time period played an important role. In the case of a change from below, then, the particular linguistic variable may serve as a reliable indicator of the chronology of BH. This seems to approach the way Hurvitz understands the shift from

---

[5] This is, of course, a more likely scenario, but it cannot be proved empirically.

EBH to LBH, which he believes was definitive and irreversible. Of course, there is an important difference between Hurvitz's understanding and ours. Whereas Hurvitz believes that the *overall* linguistic shift from EBH to LBH was irreversible, we believe that *some individual* linguistic changes were so.

On the other hand, if a particular linguistic change in BH was a change from above, that is, a change that is consciously imposed upon the users of the language, the biblical writer's choice becomes closer to, if not the same as, something that we can call "stylistic." It should be understood that the biblical writer of the later period was able to avoid the innovative form, since he (and the society also) was consciously aware of the change. At the same time, the old form was probably persistent, as is typical of a change from above. Accordingly, with the new form having to be chosen consciously and the old form recurring persistently, it should be understood that the progress was uneven, the choice was less predictable, and the trend was not irreversible. In this situation, therefore, the linguistic variable may not be considered to be a reliable indicator of the general trend of BH.

The seven authentic changes we have discussed have been categorized as follows: Three belong to changes from below: (1) תְוֹ- vs. וֹתֵיהֶם-; (2) וְהָיָה/וַיְהִי + כְּ/בְ + inf. const. vs. the proclitic וֹ + בְ/כְ + inf. const.; and (8) צעק vs. זעק. Three belong to changes from above: (5) בֵּית יהוה vs. בֵּית הָאֱלֹהִים; (6) מַמְלָכָה vs. מַלְכוּת; and (3) הַמֶּלֶךְ אאא vs. אאא הַמֶּלֶךְ (the last variable may possibly involve the Chronicler's idiolect). One case is difficult to decide as to its direction: (4) ...בֵּין...וּבֵין vs. ...בֵּין...לְ....

The result casts grave doubt on Hurvitz's overall project of the linguistic dating of biblical texts. As we remember, for those on the traditional side, the eight variables have presented strong cases for the argument for the linguistic dating of biblical texts, since all of these variables show a clear linguistic contrast and a wide linguistic distribution, and seven (except for בֵּית הָאֱלֹהִים vs. בֵּית יהוה) also provide extrabiblical attestations. However, in addition to the one variable that may not be understood as an authentic change ((7) קָהָל vs. עֵדָה), three out of the seven changes do not qualify as reliable criteria for the general chronology of BH, as they have been identified as changes from above social awareness, that is, conscious changes.

In short, Labov's distinction between two types of linguistic change suggests that linguistic changes from EBH to LBH occurred in different ways, and this situation renders some changes unreliable indicators even of the general linguistic trend of a particular period.

2.4. *Understanding EBH and LBH: Prescriptive or Descriptive?*

Therefore, as an attempt to adjudicate between Hurvitz and his followers and his challengers, the present study accepts some parts of both groups' positions and rejects other parts. On the one hand, I agree with Hurvitz and his followers that EBH and LBH should be understood in chronological terms, while rejecting the challengers' argument that all of the contrasts between EBH and LBH are explained as free stylistic choices. On the other hand, I do not accept Hurvitz's and his followers' claim that the linguistic dating of biblical texts is methodologically solid; instead, I concur with the challengers and would argue that it is hardly possible to date biblical texts solely on the basis of linguistic evidence.[6]

Therefore, I believe that the diachronic approach to BH (or EBH and LBH) should be descriptive rather than prescriptive. We may legitimately describe different chronological layers of BH inasmuch as we begin with the texts that have agreed-upon dates, but for the reasons discussed above, it is not practicable to use the resulting descriptions for the purpose of dating a chronologically problematic text.

2.5. *Further Implications*

Changes from above and scribal culture. That three of the seven authentic changes were changes from above is seemingly surprising, given that most linguistic changes discussed in historical and present-day sociolinguistics are changes from below. For example, in a massive compilation of his forty-year research, Labov presents very few cases of a change from above.[7] This apparent problem will disappear, however, when we remember that the Hebrew Bible was a religious and ideological product of the elites of Israelite and Judahite society. The Bible was written, expanded, and transmitted by the scribes, who were part of the top social classes. They must have had access to Aramaic, for example; they must have been sensitive to prestige. It can be reasonably assumed that the producers of the biblical writings established a set of norms or "standards" in their language and, by adhering to them, tried to maintain their prestige. Their language must have distinguished its users from those who did not use it

---

[6] This conclusion of ours, of course, is based on the discussion that has chosen not to consider text-critical issues. Considering them, no doubt, would work further against the validity of linguistic dating. Cf. the chapter on textual criticism in Young, Rezetko, and Ehrensvärd, *Linguistic Dating*, 1:341–60.

[7] For examples, see Labov, *Principles*, 1:321, 327, 453.

and who belonged to the lower classes of the society. This is, I believe, the reason that we see more cases of changes from above in BH than in more recent European languages that historical and present-day sociolinguists have often analyzed.[8]

Exile as the divide in BH? It seems necessary to revise the traditional understanding of the divide of BH, or the watershed moment in the history of BH. Hurvitz has consistently argued that it is the exilic period that decisively separates LBH from EBH in form and in chronology. His argument rests on linguistic and sociopolitical grounds: first, it is argued that BH entered a new phase owing to the contact with Aramaic; second, it is argued that the social upheaval during the exile influenced the language of the period.[9]

However, our empirical analysis suggests that we can no longer hold on to such an understanding of the exilic period. First, we cannot call the exilic period decisive because some changes were not irreversible, as we have identified three cases of changes from above, or consciously imposed changes. The second problem for considering the exile to be the divide of BH is that not all of the changes that we have examined have proved to anchor their critical moment in this period. Of course, of the seven authentic changes, we have seen six cases in which the use of a new form increased decisively during or after the exilic period.[10] In one case ((8) צעק vs. זעק), however, the decisive increase falls between the preexilic period and the late preexilic/early exilic period. In this particular case, it should be understood that the change had nothing to do with the disastrous

---

[8] This subject deserves a more extensive treatment. Important studies on scribal culture have multiplied recently. The most recent ones include William M. Schniedewind, *How the Bible Became a Book: The Textualization of Ancient Israel* (Cambridge: Cambridge University Press, 2004); David M. Carr, *Writing on the Tablet of the Heart: Origins of Scripture and Literature* (Oxford: Oxford University Press, 2005); Karel van der Toorn, *Scribal Culture and the Making of the Hebrew Bible* (Cambridge, Mass.: Harvard University Press, 2007); and Seth L. Sanders, *The Invention of Hebrew* (Urbana: University of Illinois Press, 2009).

[9] On the other hand, we have seen that some other scholars would place the decisive period later, that is, in the period between the dedication of the second temple and the ministry of Ezra and Nehemiah (see ch. 2 above and also Young, Rezetko, and Ehrensvärd, *Linguistic Dating*, 1:49–50). Nevertheless, even for this position, the role of the exile is deemed critical: LBH came to the fore *after* and *because of* the exile.

[10] A significant increase is discerned between the late preexilic/early exilic period and the exilic period in the cases of (2) וְהָיָה/וַיְהִי + כְ/בְ + inf. const. vs. the proclitic וְ + בְ/כְ + inf. const. and (4) ...וּבֵין...בֵין vs. ...לְ...בֵּין. A significant increase is discerned between the exilic period and the postexilic period in the cases of (1) וֹתָ- vs. וֹתֵיהֶם-; (3) הַמֶּלֶךְ אאא vs. אאא הַמֶּלֶךְ; (5) בֵית הָאֱלֹהִים vs. בֵית יְהוָה; and (6) מַלְכוּת vs. מַמְלָכָה.

events in the sixth century B.C.E. or a contact with Aramaic in the period, since the critical period predates the exile.

It is not difficult to understand why not all changes in BH decisively advanced during the exilic period. As we have seen, some changes were changes from below and should be understood to have been induced by internal causal factors. In other words, for these changes to occur, there was no need for external factors such as contact with another language (e.g., Aramaic) and a sociopolitical upheaval. Of course, the exilic period, with the aggregation of such external causal factors, must have provided a favorable context for the initiations of many changes from below. Nevertheless, internally induced changes, by definition, were able to occur anytime without these external causal factors.

In short, we cannot accept that the watershed moment of the history of BH was the exilic period. Surely, this period served as a matrix for many of the changes in BH, but not all of them. It may therefore be methodologically sounder to give up looking for a specific period that was decisive for the development of BH. We should rather examine each of the trajectories of different linguistic changes on its own.[11]

Where did Ezekiel's LBH come from? Against those who advocate the traditional division of BH into preexilic EBH and postexilic LBH, Young, Rezetko, and Ehrensvärd have raised a challenging question: where did Ezekiel's LBH come from?

> Hurvitz and Rooker have demonstrated the book of Ezekiel has a significant number of LBH features.... Ezekiel's LBH accumulation appears most significant in comparison to other prophetic books... Hurvitz and Rooker consider these LBH features as due to Ezekiel's representing transitional, exilic Hebrew. However, the book of Ezekiel itself gives a series of dates for the prophet's activity which mostly fall in the range 593–585 BCE, that is, from the last days of the preexilic period. Ezekiel is thus presented as mostly a preexilic prophet. Even if we conceive of Ezekiel as early exilic, the question arises where Ezekiel's LBH forms came from. Provided that the language of the MT book of Ezekiel actually does reflect the prophet's language to a fair degree, and provided that he actually does belong to the preexilic/exilic period, it seems reasonable to suggest that the LBH forms already existed in some strata of the language of preexilic Judah.[12]

---

[11] It is true that the present study does not exhaust all of the relevant data but examines only several samples. Nevertheless, it *can* still prove that there was no decisive point of any sort in the history of BH, inasmuch as it identifies counter examples.

[12] Young, Rezetko, and Ehrensvärd, *Linguistic Dating*, 2:90.

The traditional model of EBH before the exile and LBH after the exile cannot answer the challengers' question, since this model presupposes that a decisive change in BH occurred during (and not before) the exilic period, a situation which would enable us to distinguish one stage of BH from another unequivocally. However, if we accept that some changes were able to occur without any external causal factors, the crux disappears. These changes could have occurred any time in the development of BH, since the causal factors for them had lain latent in the language. It should not surprise us to see that some changes occurred even before the exile.

Biblical Hebrew in transition? A corollary of the preceding discussions is that we should agree with Young, Rezetko, and Ehrensvärd and also Naudé that we can no longer argue for the existence of "Biblical Hebrew in transition," or a linguistic body within BH that is considered to represent the intermediate stage between EBH and LBH (examples of which are Ezekiel as discussed by Rooker and P as discussed by Polzin; see ch. 2).[13] If we understand that there was no decisive moment in the history of BH, it is difficult to say that the Hebrew of the preexilic period was distinct from that of the postexilic period and vice versa or that there was a kind of Hebrew that was a mixture of both. The situation is much more complex and intricate, since, as we have seen, one of the changes we have examined predated the exile and a few others were not irreversible after the exile. What the evidence pictures is not two separate linguistic bodies and a mixture of both, but rather a continuum, which is multidimensional and which shows a great degree of variability.[14]

3. *Final Comments*

3.1. *Limitations of the Present Study*

As I have mentioned throughout, the present study does not exhaust all of the data that are relevant to the subject of the linguistic dating of biblical texts. For example, it does not treat the issue of loanwords from Persian

---

[13] The phrase "Biblical Hebrew in transition" is the title of Rooker's work on the language of Ezekiel, which we have consulted frequently throughout. For the position that we should give up the concept "Biblical Hebrew in transition," see Young, Rezetko, and Ehrensvärd, *Linguistic Dating*, 1:53–54; Rezetko, " 'Late' Common Nouns," 417 n. 186; Naudé, "Language of Ezekiel," 65–66; and idem, "Transitions of BH," 202, 205. For my brief treatment of Naudé, see chapter 2, p. 35 n. 103.

[14] Cf. Naudé, who emphasizes the continuity between EBH and LBH: idem, "Language of Ezekiel," 65–66; idem, "Transitions of BH," 202–3.

and Greek; it does not examine the semantic changes of particular words or expressions; it does not take into account text-critical issues such as possible alterations by later scribes (although we have decided to ignore this issue for a methodological reason); it does not fully discuss the issue of the use of extrabiblical sources; and it does not probe possible geographical or dialectal differences within BH.[15] Nevertheless, our subject matter—the variability of the evidence—is one of the most foundational, since the concept of linguistic variation as borrowed from sociolinguistics is closely related to Hurvitz's criteria of linguistic contrast (or opposition) and linguistic distribution. These two criteria are the aspects that are fundamental to Hurvitz's method and that the challengers attack most severely. Accordingly, although it does not exhaust all the relevant areas of the subject, the present study treats one of the most important aspects of the debate.

3.2. Significance of the Present Study

Finally, it is appropriate to address the advantages of a study such as this one. The present study is an empirical one, which allows other scholars to employ the same method in examining other data—either the BH variables that have not been treated here or the variables in other ancient Hebrew corpora. More importantly, the present study allows the method defined here to be fine-tuned or revised so that the results produced here may be further confirmed, adjusted, or rejected. For example, if one is dissatisfied with the periodizations of biblical books and texts which we have based on classical datings, one can redefine them and start one's own new analysis. Or, if one is not content with our divisions of texts or sources, one can revise them. Also, one can devise one's own categorization of text types or genres and see whether the results presented here need not be corrected.

Much more may be accomplished through the sociolinguistic study of ancient Hebrew. My hope, at the close of this pilot study, is that the present effort may serve as a stepping-stone for those who wish to continue the exploration.

---

[15] These critical issues have been exhaustively treated and fully documented by Young, Rezetko, and Ehrensvärd in their *Linguistic Dating*.

BIBLIOGRAPHY

Abegg, Martin G. Jr., James E. Bowley, Edward M. Cook, and Emanuel Tov. *The Dead Sea Scrolls Concordance*. Vol. 1, *The Non-Biblical Texts from Qumran*. Leiden: Brill, 2003.

Auld, A. Graeme. *Kings without Privilege: David and Moses in the Story of the Bible's Kings*. Edinburgh: T&T Clark, 1994.

——. *Samuel at the Threshold: Selected Works of Graeme Auld*. Society for Old Testament Study Monograph Series. Aldershot, England: Ashgate, 2004.

Bailey, Charles-James N. *Variation and Linguistic Theory*. Washington, D.C.: Center for Applied Linguistics, 1973.

Bar-On, Shimon. "The Festival Calendars in Exodus XXIII 14–19 and XXXIV 18–26." *Vetus Testamentum* 48 (1998): 161–95.

Bayley, Robert. "The Quantitative Paradigm." Pages 117–41 in *The Handbook of Language Variation and Change*. Edited by J. K. Chambers, Peter Trudgill, and Natalie Schilling-Estes. Malden, Mass.: Blackwell, 2002.

Bendavid, Abba. *Parallels in the Bible*. Jerusalem: Carta, 1972.

Ber, Viktor. *The Hebrew Verb HYH as a Macrosyntactic Signal: The Case of* wayhy *and the Infinitive with Prepositions* Bet *and* Kaf *in Narrative Texts*. Studies in Biblical Hebrew. Frankfurt am Main: Peter Lang, 2008.

Bergey, Ronald L. "The Book of Esther: Its Place in the Linguistic Milieu of Post-Exilic Biblical Hebrew Prose: A Study in Late Biblical Hebrew." Ph.D. diss., Dropsie College for Hebrew and Cognate Learning, 1983.

Bergs, Alexander. *Social Networks and Historical Sociolinguistics: Studies in Morphosyntactic Variation in the Paston Letters (1421–1503)*. Topics in English Linguistics 51. Berlin: M. de Gruyter, 2005.

Biber, Douglas. *Variation across Speech and Writing*. Cambridge: Cambridge University Press, 1988.

BibleWorks for Windows 7.0.018x.14. BibleWorks, 2007.

Biblia Hebraica Stuttgartensia. Stuttgart: Deutsche Bibelgesellschaft, 1967.

Blenkinsopp, Joseph. "An Assessment of the Alleged Pre-Exilic Date of the Priestly Material in the Pentateuch." *Zeitschrift für die alttestamentliche Wissenschaft* 108 (1996): 495–518.

——. *Ezra–Nehemiah: A Commentary*. Old Testament Library. Philadelphia: Westminster, 1988.

Block, Daniel I. *The Book of Ezekiel: Chapter 1–24*. New International Commentary on the Old Testament. Grand Rapids, Mich.: Eerdmans, 1997.

Blum, Erhard. *Die Komposition der Vätergeschichte*. Wissenschaftliche Monographien zum Alten und Neuen Testament 57. Neukirchen-Vluyn: Neukirchener Verlag, 1984.

——. "Das sog. 'Privilegrecht' in Exodus 34,11–26: Ein Fixpunkt der Komposition des Exodusbuches?" Pages 347–66 in *Studies in the Book of Exodus: Redaction, Reception, Interpretation*. Edited by Marc Vervenne. Bibliotheca ephemeridum theologicarum lovaniensium 126. Leuven: Leuven University Press, 1996.

——. *Studien zur Komposition des Pentateuch*. Beihefte zur Zeitschrift für die alttestamentliche Wissenschaft 189. Berlin: W. de Gruyter, 1990.

The Book of Ben Sira: Text, Concordance and an Analysis of the Vocabulary. Jerusalem: The Academy of the Hebrew Language and the Shrine of the Book, 1973.

Böttcher, Friedrich. *Ausführliches Lehrbuch der hebräischen Sprache*. Edited by Ferdinand Mühlau. 2 vols. Leipzig: J. A. Barth, 1866–1868.

Brown, Francis, S. R. Driver, and Charles A. Briggs. *The Brown-Driver-Briggs Hebrew and English Lexicon of the Old Testament*. Boston: Houghton, 1906. Repr., Peabody, Mass.: Hendrickson, 1997.

Campbell, Lyle. *Historical Linguistics: An Introduction*. 2nd ed. Edinburgh: Edinburgh University Press, 2004.

Campbell, Lyle, and Mauricio J. Mixco. *A Glossary of Historical Linguistics*. Edinburgh: Edinburgh University Press, 2007.

Carpenter, J. Estlin, and G. Harford-Battersby. *The Hexateuch according to the Revised Version*. 2 vols. London: Longmans, Green, & Co., 1900.

Carr, David M. *Writing on the Tablet of the Heart: Origins of Scripture and Literature*. Oxford: Oxford University Press, 2005.

Carroll, Robert P. *Jeremiah: A Commentary*. Old Testament Library. Philadelphia: Westminster, 1986.

Chafe, Wallace L. "Linguistic Differences Produced by Differences between Speaking and Writing." Pages 105–23 in *Literacy, Language, and Learning: The Nature and Consequences of Reading and Writing*. Edited by David R. Olson, Nancy Torrance, and Angela Hildyard. Cambridge: Cambridge University Press, 1985.

Chambers, J. K. *Sociolinguistic Theory: Linguistic Variation and Its Social Significance*. 2nd ed. Language in Society 22. Oxford: Blackwell, 2003.

Christensen, D. L. "Nahum, Book of." Pages 199–201 in vol. 2 of *Dictionary of Biblical Interpretation*. Edited by John H. Hayes. 2 vols. Nashville: Abingdon, 1999.

Clifford, Richard J. "Isaiah, Book of: Second Isaiah." Pages 490–501 in vol. 3 of *Anchor Bible Dictionary*. Edited by David Noel Freedman. 6 vols. New York: Doubleday, 1992.

Collins, John J. *Daniel: A Commentary on the Book of Daniel*. Hermeneia. Minneapolis, Minn.: Fortress, 1993.

———. *Introduction to the Hebrew Bible*. Minneapolis, Minn.: Fortress, 2004.

Conde-Silvestre, Juan Camilo. "Putting Sociolinguistics to the Test of Time" (review of Nevalainen and Raumolin-Brunberg, *Historical Sociolinguistics*). *International Journal of English Studies* 5 (2005): 211–22.

Coogan, Michael D. *The Old Testament: A Historical and Literary Introduction to the Hebrew Scriptures*. Oxford: Oxford University Press, 2006.

Corpus of Early English Correspondence. Compiled by Terttu Nevalainen, Helena Raumolin-Brunberg, Jukka Keränen, Minna Nevala, Arja Nurmi, and Minna Palander-Collin. Helsinki: Department of English, University of Helsinki, 1998.

Coulmas, Florian. "Sociolinguistics." Pages 563–81 in *The Handbook of Linguistics*. Edited by Mark Aronoff and Janie Rees-Miller. Malden, Mass.: Blackwell, 2001.

Cross, Frank Moore. "The Themes of the Book of Kings and the Structure of the Deuteronomistic History." Pages 274–89 in idem, *Canaanite Myth and Hebrew Epic: Essays in the History of the Religion of Israel*. Cambridge, Mass.: Harvard University Press, 1973.

Cryer, Frederick H. "The Problem of Dating Biblical Hebrew and the Hebrew of Daniel." Pages 185–98 in *In the Last Days: On Jewish and Christian Apocalyptic and Its Period*. Edited by Knud Jeppesen, Kirsten Nielsen, and Bent Rosendal. Aarhus: Aarhus University Press, 1994.

Davies, Philip R. "Biblical Hebrew and the History of Ancient Judah: Typology, Chronology and Common Sense." Pages 150–63 in *Biblical Hebrew: Studies in Chronology and Typology*. Edited by Ian Young. Journal for the Study of the Old Testament: Supplement Series 369. London: T&T Clark, 2003.

———. *In Search of 'Ancient Israel'*. 2nd ed. London: Sheffield Academic Press, 1995.

Dietrich, Walter. *Prophetie und Geschichte: Eine redaktionsgeschichtliche Untersuchung zum deuteronomistischen Geschichtswerk*. Forschungen zur Religion und Literatur des Alten und Neuen Testaments 108. Göttingen: Vandenhoeck & Ruprecht, 1972.

Dobbs-Allsopp, F. W. "Linguistic Evidence for the Date of Lamentations." *Journal of the Ancient Near Eastern Society* 26 (1998): 1–36.

Driver, S. R. *An Introduction to the Literature of the Old Testament*. New edition revised 1913. New York: Charles Scribner's Sons, 1914.

Ehrensvärd, Martin. "Linguistic Dating of Biblical Texts." Pages 164–88 in *Biblical Hebrew: Studies in Chronology and Typology*. Edited by Ian Young. Journal for the Study of the Old Testament: Supplement Series 369. London: T&T Clark, 2003.

———. "Once Again: The Problem of Dating Biblical Hebrew." *Scandinavian Journal of the Old Testament* 11 (1997): 29–40.

———. "Why Biblical Texts Cannot Be Dated Linguistically." *Hebrew Studies* 47 (2006): 177–89.

Eskhult, Mats. "The Importance of Loanwords for Dating Biblical Hebrew Texts." Pages 8–23 in *Biblical Hebrew: Studies in Chronology and Typology*. Edited by Ian Young. Journal for the Study of the Old Testament: Supplement Series 369. London: T&T Clark, 2003.

———. "Markers of Text Type in Biblical Hebrew from a Diachronic Perspective." Pages 153–64 in *Hamlet on a Hill: Semitic and Greek Studies Presented to Professor T. Muraoka on the Occasion of His Sixty-Fifth Birthday*. Edited by M. F. J. Baasten and W. Th. van Peursen. Orientalia lovaniensia analecta 118. Leuven: Peeters, 2003.

———. "Traces of Linguistic Development in Biblical Hebrew." *Hebrew Studies* 46 (2005): 353–70.

———. "Verbal Syntax in Late Biblical Hebrew." Pages 84–93 in *Diggers at the Well: Proceedings of a Third International Symposium on the Hebrew of the Dead Sea Scrolls and Ben Sira*. Edited by T. Muraoka and J. F. Elwolde. Studies on the Texts of the Desert of Judah 36. Leiden: Brill, 2000.

Fischer, Olga. "Syntax." Pages 207–408 in *The Cambridge History of the English Language*, vol. 2, *1066–1476*. Edited by Norman Blake. Cambridge: Cambridge University Press, 1992.

Galambush, J. G. "Ezekiel, Book of." Pages 372–75 in vol. 1 of *Dictionary of Biblical Interpretation*. Edited by John H. Hayes. 2 vols. Nashville: Abingdon, 1999.

Garbell, Irene. "Gesenius, Heinrich Friedrich Wilhelm." Page 562 in vol. 7 of *Encyclopaedia Judaica*. Edited by Michael Berenbaum and Fred Skolnik. 22 vols. 2nd ed. Detroit: Macmillan, 2007.

Gelderen, Elly van. *A History of the English Language*. Amsterdam: John Benjamins, 2006.

Gesenius, Wilhelm. *Geschichte der hebräischen Sprache und Schrift: Eine philologisch-historische Einleitung in die Sprachlehren und Wörterbücher der hebräischen Sprache*. Leipzig: F. C. W. Vogel, 1815. Repr., New York: G. Olms, 1973.

———. *Gesenius' Hebrew Grammar*. Edited and enlarged by E. Kautzsch. Translated and revised by A. E. Cowley. 2nd ed. Oxford: Clarendon, 1910.

Gianto, Agustinus. "Variations in Biblical Hebrew." *Biblica* 77 (1996): 493–508.

Goody, Jack. *The Interface between the Written and the Oral*. Cambridge: Cambridge University Press, 1987.

Görlach, Manfred. *Introduction to Early Modern English*. Cambridge: Cambridge University Press, 1991.

Greenberg, Moshe. "The Design and Themes of Ezekiel's Program of Restoration." *Interpretation* 38 (1984): 181–208.

———. *Ezekiel 1–20: A New Translation with Introduction and Commentary*. Anchor Bible 22. Garden City, N.Y.: Doubleday, 1983.

Groom, Susan Anne. *Linguistic Analysis of Biblical Hebrew*. Carlisle, Cumbria: Paternoster, 2003.

Guenther, Allen R. "A Diachronic Study of Biblical Hebrew Prose Syntax: An Analysis of the Verbal Clause in Jeremiah 37–45 and Esther 1–10." Ph.D. diss., University of Toronto, 1977.

Guy, Gregory R. "Variationist Approaches to Phonological Change." Pages 369–400 in *The Handbook of Historical Linguistics*. Edited by Brian D. Joseph and Richard D. Janda. Malden, Mass.: Blackwell, 2004.

Hannemann, Gideon. "On the Preposition בין in the Mishnah and in the Bible." *Leshonenu* 40 (1975–1976): 33–53 [Hebrew].

Helsinki Corpus of English Texts. Compiled by the Helsinki Corpus project team. Helsinki: Department of English, University of Helsinki, 1991.

Hill, Andrew E. "The Book of Malachi: Its Place in Post-Exilic Chronology Linguistically Reconsidered." Ph.D. diss., University of Michigan, 1981.

——. "Dating Second Zechariah: A Linguistic Reexamination." *Hebrew Annual Review* 6 (1982): 105–34.

——. "Dating the Book of Malachi: A Linguistic Reexamination." Pages 77–89 in *The Word of the Lord Shall Go Forth: Essays in Honor of David Noel Freedman in Celebration of His Sixtieth Birthday.* Edited by Carol L. Meyers and M. O'Connor. Winona Lake, Ind.: Eisenbrauns, 1983.

Hillers, Delbert R. "Micah, Book of." Pages 807–10 in vol. 4 of *Anchor Bible Dictionary.* Edited by David Noel Freedman. 6 vols. New York: Doubleday, 1992.

Ho, Craig Y. S. "Conjectures and Refutations: Is 1 Samuel XXXI 1–13 Really the Source of 1 Chronicles X 1–12?" *Vetus Testamentum* 45 (1995): 82–106.

Hurvitz, Avi. "Can Biblical Texts Be Dated Linguistically? Chronological Perspectives in the Historical Study of Biblical Hebrew." Pages 143–60 in *Congress Volume, Oslo 1998.* Edited by André Lemaire and Magne Saebø. Supplements to Vetus Testamentum 80. Leiden: Brill, 2000.

——. "Continuity and Innovation in Biblical Hebrew: The Case of 'Semantic Change' in Post-Exilic Writing." Pages 1–10 in *Studies in Ancient Hebrew Semantics.* Edited by T. Muraoka. Abr-Nahrain: Supplement Series 4. Leuven: Peeters, 1995.

——. "The Date of the Prose-Tale of Job Linguistically Reconsidered." *Harvard Theological Review* 67 (1974): 17–34.

——. "Hebrew and Aramaic in the Biblical Period: The Problem of 'Aramaisms' in Linguistic Research on the Hebrew Bible." Pages 24–37 in *Biblical Hebrew: Studies in Chronology and Typology.* Edited by Ian Young. Journal for the Study of the Old Testament: Supplement Series 369. London: T&T Clark, 2003.

——. "Historical Linguistics and the Hebrew Bible: The Formation and Emergence of Late Biblical Hebrew." Pages 15–28 in *Hebrew through the Ages: In Memory of Shoshanna Bahat.* Edited by Moshe Bar-Asher. Studies in Language 2. Jerusalem: The Academy of the Hebrew Language, 1997 [Hebrew].

——. "The Historical Quest for 'Ancient Israel' and the Linguistic Evidence of the Hebrew Bible: Some Methodological Observations." *Vetus Testamentum* 47 (1997): 301–15.

——. "The Language of Qoheleth and Its Historical Setting within Biblical Hebrew." Pages 23–34 in *The Language of Qohelet in Its Context: Essays in Honour of Prof. A. Schoors on the Occasion of His Seventieth Birthday.* Edited by Angelika Berlejung and Pierre Van Hecke. Orientalia lovaniensia analecta 164. Leuven: Peeters, 2007.

——. "The Language of the Priestly Source and Its Historical Setting: The Case for an Early Date." Pages 83–94 in *Proceedings of the Eighth World Congress of Jewish Studies, Jerusalem, August 16–21, 1981: Panel Sessions: Bible Studies and Hebrew Language.* Jerusalem: World Union of Jewish Studies, 1983.

——. "Linguistic Criteria for Dating Problematic Biblical Texts." *Hebrew Abstracts* 14 (1973): 74–79.

——. *A Linguistic Study of the Relationship between the Priestly Source and the Book of Ezekiel: A New Approach to an Old Problem.* Cahiers de la Revue biblique 20. Paris: J. Gabalda, 1982.

——. "Once Again: The Linguistic Profile of the Priestly Material in the Pentateuch and Its Historical Age: A Response to J. Blenkinsopp." *Zeitschrift für die alttestamentliche Wissenschaft* 112 (2000): 180–91.

——. "The Recent Debate on Late Biblical Hebrew: Solid Data, Experts' Opinions, and Inconclusive Arguments." *Hebrew Studies* 47 (2006): 191–210.

——. "The Relevance of Biblical Hebrew Linguistics for the Historical Study of Ancient Israel." Pages 21*–33* in *Proceedings of the Twelfth World Congress of Jewish Studies, Jerusalem, July 29–August 5, 1997: Division A: The Bible and Its World.* Edited by Ron Margolin. Jerusalem: World Union of Jewish Studies, 1999.

——. *The Transition Period in Biblical Hebrew: A Study in Post-Exilic Hebrew and Its Implications for the Dating of Psalms.* Jerusalem: Bialik, 1972 [Hebrew].

——. "The Usage of שש and בוץ in the Bible and Its Implications for the Date of P." *Harvard Theological Review* 60 (1967): 117–21.

Japhet, Sara. *I and II Chronicles: A Commentary.* Old Testament Library. Louisville, Ky.: Westminster/John Knox, 1993.

——. "The Supposed Common Authorship of Chronicles and Ezra–Nehemiah Investigated Anew." *Vetus Testamentum* 18 (1968): 330–71.

Joosten, Jan. "The Distinction between Classical and Late Biblical Hebrew as Reflected in Syntax." *Hebrew Studies* 46 (2005): 327–39.

Joüon, Paul, and T. Muraoka. *A Grammar of Biblical Hebrew.* Rev. ed. Subsidia biblica 27. Rome: Editrice Pontificio Istituto Biblico, 2006.

Kasovsky, Chayim Y. (Kasowski, Chaim Josua.) *Thesaurus Mishnae: concordantiae verborum quae in sex Mishnae ordinibus repreiuntur.* 4 vols. Jerusalem: Massadah, 1956–1960.

Knauf, Ernst Axel. "War 'Biblisch-Hebräisch' eine Sprache? Empirische Gesichtspunkte zur linguistischen Annäherung an die Sprache der althebräischen Literatur." *Zeitschrift für Althebräistik* 3 (1990): 11–23.

Knoppers, Gary N. *I Chronicles 1–9: A New Translation with Introduction and Commentary.* Anchor Bible 12. New York: Doubleday, 2004.

Koehler, Ludwig, Walter Baumgartner, and Johann Jakob Stamm. *The Hebrew and Aramaic Lexicon of the Old Testament.* Translated and edited under the supervision of M. E. J. Richardson. 5 vols. Leiden: Brill, 1994–2000.

Kofoed, Jens Bruun. "Using Linguistic Difference in Relative Text Dating: Insights from Other Historical Linguistic Case Studies." *Hebrew Studies* 47 (2006): 93–114.

Kohlenberger, John R., III, and James A. Swanson. *The Hebrew-English Concordance of the Old Testament with the New International Version.* Grand Rapids, Mich.: Zondervan, 1998.

Kropat, Arno. *Die Syntax des Autors der Chronik verglichen mit der seiner Quellen: Ein Beitrag zur historischen Syntax des Hebräischen.* Beihefte zur Zeitschrift für die alttestamentliche Wissenschaft 16. Giessen: Alfred Töpelmann, 1909.

Kutscher, E. Y. "Hebrew Language, the Dead Sea Scrolls." Pages 634–39 in vol. 8 of *Encyclopaedia Judaica.* Edited by Michael Berenbaum and Fred Skolnik. 22 vols. 2nd ed. Detroit: Macmillan, 2007.

——. *A History of the Hebrew Language.* Edited by Raphael Kutscher. Jerusalem: Magnes, 1982.

——. *The Language and Linguistic Background of the Isaiah Scroll (1QIsaᵃ).* Studies on the Texts of the Desert of Judah 6. Leiden: Brill, 1974.

Kytö, Merja. *Manual to the Diachronic Part of the Helsinki Corpus of English Texts: Coding Conventions and Lists of Source Texts.* 3rd ed. Helsinki: Department of English, University of Helsinki, 1996. Online: http://icame.uib.no/hc/.

——. "Third-Person Present Singular Verb Inflection in Early British and American English." *Language Variation and Change* 5 (1993): 113–39.

——. *Variation and Diachrony, with Early American English in Focus: Studies on Can/May and Will/Shall.* Bamberger Beiträge zur englischen Sprachwissenschaft 28. Frankfurt am Main: Peter Lang, 1991.

Labov, William. *Principles of Linguistic Change.* Vol. 1, *Internal Factors.* Language in Society 20. Oxford: Blackwell, 1994.

——. *Principles of Linguistic Change.* Vol. 2, *Social Factors.* Language in Society 29. Oxford: Blackwell, 2001.

——. "The Social Motivation of a Sound Change." *Word* 19 (1963): 273–309.

———. *The Social Stratification of English in New York City*. Urban Language Series. Washington, D.C.: Center for Applied Linguistics, 1966.

Lemaire, André. "Résponse à J. H. Hospers." *Zeitschrift für Althebräistik* 6 (1993): 124–27.

Levin, Christoph. *Der Jahwist*. Forschungen zur Religion und Literatur des Alten und Neuen Testaments 157. Göttingen: Vandenhoeck & Ruprecht, 1993.

———. Review of Wright, *Yahwistic Source*. *Review of Biblical Literature* 8 (2006). Online: http://bookreviews.org/pdf/4860_5055.pdf.

Levine, Baruch A. "Late Language in the Priestly Source: Some Literary and Historical Observations." Pages 69–82 in *Proceedings of the Eighth World Congress of Jewish Studies, Jerusalem, August 16–21, 1981: Panel Sessions: Bible Studies and Hebrew Language*. Jerusalem: World Union of Jewish Studies, 1983.

Levinson, Bernard M. "Goethe's Analysis of Exodus 34 and Its Influence on Wellhausen: The *Pfropfung* of the Documentary Hypothesis." *Zeitschrift für die alttestamentliche Wissenschaft* 114 (2002): 212–23.

MacDonald, J. "Some Distinctive Characteristics of Israelite Spoken Hebrew." *Bibliotheca orientalis* 32 (1975): 162–75.

Malamat, Abraham. "Organs of Statecraft in the Israelite Monarchy." *Biblical Archaeologist* 28 (1965): 33–65.

Mayes, A. D. H. "Deuteronomistic History." Pages 268–73 in vol. 1 of *Dictionary of Biblical Interpretation*. Edited by John H. Hayes. 2 vols. Nashville: Abingdon, 1999.

McBride, S. D. "Deuteronomy." Pages 273–94 in vol. 1 of *Dictionary of Biblical Interpretation*. Edited by John H. Hayes. 2 vols. Nashville: Abingdon, 1999.

McKane, W. "Jeremiah, Book of (Twentieth-Century Interpretation)." Pages 570–74 in vol. 1 of *Dictionary of Biblical Interpretation*. Edited by John H. Hayes. 2 vols. Nashville: Abingdon, 1999.

McKenzie, Steven L. "The Chronicler as Redactor." Pages 70–90 in *The Chronicler as Author: Studies in Text and Texture*. Edited by M. Patrick Graham and Steven L. McKenzie. Journal for the Study of the Old Testament: Supplement Series 263. Sheffield: Sheffield Academic Press, 1999.

———. "Deuteronomistic History." Pages 160–68 in vol. 2 of *Anchor Bible Dictionary*. Edited by David Noel Freedman. 6 vols. New York: Doubleday, 1992.

Merwe, C. H. J. van der. "The Elusive Biblical Hebrew Term ויהי: A Perspective in terms of Its Syntax, Semantics, and Pragmatics in 1 Samuel." *Hebrew Studies* 40 (1999): 83–114.

Milgrom, Jacob. "The Antiquity of the Priestly Source: A Reply to Joseph Blenkinsopp." *Zeitschrift für die alttestamentliche Wissenschaft* 111 (1999): 10–22.

———. *Leviticus 1–16: A New Translation with Introduction and Commentary*. Anchor Bible 3. New York: Doubleday, 1991.

———. "Priestly Terminology and the Political and Social Structure of Pre-Monarchic Israel." *Jewish Quarterly Review* (new series) 69 (1978): 65–81.

Millar, William R. "Isaiah, Book of: Isaiah 24–27 (Little Apocalypse)." Pages 488–90 in vol. 3 of *Anchor Bible Dictionary*. Edited by David Noel Freedman. 6 vols. New York: Doubleday, 1992.

Miller, Cynthia L. *The Representation of Speech in Biblical Hebrew Narrative: A Linguistic Analysis*. Harvard Semitic Monographs 55. Atlanta: Scholars, 1996.

Milroy, James. *Linguistic Variation and Change: On the Historical Sociolinguistics of English*. Language in Society 19. Oxford: Blackwell, 1992.

Moberly, Robert W. L. "The Earliest Commentary on the Akedah." *Vetus Testamentum* 38 (1988): 302–23.

Naudé, Jacobus A. "The Language of the Book of Ezekiel: Biblical Hebrew in Transition?" *Old Testament Essays* 13 (2000): 46–71.

———. "The Transitions of Biblical Hebrew in the Perspective of Language Change and Diffusion." Pages 189–214 in *Biblical Hebrew: Studies in Chronology and Typology*. Edited by Ian Young. Journal for the Study of the Old Testament: Supplement Series 369. London: T&T Clark, 2003.

Nevalainen, Terttu. "Gender Differences in the Evolution of Standard English: Evidence from the *Corpus of Early English Correspondence*." *Journal of English Linguistics* 28 (2000): 38–59.

——. "Social Mobility and the Decline of Multiple Negation in Early Modern English." Pages 263–91 in *Advances in English Historical Linguistics (1996)*. Edited by Jacek Fisiak and Marcin Krygier. Trends in Linguistics: Studies and Monographs 112. Berlin: M. de Gruyter, 1998.

Nevalainen, Terttu, and Helena Raumolin-Brunberg. *Historical Sociolinguistics: Language Change in Tudor and Stuart England*. Longman Linguistics Library. London: Longman, 2003.

New Revised Standard Version Bible. Division of Christian Education of the National Council of Churches of Christ in the United States of America, 1989.

Newsom, C. A., and S. E. Schreiner. "Job, Book of." Pages 587–99 in vol. 1 of *Dictionary of Biblical Interpretation*. Edited by John H. Hayes. 2 vols. Nashville: Abingdon, 1999.

Nicholson, Ernest. *The Pentateuch in the Twentieth Century: The Legacy of Julius Wellhausen*. Oxford: Oxford University Press, 1998.

Noth, Martin. *The Deuteronomistic History*. Translated by David J. A. Clines et al. Journal for the Study of the Old Testament Supplement Series 15. Sheffield: JSOT Press, 1981. Translation of pages 1–110 of *Überlieferungsgeschichtliche Studien: Die sammelnden und bearbeiten Geschichtswerke im Alten Testament*. 2nd ed. Tübingen: M. Niemeyer, 1957.

——. *A History of Pentateuchal Traditions*. Translated by Bernhard W. Anderson. Englewood Cliffs, N.J.: Prentice-Hall, 1972.

Ólafsson, Sverrir. "Late Biblical Hebrew: Fact or Fiction?" Pages 135–47 in *Intertestamental Essays: In Honour of Józef Tadeusz Milik*. Edited by Zdzislaw J. Kapera. Qumranica mogilanensia 6. Kraców: Enigma, 1992.

Petersen, David L. *Zechariah 9–14 and Malachi: A Commentary*. Old Testament Library. Louisville, Ky.: Westminster John Knox, 1995.

Peursen, W. Th. van. *The Verbal System in the Hebrew Text of Ben Sira*. Studies in Semitic Languages and Linguistics 41. Leiden: Brill, 2004.

Polak, Frank H. "The Oral and the Written: Syntax, Stylistics and the Development of Biblical Prose." *Journal of the Ancient Near Eastern Society* 26 (1998): 59–105.

——. "Parameters for Stylistic Analysis of Biblical Hebrew Prose Texts." Pages 259–81 in *Bible and Computer: The Stellenbosch AIBI-6 Conference: Proceedings of the Association Internationale Bible et Informatique, "From Alpha to Byte": University of Stellenbosch, 17–21 July, 2000*. Edited by Johann Cook. Leiden: Brill, 2002.

——. "Sociolinguistics: A Key to the Typology and the Social Background of Biblical Hebrew." *Hebrew Studies* 47 (2006): 115–62.

——. "Sociolinguistics and the Judean Speech Community in the Achaemenid Empire." Pages 589–628 in *Judah and the Judeans in the Persian Period*. Edited by Oded Lipschits and Manfred Oeming. Winona Lake, Ind.: Eisenbrauns, 2006.

——. "Style is More Than the Person: Sociolinguistics, Literary Culture and the Distinction between Written and Oral Narrative." Pages 38–103 in *Biblical Hebrew: Studies in Chronology and Typology*. Edited by Ian Young. Journal for the Study of the Old Testament: Supplement Series 369. London: T&T Clark, 2003.

——. "The Style of the Dialogue in Biblical Prose Narrative." *Journal of the Ancient Near Eastern Society* 28 (2001): 53–95.

Polzin, Robert. *Late Biblical Hebrew: Toward an Historical Typology of Biblical Hebrew Prose*. Harvard Semitic Monographs 12. Missoula, Mont.: Scholars, 1976.

Qimron, Elisha. *The Hebrew of the Dead Sea Scrolls*. Harvard Semitic Studies 29. Atlanta: Scholars, 1986.

Raumolin-Brunberg, Helena. "The Diffusion of Subject *You*: A Case Study in Historical Sociolinguistics." *Language Variation and Change* 17 (2005): 55–73.

——. "Historical Sociolinguistics." Pages 11–37 in *Sociolinguistics and Language History: Studies Based on the Corpus of Early English Correspondence*. Edited by Terttu Nevalainen and Helena Raumolin-Brunberg. Language and Computers: Studies in Practical Linguistics 15. Amsterdam: Rodopi, 1996.

———. "Prototype Categories and Variation Studies." Pages 287–303 in *English Historical Linguistics 1992: Papers from the 7th International Conference on English Historical Linguistics, Valencia, 22–26 September 1992*. Edited by Francisco Fernández, Miguel Fuster, and Juan José Calvo. Current Issues in Linguistic Theory 133. Amsterdam: John Benjamins, 1994.

Rendsburg, Gary A. "Aramaic-Like Features in the Pentateuch." *Hebrew Studies* 47 (2006): 163–76.

———. *Diglossia in Ancient Hebrew*. American Oriental Series 72. New Haven, Conn.: American Oriental Society, 1990.

———. "Hurvitz Redux: On the Continued Scholarly Inattention to a Simple Principle of Hebrew Philology." Pages 104–28 in *Biblical Hebrew: Studies in Chronology and Typology*. Edited by Ian Young. Journal for the Study of the Old Testament: Supplement Series 369. London: T&T Clark, 2003.

———. "Israelian Hebrew Features in Genesis 49." *Maarav* 8 (1992): 161–70.

———. *Israelian Hebrew in the Book of Kings*. Occasional Publications of the Department of Near Eastern Studies and the Program of Jewish Studies, Cornell University 5. Bethesda, Md.: CDL Press, 2002.

———. "Israelian Hebrew in the Song of Songs." Pages 315–23 in *Biblical Hebrew in Its Northwest Semitic Setting: Typological and Historical Perspectives*. Edited by Steven E. Fassberg and Avi Hurvitz. Publication of the Institute for Advanced Studies, the Hebrew University of Jerusalem 1. Jerusalem: Hebrew University Magnes Press, 2006.

———. "Late Biblical Hebrew and the Date of 'P'" (review of Polzin, *Late Biblical Hebrew*). *Journal of the Ancient Near Eastern Society of Columbia University* 12 (1980): 65–80.

———. *Linguistic Evidence for the Northern Origin of Selected Psalms*. Society of Biblical Literature Monograph Series 43. Atlanta: Scholars, 1990.

———. "Morphological Evidence for Regional Dialects in Ancient Hebrew." Pages 65–88 in *Linguistics and Biblical Hebrew*. Edited by Walter R. Bodine. Winona Lake, Ind.: Eisenbrauns, 1992.

———. "The Northern Origin of 'The Last Words of David' (2 Sam 23,1–7)." *Biblica* 69 (1988): 113–21.

———. "The Northern Origin of Nehemiah 9." *Biblica* 72 (1991): 348–66.

———. "Once More the Dual: With Replies to J. Blau and J. Blenkinsopp." *Ancient Near Eastern Studies* 38 (2001): 28–41.

Rendtorff, Rolf. *The Problem of the Process of Transmission in the Pentateuch*. Translated by John J. Scullion. Journal for the Study of the Old Testament: Supplement Series 89. Sheffield: JSOT Press, 1990.

Rezetko, Robert. "Dating Biblical Hebrew: Evidence from Samuel–Kings and Chronicles." Pages 215–50 in *Biblical Hebrew: Studies in Chronology and Typology*. Edited by Ian Young. Journal for the Study of the Old Testament: Supplement Series 369. London: T&T Clark, 2003.

———. "'Late' Common Nouns in the Book of Chronicles." Pages 379–417 in *Reflection and Refraction: Studies in Biblical Historiography in Honour of A. Graeme Auld*. Edited by Robert Rezetko, Timothy H. Lim, and W. Brian Aucker. Supplements to Vetus Testamentum 113. Leiden: Brill, 2007.

———. *Source and Revision in the Narratives of David's Transfer of the Ark: Text, Language, and Story in 2 Samuel 6 and 1 Chronicles 13, 15–16*. Library of Hebrew Bible/Old Testament Studies 470. London: T&T Clark, 2007.

———. "The Spelling of 'Damascus' and the Linguistic Dating of Biblical Texts." *Scandinavian Journal of the Old Testament* 24 (2010): 110–28.

Rissanen, Matti. "Syntax." Pages 187–331 in *The Cambridge History of the English Language*. Vol. 3, *1476–1776*. Edited by Roger Lass. Cambridge: Cambridge University Press, 1999.

Rissanen, Matti, Matti Kilpiö, Merja Kytö, Anneli Meurman-Solin, Saara Nevanlinna, Päivi Pahta, and Irma Taavitsainen. "Introduction." Pages 1–15 in *English in Transition: Corpus-Based Studies in Linguistic Variation and Genre Styles.* Edited by Matti Rissanen, Merja Kytö, and Kirsi Heikkonen. Topics in English Linguistics 23. Berlin: M. de Gruyter, 1997.

Roberts, J. J. M. *Nahum, Habakkuk, and Zephaniah: A Commentary.* Old Testament Library. Louisville, Ky.: Westminster/John Knox, 1991.

Rofé, Alexander. *Introduction to the Composition of the Pentateuch.* Translated by Harvey N. Bock. Biblical Seminar 58. Sheffield: Sheffield Academic Press, 1999.

Romaine, Suzanne. *Socio-Historical Linguistics: Its Status and Methodology.* Cambridge Studies in Linguistics 34. Cambridge: Cambridge University Press, 1982.

Rooker, Mark F. *Biblical Hebrew in Transition: The Language of the Book of Ezekiel.* Journal for the Study of the Old Testament: Supplement Series 90. Sheffield: JSOT Press, 1990.

——. "Dating Isaiah 40–66: What Does the Linguistic Evidence Say?" *Westminster Theological Journal* 58 (1996): 303–12. Repr. pages 59–73 in *Studies in Hebrew Language, Intertextuality, and Theology.* Texts and Studies in Religion 98. Lewiston, N.Y.: Edwin Mellen, 2003.

Rose, Martin. *Deuteronomist und Jahwist: Untersuchungen zu den Berührungspunkten beider Literaturwerke.* Abhandlungen zur Theologie des Alten und Neuen Testaments 67. Zürick: Theologischer Verlag, 1981.

Sáenz-Badillos, Angel. *A History of the Hebrew Language.* Translated by John Elwolde. Cambridge: Cambridge University Press, 1993.

Sanders, Seth L. *The Invention of Hebrew.* Urbana: University of Illinois Press, 2009.

Schmid, Hans Heinrich. *Der sogenannte Jahwist: Beobachtungen und Fragen zur Pentateuchforschung.* Zürich: Theologischer Verlag, 1976.

Schmidt, Werner H. *Old Testament Introduction.* Translated by Matthew J. O'Connell with David J. Reimer. 2nd ed. Berlin: W. de Gruyter; Louisville, Ky.: Westminster John Knox, 1999.

Schneider, Edgar W. "Investigating Variation and Change in Written Documents." Pages 67–96 in *The Handbook of Language Variation and Change.* Edited by J. K. Chambers, Peter Trudgill, and Natalie Schilling-Estes. Malden, Mass.: Blackwell, 2002.

Schniedewind, William M. *How the Bible Became a Book: The Textualization of Ancient Israel.* Cambridge: Cambridge University Press, 2004.

——. "Linguistic Ideology in Qumran Hebrew." Pages 245–55 in *Diggers at the Well: Proceedings of a Third International Symposium on the Hebrew of the Dead Sea Scrolls and Ben Sira.* Edited by T. Muraoka and J. F. Elwolde. Studies on the Texts of the Desert of Judah 36. Leiden: Brill, 2000.

——. "Prolegomena for the Sociolinguistics of Classical Hebrew." *Journal of Hebrew Scriptures* 5 (2004–2005): Article 6. Online: http://www.jhsonline.org/Articles/article_36.pdf.

——. "Qumran Hebrew as an Antilanguage." *Journal of Biblical Literature* 118 (1999): 235–52.

——. "Steps and Missteps in the Linguistic Dating of Biblical Hebrew" (review of Young [ed.], *Biblical Hebrew*). *Hebrew Studies* 46 (2005): 377–84.

Seitz, Christopher R. "Isaiah, Book of: First Isaiah." Pages 472–88 in vol. 3 of *Anchor Bible Dictionary.* Edited by David Noel Freedman. 6 vols. New York: Doubleday, 1992.

Seow, C. L. "Hosea, Book of." Pages 291–97 in vol. 3 of *Anchor Bible Dictionary.* Edited by David Noel Freedman. 6 vols. New York: Doubleday, 1992.

Smend, Rudolf. "Das Gesetz und die Völker: Ein Beitrag zur deuteronomistischen Redaktionsgeschichte." Pages 494–509 in *Probleme biblischer Theologie: Gerhard von Rad zum 70. Geburtstag.* Edited by Hans Walter Wolff. Munich: C. Kaiser, 1971.

Swann, Joan, Ana Deumert, Theresa Lillis, and Rajend Mesthrie. *A Dictionary of Sociolinguistics.* Edinburgh: Edinburgh University Press, 2004.

Talshir, David. "The Habitat and History of Hebrew during the Second Temple Period." Pages 251–75 in *Biblical Hebrew: Studies in Chronology and Typology.* Edited by Ian

Young. Journal for the Study of the Old Testament: Supplement Series 369. London: T&T Clark, 2003.

Talshir, Zipora. "The Reign of Solomon in the Making: Pseudo-Connections between 3 Kingdoms and Chronicles." *Vetus Testamentum* 50 (2000): 233–49.

———. "Synchronic and Diachronic Approaches in the Study of the Hebrew Bible: Text Criticism within the Frame of Biblical Philology." *Textus* 23 (2007): 1–32.

Thiel, Winfried. *Die deuteronomistische Redaktion von Jeremia 1–25*. Wissenschaftliche Monographien zum Alten und Neuen Testament 41. Neukirchen-Vluyn: Neukirchener Verlag, 1973.

———. *Die deuteronomistische Redaktion von Jeremia 26–45*. Wissenschaftliche Monographien zum Alten und Neuen Testament 52. Neukirchen-Vluyn: Neukirchener Verlag, 1981.

Thompson, Thomas L. "The Intellectual Matrix of Early Biblical Narrative: Inclusive Monotheism in Persian Period Palestine." Pages 107–24 in *The Triumph of Elohim: From Yahwism to Judaism*. Edited by Diana V. Edelman. Contributions to Biblical Exegesis and Theology 13. Kampen: Kok Pharos, 1995.

Toorn, Karel van der. *Scribal Culture and the Making of the Hebrew Bible*. Cambridge, Mass.: Harvard University Press, 2007.

Tov, Emanuel. *Textual Criticism of the Hebrew Bible*. 2nd rev. ed. Minneapolis, Minn.: Fortress, 2001.

Trask, R. L. *Historical Linguistics*. London: Arnold, 1996.

Trudgill, Peter. *The Social Differentiation of English in Norwich*. Cambridge Studies in Linguistics 13. Cambridge: Cambridge University Press, 1974.

Ullendorff, Edward. "Is Biblical Hebrew a Language?" *Bulletin of the School of Oriental and African Studies* 34 (1971): 241–55. Repr. pages 3–17 in *Is Biblical Hebrew a Language? Studies in Semitic Languages and Civilizations*. Wiesbaden: Otto Harrassowitz, 1977.

Ulrich, Eugene. *The Dead Sea Scrolls and the Origins of the Bible*. Studies in the Dead Sea Scrolls and Related Literature. Grand Rapids, Mich.: Eerdmans, 1999.

Van Seters, John. *Abraham in History and Tradition*. New Haven: Yale University Press, 1975.

———. *In Search of History: Historiography in the Ancient World and the Origins of Biblical History*. New Haven: Yale University Press, 1983.

———. *Prologue to History: The Yahwist as Historian in Genesis*. Louisville, Ky.: Westminster/John Knox, 1992.

Veijola, Timo. *Die ewige Dynastie: David und die Entstehung seiner Dynastie nach der deuteronomistischen Darstellung*. Suomalainen Tiedeakatemian Toimituksia (= Annales Academiae Scientiarum Fennicae) 193. Helsinki: Suomalainen Tiedeakatemia, 1975.

———. *Das Königtum in der Beurteilung der deuteronomistischen Historiographie: Eine redaktionsgeschichtliche Untersuchung*. Suomalainen Tiedeakatemian Toimituksia 198. Helsinki: Suomalainen Tiedeakatemia, 1977.

Vern, Robyn C. *Dating Archaic Biblical Hebrew Poetry: A Critique of the Linguistic Arguments*. Perspectives on Hebrew Scriptures and Its Contexts 10. Piscataway, N.J.: Gorgias, 2011.

Vörlander, Hermann. *Die Entstehungszeit des jehowistischen Geschichtswerkes*. Europäische Hochschulschriften: Reihe 23, Theologie 109. Frankfurt am Main: Lang, 1978.

Weinreich, Uriel, William Labov, and Marvin I. Herzog. "Empirical Foundations for a Theory of Language Change." Pages 95–195 in *Directions for Historical Linguistics: A Symposium*. Edited by W. P. Lehmann and Yakov Malkiel. Austin, Tex.: University of Texas Press, 1968.

Williamson, H. G. M. *1 and 2 Chronicles*. New Century Bible. Grand Rapids, Mich.: Eerdmans, 1982.

———. "Ezra and Nehemiah, Books of." Pages 375–82 in vol. 1 of *Dictionary of Biblical Interpretation*. Edited by John H. Hayes. 2 vols. Nashville: Abingdon, 1999.

———. *Ezra, Nehemiah*. Word Biblical Commentary 16. Waco, Tex.: Word, 1985.

Willoughby, Bruce E. "Amos, Book of." Pages 203–12 in vol. 1 of *Anchor Bible Dictionary*. Edited by David Noel Freedman. 6 vols. New York: Doubleday, 1992.

Wolfram, Walt, and Natalie Schilling-Estes. "Dialectology and Linguistic Diffusion." Pages 713–35 in *Handbook of Historical Linguistics*. Edited by Brian D. Joseph and Richard D. Janda. Malden, Mass.: Blackwell, 2004.

Wright, Richard M. "Further Evidence for North Israelite Contributions to Late Biblical Hebrew." Pages 129–48 in *Biblical Hebrew: Studies in Chronology and Typology*. Edited by Ian Young. Journal for the Study of the Old Testament: Supplement Series 369. London: T&T Clark, 2003.

———. *Linguistic Evidence for the Pre-Exilic Date of the Yahwistic Source*. Library of Hebrew Bible/Old Testament Studies 419. London: T&T Clark, 2005.

Yeivin, Israel. *Introduction to the Tiberian Masorah*. Translated and edited by E. J. Revell. Society of Biblical Literature Masoretic Studies 5. Missoula, Mont.: Scholars, 1980.

Young, Ian. "Biblical Texts Cannot Be Dated Linguistically." *Hebrew Studies* 46 (2005): 341–51.

———. "Concluding Reflections." Pages 312–17 in *Biblical Hebrew: Studies in Chronology and Typology*. Edited by Ian Young. Journal for the Study of the Old Testament: Supplement Series 369. London: T&T Clark, 2003.

———. *Diversity in Pre-Exilic Hebrew*. Forschungen zum Alten Testament 5. Tübingen: J. C. B. Mohr, 1993.

———. "Introduction: The Origin of the Problem." Pages 1–6 in *Biblical Hebrew: Studies in Chronology and Typology*. Edited by Ian Young. Journal for the Study of the Old Testament: Supplement Series 369. London: T&T Clark, 2003.

———. "Is the Prose Tale of Job in Late Biblical Hebrew?" *Vetus Testamentum* 59 (2009): 606–29.

———. "Late Biblical Hebrew and Hebrew Inscriptions." Pages 276–311 in *Biblical Hebrew: Studies in Chronology and Typology*. Edited by Ian Young. Journal for the Study of the Old Testament: Supplement Series 369. London: T&T Clark, 2003.

———. "Textual Stability in Gilgamesh and the Dead Sea Scrolls." Pages 173–84 in *Gilgameš and the World of Assyria: Proceedings of the Conference Held at Mandelbaum House, The University of Sydney, 21–23 July 2004*. Edited by Joseph Azize and Noel Weeks. Ancient Near Eastern Studies Supplement 21. Leuven: Peeters, 2007.

———, ed. *Biblical Hebrew: Studies in Chronology and Typology*. Journal for the Study of the Old Testament: Supplement Series 369. London: T&T Clark, 2003.

Young, Ian, Robert Rezetko, and Martin Ehrensvärd. *Linguistic Dating of Biblical Texts*. 2 vols. London: Equinox, 2008.

Zevit, Ziony. "Converging Lines of Evidence Bearing on the Date of P." *Zeitschrift für die alttestamentliche Wissenschaft* 94 (1982): 481–511.

———. "Introductory Remarks: Historical Linguistics and the Dating of Hebrew Texts ca. 100–300 B.C.E." *Hebrew Studies* 46 (2005): 321–26.

———. Review of Young (ed.), *Biblical Hebrew*. *Review of Biblical Literature* 6 (2004): 1–15. Online: http://bookreviews.org/pdf/4084_3967.pdf.

———. "Symposium Discussion Session: An Edited Transcription." *Hebrew Studies* 46 (2005): 371–76.

———. "What a Difference a Year Makes: Can Biblical Texts Be Dated Linguistically?" *Hebrew Studies* 47 (2006): 83–91.

Zimmerli, Walther. *Ezekiel 1: A Commentary on the Book of the Prophet Ezekiel, Chapter 1–24*. Translated by Ronald E. Clements. Hermeneia. Philadelphia: Fortress, 1979.

INDEX OF AUTHORS

INDEX OF SCRIPTURAL REFERENCES